ON NOT SPEAKING

In this major new book, leading cultural thinker Ien Ang engages with urgent questions of identity in an age of globalization and diaspora. The starting-point for Ang's discussion is the experience of visiting Taiwan. Ang, a person of Chinese descent, born in Indonesia and raised in the Netherlands, found herself 'faced with an almost insurmountable difficulty' – surrounded by people who expected her to speak to them in Chinese. She writes: 'It was the beginning of an almost decade-long engagement with the predicaments of "Chineseness" in diaspora. In Taiwan I was different because I couldn't speak Chinese; in the West I was different because I looked Chinese.'

From this autobiographical beginning, Ang goes on to reflect upon tensions between 'Asia' and 'the West' at a national and global level, and to consider the disparate meanings of 'Chineseness' in the contemporary world. She offers a critique of the increasingly aggressive construction of a global Chineseness, and challenges Western tendencies to equate 'Chinese' with 'Asian' identity.

Ang then turns to 'the West', exploring the paradox of Australia's identity as a 'Western' country in the Asian region, and tracing Australia's uneasy relationship with its Asian neighbours, from the White Australia policy to contemporary multicultural society. Finally, Ang draws together her discussion of 'Asia' and 'the West' to consider the social and intellectual space of the 'in-between', arguing for a theorizing not of 'difference' but of 'togetherness' in contemporary societies.

Ien Ang is Professor of Cultural Studies and Director of the Institute for Cultural Research at the University of Western Sydney, Australia. She is the author of a number of books, including *Watching Dallas* (1985), *Desperately Seeking the Audience* (1991) and *Living Room Wars* (1996), and recently co-edited *Alter/ Asians: Asian Australian Identities in Art, Media and Popular Culture* (2000).

ON NOT SPEAKING CHINESE

Living between Asia and the West

Ien Ang

London and New York

First published 2001
by Routledge
11 New Fetter Lane, London EC4P 4EE

Simultaneously published in the USA and Canada
by Routledge
29 West 35th Street, New York, NY 10001

*Routledge is an imprint of the
Taylor & Francis Group*

© 2001 Ien Ang

Typeset in Galliard by Keystroke, Jacaranda Lodge,
Wolverhampton
Printed and bound in Great Britain by
MPG Books Ltd, Bodmin

British Library Cataloguing in Publication Data
A catalogue record for this book is available from
the British Library

Library of Congress Cataloging in Publication Data
A catalog record for this book has been requested

ISBN 0–415–25912–6 (hbk)
ISBN 0–415–25913–4 (pbk)

CONTENTS

CONTENTS

PREFACE

'On not speaking Chinese', the opening chapter of this book, was first presented in 1992 at a conference in Taiwan. The conference organizers said it was up to me what I wanted to talk about. I was elated, of course, for I had never been to Taiwan before, but when I started to prepare for the event I was suddenly faced with an almost insurmountable difficulty. Imagining my Taiwanese audience, I felt I couldn't open my mouth in front of them without explaining why I, a person with stereotypically Chinese physical characteristics, could not speak to them in Chinese. In anticipation, I wrote this essay, which is now also the title of this book.

My scholarly work until then had mainly focused on mass media and popular culture – globally ubiquitous phenomena which fascinated me deeply but the analysis of which did not really implicate my personal identity (although I did make it a point, in the mid-1980s, that I liked watching *Dallas*). To all intents and purposes it was an academic pursuit which I could articulate in an 'objective' voice. In Taiwan, however, I felt that I couldn't speak without recognizing explicitly who I was and responding to how I was likely to be perceived by the people in this country. I expected much questioning, which turned out to be more than warranted: again and again, people on the streets, in shops, restaurants and so on were puzzled and mystified that I couldn't understand them when they talked to me in Chinese. So my decision to present a semi-autobiographical paper on the historical and cultural peculiarities of 'not speaking Chinese' resonated intimately with this experience. It was the beginning of an almost decade-long engagement with the predicaments of 'Chineseness' in diaspora. In Taiwan I was different because I couldn't speak Chinese; in the West I was different because I looked Chinese.

The politics of identity and difference has been all the rage in the 1990s. All over the world, people have become increasingly assertive in claiming and declaring 'who they are'. This book is perhaps a symptom of this trend, but it is also a critique – not in the sense of dismissing identity politics altogether, but by pointing to 'identity' as a double-edged sword: many people obviously need identity (or think they do), but identity can just as well be a strait-jacket. 'Who I am' or 'who we are' is never a matter of free choice.

In the past decade, identity politics has also been extremely salient for me in my newly adopted country, Australia. As a person of Chinese background I became identified as 'Asian' in a white country which has come to define itself increasingly as 'multicultural'. But while I am of Chinese descent, I was born in Indonesia and grew up in the Netherlands, before relocating to Australia as an adult. Coming from Europe to this part of the world, I did feel somehow reconnected with 'Asia', but only obliquely. The plane flew over my country of birth but landed thousands of kilometres further south, in the only corner of the 'Western' world which has ever imagined itself as 'part of Asia'. Identity politics – including that of nations – can take strange turns!

To a certain extent then, any identity is always mistaken, and this may be taken as the overall motto of this book. My personal biographical trajectory compels me to identify myself neither as fully 'Asian' nor as completely 'Western'. It is from this hybrid point of view – the ambiguous position of neither/nor, or both/and – that this book has been written. It is also from this point of view that I argue beyond identity and difference toward a more dynamic concern for togetherness-in-difference – a crucial issue for cultural politics in the twenty-first century.

ACKNOWLEDGEMENTS

Much of this work has been made possible by an Australian Research Council Large Grant on 'Reimagining Asians in Multicultural Australia', which I received jointly with Jon Stratton. I thank Jon for being such a stimulating and searching intellectual companion throughout the decade. Short-term residencies at the Obermann Center for Advanced Studies, University of Iowa, the Center for Cultural Studies, University of California, Santa Cruz and the Centre for Advanced Studies, National University of Singapore at different times during the past decade have enabled me to concentrate on reflecting and writing. I thank all those involved for making this possible. I also thank all those who have over the years invited me to numerous conferences, seminars, workshops, etc., where I had the opportunity to present early versions of the essays collected in this book.

Over the years, many friends and colleagues, old and new, have been around for conversation, discussion, camaraderie, guidance, the sharing of work, fun and frustration, discovery of new horizons, or simply getting my act together. I cannot mention them all, but here I wish to especially thank (for reasons I hope they know): Jody Berland, Michael Bérubé, Charlotte Brunsdon, Rey Chow, Chua Beng-huat, James Clifford, Jane Desmond, Virginia Dominguez, Rita Felski, Simryn Gill, Mitzi Goldman, Helen Grace, Ghassan Hage, Koichi Iwabuchi, Elaine Lally, Lisa Law, Jeannie Martin, Iain McCalman, Dave Morley, Meaghan Morris, Tessa Morris-Suzuki, Bruce Robinson, Mandy Thomas, Zoë Sofoulis, Yao Souchou and Anna Yeatman. I also thank Rebecca Barden from Routledge – now Taylor and Francis – for her always reliable support. The University of Western Sydney, especially through my colleagues at the Research Centre in Intercommunal Studies – now the Institute for Cultural Research – has been a wonderful place for pursuing new intellectual avenues in a time of rampant restructuring and diminishing resources. Last but not least, I thank Ian Johnson for distracting me from finishing this book, if only by taking me in entirely different directions . . .

Earlier versions of some chapters were published in the following places. I remain grateful to the editors who first included my work in their publications:

Chapter 1 was first published as 'To Be or Not to Be Chinese: Diaspora, Culture and Postmodern Ethnicity', in *South-East Asian Journal of Social Science*, vol. 21, no. 1, 1993, pp. 1–17 and subsequently as 'On not speaking Chinese' in *New Formations*, no. 24, December 1994, pp. 1–18; Chapter 2 was first published in *boundary 2: International Journal of Literature and Culture*, vol. 25, no. 3, 1998, pp. 223–242 (guest-edited by Rey Chow); Chapter 5 in *Topia: Canadian Journal of Cultural Studies*, no. 2, Spring 1998, pp. 22–41; Chapter 6 in John Docker and Gerhard Fischer (eds), *Race, Colour, Identity: Constructing the Multicultural Subject in Australia and New Zealand*. Tübingen: Stauffenburg Verlag and Sydney: UNSW Press, 2000, pp. 115–130; Chapter 7 in Ghassan Hage and Rowanne Couch (eds), *The Future of Australian Multiculturalism*. Sydney: Research Institute for Humanities and Social Sciences, University of Sydney, 1999, pp. 189–204; Chapter 8 in *Feminist Review*, no. 52, Spring 1996, pp. 36–49; Chapter 9 in Paul Gilroy, Lawrence Grossberg and Angela McRobbie (eds), *Without Guarantees: In Honour of Stuart Hall*. London: Verso, 2000, pp. 1–13; Chapter 10 in *European Journal for Cultural Studies*, vol. 1, no. 1, 1998, pp. 13–32; and Chapter 11 in Barbara Caine and Rosemary Pringle (eds), *Transitions: New Australian Feminisms*. St. Leonards: Allen & Unwin, 1995, pp. 57–73. Chapters 3, 4 and 12 appear in this volume for the first time. All chapters have been updated or revised, and freshly copy-edited for this book. The connections between the chapters are clarified for the first time in the Introduction.

Ien Ang
Sydney
March 2001

INTRODUCTION

Between Asia and the West
(In complicated entanglement)

The figure of the postcolonial diasporic intellectual – born in the Third World and educated and living and working in the West – has become the subject of much controversy in recent years. This is especially the case as some diasporic intellectuals – one thinks of Edward Said, Homi Bhabha, Gayatri Spivak and Stuart Hall, to name but a few – have gained international celebrity status in the halls of the Western academy. As Caren Kaplan (1996: 123) has observed, 'the cosmopolitan intellectual as migrant figure signals for many either the liberatory or negative effects of an increasingly transnational world'. As such, the figure of the diasporic intellectual operates as a metaphor that condenses the current intellectual discomfort and sense of crisis thrown up by the new world (dis)order created by the end of the Cold War, the accelerated globalization of capitalism, and the increasingly assertive presence of 'the Rest' in 'the West'. What is it then about the distinctive voice of the diasporic intellectual that generates so much contention?

Rey Chow, who grew up in Hong Kong and now lives and works in the United States, has this to say about her own work:

> If there is something from my childhood and adolescent years that remains a chief concern in my writing, it is the tactics of dealing with and dealing in dominant cultures that are so characteristic of living in Hong Kong. These are the tactics of those who do not have claims to territorial propriety or cultural centrality.
>
> (1993: 25)

For Chow, 'Hong Kong' operates as a kind of interstitial location which impels her to engage in what she calls 'tactics of intervention'. According to Chow:

> The history of Hong Kong predisposes one to a kind of 'border' or 'parasite' practice – an identification with 'Chinese culture' but a distantiation from the Chinese Communist regime; a resistance against colonialism but an unwillingness to see the community's prosperity disrupted.
>
> (ibid.: 22)

1

Hong Kong's unsettled and unsettling location between China and the West produces the multiple ambivalences Chow sums up, in which a desire to have it both ways is continually undercut by the refusal or inability to identify with either. Chow wishes to hold on to this unstable, ambivalent, doubly marginalized positionality as the very place from where she can enact 'a specific kind of social power' (ibid.), the power to interrupt, to trouble, to intervene tactically rather than strategically in the interrogation of dominant discourses. Tactical interventions never make counter-hegemonic claims to alternative truths but are limited to bringing out the contradictions and the violence inherent in all posited truths. The tactical interventionist forever remains on the border: her agency is not in anticipation of or in preparation for the occupation of a new field by destroying and replacing existing ones. It is 'para-sitical' in that it never takes over a field in its entirety, but erodes it slowly and insidiously, making space for itself surreptitiously. Chow's position here echoes Homi Bhabha's (1990b) enunciation of a 'third space', the in-between space of hybridity from where cultural change can be brought about quietly, without revolutionary zeal, by 'contaminating' established narratives and dominant points of view.

To be sure, it is the diasporic intellectual's affirmation of this essentially 'negative' agency of hybridity, as exemplified by Chow, that is so disturbing to their critics. Aijaz Ahmad (1992), for example, in a scathing critique, argues that the politics of hybridity never moves beyond the ephemeral and the contingent, failing to produce stable commitment to a political cause, a sustained politics of radical structural change. In a different context, Ella Shohat (1992) has similarly criticized postcolonial theory – a body of work mostly elaborated by diasporic intellectuals – for its theoretical and political ambivalence because it 'posits no clear domination and calls for no clear opposition'. Such critiques relate to a call for conscious partisanship and unflinching commitment (to one's class, gender, race or nation) as a prerequisite to radical politics and knowledge. The diasporic intellectual acts as a perpetual party-pooper here because her impulse is to point to ambiguities, complexities and contradictions, to complicate matters rather than provide formulae for solutions, to blur distinctions between colonizer and colonized, dominant and subordinate, oppressor and oppressed. In short, the diasporic intellectual is declared suspect because her emphasis on undecidability and ambivalence leads arguably to a valuation of hybridity, which does not lend itself to the development of revolutionary strategies of structural progressive change and systematic radical resistance.

I must warn the reader that the spirit of the diasporic intellectual's tactical interventionism runs throughout this book: the space from which these chapters were written was precisely the space of hybridity, between Asia and the West. At the same time, I hope to contribute to a reappreciation of the politics of hybridity – and its emphasis on multiplicity, uncertainty and ambivalence – which always seems to be at the heart of criticisms of the diasporic intellectual's discourse. In a riposte to these criticisms, Stuart Hall (1996f: 244) has remarked that 'a certain nostalgia runs through some of these arguments for a return to a clear-cut politics

2

of binary oppositions'. Hall notes that the current crisis of the left can be understood precisely as a sign that there are no longer, if there ever were, simple lines to be drawn between goodies and baddies. This doesn't mean that there are no hard political choices to be made, but, he asks, 'isn't the ubiquitous, the soul-searing, lesson of our times the fact that political binaries do not (do not any longer? did they ever?) either stabilise the field of political antagonism in any permanent way or render it transparently intelligible?' And, so Hall continues, 'Are we not all, in different ways, . . . desperately trying to understand what making an ethical political choice and taking a political position in a necessarily contingent political field is like, what sort of "politics" it adds up to?' (1996f: 244).

'Hybridity' captures in a shorthand fashion the complexities and ambiguities of any politics in an increasingly globalized, postcolonial and multicultural world, a world in which heroic, utopian ideas of revolutionary transformation seem seriously out of touch even as sites of social struggle and political conflict have multiplied. In this light, Chow's emphasis on 'tactics' rather than 'strategies' signifies a realistic recognition of the *limits* to radical political intervention in the contemporary world. These tactics should be taken more rather than less seriously as the very concrete instances in which people work out specific, situationally determined modes of 'hybrid accommodation with national and transnational forces' (Clifford 1998: 367). Hybridity, here, should not be dismissed pejoratively as the merely contingent and ephemeral, equated with lack of commitment and political resoluteness, but should be valued, in James Clifford's (ibid.: 366) words, as 'a pragmatic response, making the best of given (often bad) situations . . . in limited historical conjunctures'.

In the course of this book, I will argue for the importance of hybridity as a basis for cultural politics in a world in which we no longer have the secure capacity to draw the line between us and them, between the different and the same, here and there, and indeed, between Asia and the West. We now live in a world of what anthropologist Clifford Geertz (1988: 148) has characterized as 'a gradual spectrum of mixed-up differences'. This is a globalized world in which 'people quite different from one another in interest, outlook, wealth, and power' are 'contained in a world where, tumbled as they are into endless connection, it is increasingly difficult to get out of each other's way' (ibid.: 147). Hybridity is a necessary concept to hold onto in this condition, because unlike other key concepts in the contemporary politics of difference – such as diaspora and multiculturalism – it foregrounds complicated entanglement rather than identity, togetherness-in-difference rather than virtual apartheid. The diasporic intellectual may in fact be especially well placed to analyse this complicated entanglement beause it is embodied in her own life trajectory.

From Asia to the West

As an ethnic Chinese, Indonesian-born and European-educated academic who now lives and works in Australia, I sort of fit into the category of the 'diasporic intellectual', although I prefer the more neutral term 'migrant intellectual'. This book is to a certain extent auto-biographical, in that it is in large part a reflection on my own experiences as a multiple migrant. Migrants always inevitably undergo a process of cross-cultural translation when they move from one place to another, from one regime of language and culture to another. Salman Rushdie (1991), the famous diasporic Indian writer, calls himself a 'translated man'. But the process of cultural translation is not a straightforward and teleological one: from the 'old' to the 'new'. As Clifford (1997: 182) has put it, 'One enters the translation process from a specific location, from which one only partly escapes.' Hall (1996a: 399) remarks that diasporic intellectuals are 'transitional figures', 'constantly translating between different languages, different worlds'. It is this condition of transitionality that characterizes the lives of migrant intellectuals, also aptly described as 'living in translation', to borrow a term from Tejaswini Niranjana (1992: 46).

This book draws on my own particular experiences with living in translation between Asia and the West, as it were, although more specific geo-historical coordinates will need to be elaborated below. After all, 'Asia' and 'the West' are not natural entities but historically produced, homogenizing categories. The idea of 'Asia' as a distinct, demarcatable region of the world originated in a very Eurocentric system of geographical classification. In their book *The Myth of Continents*, Martin Lewis and Kären Wigen (1997: 37) remark that 'of all the so-called continents, Asia is not only the largest but also the most fantastically diversified, a vast region whose only commonalities – whether human or physical – are so general as to be trivial'. This is true, but it does not do away with the reality that in the contemporary world, 'Asia' and 'Asians' are powerful terms of identification for many cultures, societies and peoples who are somehow subsumed under these terms. We know, commonsensically, which are Asian countries, and millions of people living in these countries – as well as in the West – would call themselves Asians (as well as Singaporeans, Chinese, Thai, Indian, and so on), even though this may not always be a strongly or unambiguously felt identification.

'The West', for its part, may be an internally diverse category but it is evidently, as Naoki Sakai (1989: 95) remarks, 'a name always associating itself with those regions, communities, and peoples that appear politically and economically superior to other regions, communities and peoples'. Indeed, it is the very entrenched hegemony of this asymmetrical relationship between the West and the Rest which reinforces the potency of 'Asia' and 'Asians' as categories which represent a *difference* from the West, whether imposed or self-declared. Being Asian means being non-Western, at least from the dominant point of view, and this in itself has strong implications for one's sense of self, especially if one is (positioned as) Asian in the West. The fact that identification with being Asian – sometimes in hyphenated form such as 'Asian-American' – is so ubiquitous across Western nation–states reveals much about the tension that exists between the two categories. Paul Gilroy (1993: 1) once remarked that 'striving to be both European and black requires some specific forms of double consciousness', pointing to the presumably unnatural quality of such an identity. The same can be said about being both Western and

4

Asian, even though no *a priori* similarity in the forms of double consciousness can be assumed between blacks of the African diaspora (of which Gilroy speaks) and Asians in the West, given the vastly different historical conditions under which Africans and Asians have entered Western space, in Europe, the Americas, and in Australasia (Chun 2001).

The themes I focus on in this book are not merely personal, but coincide with some major cultural and historical developments which have taken place in the past thirty to forty years or so, a period in which the configuration of the world has changed dramatically. Specifically, what we have experienced in the past few decades is a transition from a world of nation–states who organize themselves more or less effectively as socially distinct, culturally homogeneous and politically sovereign (and in which there is no real place for migrants who are considered too different), to an interconnected, intermingled world in which virtually all nation–states have become territories where various economies, cultures and peoples intersect and interact. In the latter part of the twentieth century, in other words, nation–states have become spaces of global flows, in which the confluence of cultural difference and diversity has become increasingly routinized. At the same time, the process of globalization has also routinized the transnational interconnections and interdependencies which erode and transcend the separateness of nation–states. In short, the world is now a space of complicated entanglement, of togetherness-in-difference.

My own personal history as a migrant and as a migrant intellectual has been marked in quite interesting ways by this enormous world-historical transformation. As an Asian migrant in the West, my positioning in the world has changed dramatically in the past thirty years or so, not least because the global meaning of 'Asia' has undergone major shifts in the postcolonial period. In the 1960s, when I migrated from Asia to Europe as a child, Asianness – in whatever national embodiment: Chinese, Japanese, Indian, Malay, Filipino, and so on – was still firmly associated with Third World backwardness in the Western imagination. China had become communist and was totally out of bounds. Japanese economic progress, actively supported by the United States, was routinely dismissed as the result of the dumb Japanese skill at imitating and copying the West, not the reward of their own creativity, innovativeness and hard work. South-East Asian nations such as Indonesia, Malaysia and Singapore were still in the throws of the decolonization process. The Vietnam War, which more than any event brought Asia into the everyday lifeworld of people living in the West, produced TV images of violence, cruelty and sheer human despair. When thousands of 'boat people' from Indochina were allowed to settle in Western countries after 1975, their refugee status did not exactly enhance the standing of the category 'Asian' in Western minds.

By the 1990s, however, Asianness is no longer linked exclusively to lamentable Third World connotations. One important reason for this has been the highly contested, spectacular rise of East and South-East Asian 'dragons' and 'tigers' in the global economy in the 1980s and 1990s, a development which managed to make the advanced, Western world extremely nervous and jittery. For the first time in modern world history the West, 'symbolically at the heart of global power' (Keith and Pile 1993: 22), faced the prospect of being outperformed by the East. The spectre of a coming Asian Century – which would supplant the previous, American Century – loomed large, symbolized most traumatically by the high-profile Japanese take-overs of companies that represent the 'soul of America', Hollywood, in the late 1980s (see e.g. Morley and Robins 1995, Chapter 8). In the transnational corporate world, there was a flurry of interest in the success formulae of Japanese management style, Chinese business culture and, more generally, in the principles behind the dynamism of 'confucian capitalism'.[1] At the same time, leaders of previously 'unimportant' – due to their smallness and lack of visibility on the world stage – Asian nations such as Singapore's Lee Kuan Yew and Malaysia's Prime Minister Mahathir Mohammad had begun to boast about the superiority of so-called 'Asian values': their societies were supposedly more harmonious, more morally upright, and more efficient and disciplined than those of the West, which they painted as increasingly violent, decadent and disorderly. In this discourse, 'Asia' – Asian capitalism, Asian modernity, Asian culture – is touted as the model for an affluent, hypermodern future, not the residue of a traditional and backward past, as classic Orientalism would have it. Some even entertained the – distinctly postcolonial – fantasy that Asia, imagined as a fictive, civilizational historical subject, would finally turn the tables on the West, as reflected in book titles by high profile Asian leaders such as *The Japan that Can Say No* (Ishihara 1991), *The Voice of Asia* (Mahathir and Ishihara 1995), *The Asian Renaissance* (Anwar 1996), the provocative *Can Asians Think?* (Mahbubani 1998) and *A New Deal for Asia* (Mahathir 1999). These Asians were telling the world that they were no longer the deferential followers of the West, but have created alternative (and arguably, for some, superior) *Asian* styles of modernity. In the West, the mood was mirrored in the publication of Harvard Professor Samuel Huntington's famous article 'The Clash of Civilizations' in 1993, in which he projects a decline of Western power and a 'resurgence of non-Western cultures', with Asia, in Huntington's view, likely to pose the most formidable challenge to the West in the first decades of the twenty-first century (Huntington 1993; 1997).

Of course this whole scenario was dealt a severe blow when the successful Asian economies were thrown into crisis in 1997, causing widespread chaos and hardship across the region as the value of local currencies tumbled, unemployment rose and, in the wake of economic downturn, long-standing political powers-that-be were destabilized – the most dramatic of which was the forced resignation of President Suharto in Indonesia in May 1998 after months of student protests and mass rioting. The 'Asian meltdown' led many Western observers to claim that the very basis of Asian economic success – represented by the dubious phenomenon of 'crony capitalism' – was unsound and that Western (read: US-style neoliberal) economic policies were still superior after all. There is a triumphalist subtext to such Western responses to the crisis: 'Asian values' could now be declared a myth and the West has emerged, once again, on top (Fukuyama 1998; see also Sheridan 1999).

Nevertheless, Asia's standing has not been completely wiped out by the loss of its economic face. Too many decades have passed in which Westerners have had to deal with Asians – from Japanese corporate managers to Chinese Communist Party leaders, from Hong Kong entrepreneurs to Singaporean and Malaysian diplomats – on the basis of presumed equality, that is, on the basis of the assumed *modernity* of Asia.[2] While there may be differences among moderns, moderns cannot relegate one another to the realm of absolute Otherness. Whatever their differences, moderns share the same world, the *modern* world, and therefore are expected to treat each other, at least in principle, as equals. Thus, modern Asians can generally no longer be represented unproblematically as primitives or exotics – two versions of the absolute Other – by their Western counterparts. They may perhaps be called 'recalcitrant' (indicating at most the irritation felt by the older brother in a quarrel among siblings),[3] but they cannot be dismissed as 'backward'. Modern Asia, in other words, unlike, say, Africa – too afflicted by endless poverty and disaster – or the Arabs – too insistent on their fundamental difference – has acquired a position of symbolic equipoise with the West.[4] Malaysia's Prime Minister Mahathir Mohamad expresses the sentiments best when he exclaims: 'Asians will certainly not dominate the world. But Asians or the mixed people living in Asia will take their rightful place, their rightful share of the World Century' (Mahathir 1999: 151).

In Australia, a country geographically tucked away at the far south end of the so-called Asia-Pacific region and therefore the western nation most directly exposed to changes and developments occurring among its northern neighbours, the 1980s and 1990s were marked by an increasingly loud chorus of clamours for Australia to 'engage', 'enmesh' and 'integrate' with Asia. The need for an 'Asianization' of Australia, as perceived by government and business leaders and by influential economists, policy analysts and journalists, was based on the observation that if Australia did not, it would be hopelessly left behind in the global economy and become a parochial backwater in world society, a 'banana republic'. I came to live and work in Australia in 1991 after having spent twenty-five years in Western Europe. I left a Europe that had just undergone massive upheaval after the fall of the Berlin Wall in 1989, and where international discussion was immersed by excitement about the prospect of a unified Europe – something worked upon assiduously by powerful European leaders such as Helmut Kohl and François Mitterand (though not Margaret Thatcher). When I arrived in Australia, however, I soon realized how geoculturally specific this 'desire for Europe' was (see Ang 1998). Nothing of it was evident in Australia; instead, to my amazement, the country was engrossed in a 'desire for Asia'. Paul Keating, the flamboyant political leader who 'pushed Australia further into Asia than any other prime minister' (Sheridan 1995: xix), stated that by the year 2000 Australia should be a country in which 'our national culture is shaped by, and helps to shape, the cultures around us' (quoted in ibid.). For me, as a new migrant into Australia, this was a puzzling as well as exciting experience: this Australian infatuation with Asia – after more than a century-long rejection – rearticulated and recontextualized my own Asianness in unprecedented ways.

At the same time, the great number of other migrants from Asian countries in Australia has meant that Asians – people who look like me – were no longer an anomaly but a regular presence in this Western country, a presence to be reckoned with (as in some other parts in the Western world such as California, but certainly not in Europe). This has had a tremendous impact on my *experience* of being Asian in the West. Over the years I had become used to the awkward position of being one of the only or, at most, one of the few Asians in an otherwise white environment. This was so much the case that I always impulsively reacted pleased when I encountered another Chinese-looking person, presuming a 'we are in the same boat' sense of empathy. For example, when I first went to San Francisco in the mid-1980s I was so pleased to be served by a Chinese-American clerk in a department store that I was disappointed that he didn't seem to treat me with any sign of special recognition, but as just another customer. Of course, unlike Amsterdam (which was my experiential yardstick at that time) San Francisco has long had a large and highly visible Chinese-American population, so being Asian was nothing exceptional. Today, living in Sydney, I similarly take it for granted that there are many other Asians around. I routinely encounter them as shop assistants, taxi drivers, students, doctors, even colleagues (though not, I have to say, as senior managers or political representatives). In other words, there are now so many Asians *in* the West that the West itself is slowly becoming, to all intents and purposes, 'Asianized'.

It is in response to this shifting context of the Westernization of Asia and the Asianization of the West – two complex, uneven and asymmetrical processes to be sure – that this book should be read. The book is also a critical engagement with some major strands of cultural politics which have emerged in the West in parallel with the world-historical transformations I have outlined: identity politics, as well as those of diaspora and multiculturalism.

From assimilation to identity politics

My formative years were spent in Europe, in the Netherlands to be more precise, where I received a throroughly westernized education. Indeed, since I was 12, when my family relocated from Indonesia to the Netherlands, I was brought up in an assimilationist European environment in which my Asianness (or Chineseness) was rendered virtually irrelevant. The most memorable exception was the dubious special attention I occasionally received as a young woman from European men who were fascinated by my long, straight black hair – a fatuous but still all-too-common manifestation of the erotic exoticization of Asian femininity which has long been part of western Orientalism. In general, however, my Asianness tended to be treated as non-existent; for many years I went through life (in Europe) in the belief that my Asian background was of no real significance to my social identity. We ate Asian food at home – our tastebuds couldn't really get used to the blandness of northern European cuisine – but we spoke Dutch. All my friends treated me as if I were Dutch (although none of them would ever have assumed that I was born there). I lived in a thoroughly European world. Today, several decades later and in an era of liberal multiculturalism and ethnic revivalism, such an assimilated existence would probably be disapproved of as 'self-denial'. But this was a time before the coming into dominance of 'identity politics'.

Until the 1970s, many postcolonial immigrants like us diligently pursued their own assimilation into the dominant culture of the modern West – an ideology my parents firmly believed in – not only because it held the promise of access into a secure world of comfort, affluence and, most importantly, the possibility of upward mobility. (Hence, of course, my parents' insistence on the importance of learning the language and culture of the West.) It was also simply a necessity, a survival strategy, given the fact that when we first moved into the Netherlands, in the 1960s, there were only few migrants like us with whom we could form what would now be called an 'ethnic (or diasporic) community', which would celebrate its cultural origins and protect/police its boundaries by insisting on maintaining its linguistic and cultural *difference* from the dominant culture. This was not the kind of aspirational environment I grew up in. Instead, for my family 'out of Asia into the West' meant the utopian hope and the dogged determination to fully westernize, and to *claim* the West as our destiny and our eventual site of belonging.

But assimilation, as Zygmunt Bauman (1991) has forcefully shown, can never be fully successful. The modern project of assimilation, which literally means 'making alike', is inherently contradictory, because the very *acquired* – rather than inherited or ascribed – character of cultural traits gained in the process of assimilation turns the assimilating subject into a less than real, and thus somehow inferior Westerner (Bauman's discussion focuses on the German Jews before Hitler rose to power). Even the most westernized non-Western subject can never become truly, authentically Western. The traces of Asianness cannot be erased completely from the westernized Asian: we will always be 'almost the same but not quite', because we are 'not white' (Bhabha 1994: 89). As Bauman (1991: 105) remarks, 'The acceptance of assimilation as a vision and as a framework for a life strategy was tantamount to the recognition of the extant hierarchy, its legitimacy, and above all its immutability.'

Indeed, assimilationism was long an official government goal in immigrant nation–states such as the United States and Australia, and a tacit expectation inflicted on 'newcomers' in old-world European countries. The idea was that all immigrants would be incorporated smoothly within the dominant national culture, leaving their original cultures happily behind. In the USA, the idea of the 'melting pot', popularized by the Jewish playwright Israel Zangwill who wrote his play *The Melting Pot* in 1908,[5] was often taken to mean the absorption of newcomers into the established, white Anglo-Saxon order until they became invisible in the national scene, both physically and culturally. This process was thought to be achievable especially for white European migrants (including European Jews), but not, of course, for blacks and other non-white races such as the Chinese (against whom there were exclusionary anti-immigration laws in both the USA and Australia). The ultimate failure of the assimilation project could no longer be denied when, by the late 1960s, even the (descendants of) European migrants such as Italians,

Poles, and Jews turned out to distinguish themselves more from the WASPS than expected, as reflected pointedly in a 1972 book entitled *The Rise of the Unmeltable Ethnics* (Novak 1972). A similar process took place in Australia, where incidentally mass European immigration only began in the late 1940s, at least half a century later than in the USA. At the same time, those previously excluded from national belonging on the grounds of their 'race' – for example, black descendants of African slaves in the USA and indigenous Aboriginal people in Australia – were at the forefront of the struggle against racial discrimination and for their social, political and cultural rights. In this ferment, any ideal or illusion of national-cultural homogeneity – for which assimilation was thought to be a perfect mechanism – could no longer be sustained. This process of unravelling was further accelerated when the number of non-western, postcolonial migrants throughout Western countries reached a critical mass.

Afro-Caribbeans, South Asians and other former members of the Empire had started to enter Britain in the 1950s, resulting in substantial populations of what are now called 'Blacks and Asians' in that country. Similar postcolonial migrations have changed the make-up of other former colonial powers such as France and the Netherlands. In European countries such as Germany and the Netherlands, the demand for cheap labour led them to import so-called 'guest workers' from the peripheries of Europe such as Turkey and North Africa, many of whom have become, several decades on, permanent residents with growing families. From the mid-1960s onwards, New World countries such as the USA, Canada and Australia progressively removed their racially discriminatory immigration laws, opening their doors for non-whites, many of whom are from Asian countries. The end of the Vietnam War propelled the exodus of hundreds of thousands of Indochinese refugees, most of whom were given permission to start a new life in diverse parts of the West. All these developments have massively altered the population make-up of most Western countries: in no way could all these migrants, with all their different languages, cultures, and looks, be absorbed into the dominant culture without changing the latter irrevocably. Assimilation was dead. All these countries – the wealthiest, most developed and powerful countries in the world – are today, whether they officially acknowledge it or not, 'multicultural states' (Bennett 1998): they all have to deal with the question of how to manage the difference and diversity within their borders – as migrants from all corners of the globe continue to seek entry precisely in a bid to get their share of Western prosperity.

It is in this *de facto* multiracial and multicultural West that the politics of 'identity' – which, after all, can only be enunciated in a world of difference – has acquired an unprecedented currency. It was in the 1980s, when I was still living in Europe, that my own notional Asianness had started to haunt me, as it were. In a social atmosphere in which 'who you are' – in terms of gender, sexual orientation, ethnicity or race – became an increasingly prominent pretext and motive for political association and cultural self-assertion, it became inescapable for me to 'declare my interest', so to speak. More and more people had begun to enquire about my background. Despite my perfect Dutch and my assimilated lifestyle, people wanted to know 'where are you from?', and were never satisfied when I answered simply, 'from Holland'. Implied in the very question was always the expectation, the requirement even, that I would mention *another* space. That space, in very general terms, is somewhere in 'Asia' – or more precisely, 'China', the Asian land/nation/culture that has loomed largest in the European imagination as *the* embodiment of the mysterious, inscrutable other – presumably the 'natural' land of origin for people with my 'racial' features. More annoyingly, the question, 'Do you speak Chinese?' was put to me *ad nauseam*. My answer, a resounding negative, was easy enough to blurt out, but as I contemplated on the question itself – and the very frequency with which I was confronted with it – I became aware of its precarious cultural-political presumptions and implications, many of which I reflect on in this book.

The title of this book, *On Not Speaking Chinese*, articulates the subjective position from which the chapters collected here have been written: it signals a somewhat awkward, oblique relationship to a socially assigned 'identity' in a time when both identity claims and identity impositions of the essentializing kind are the order of the day. If there is an overarching theme throughout this book, then, it revolves around the multiple disjunctures and tensions between large-scale, publicly reproduced categorical identities – 'Chinese', 'Asian' – and the concrete social subjectivities and experiences which are shaped and circumscribed by these identity categories but at the same time always exceed their reified boundaries. In other words, there can never be a perfect fit between fixed identity label and hybrid personal experience; indeed, while the rhetoric of identity politics generally emphasizes the liberating force of embracing a collective identity, especially if that identity was previously repressed or oppressed, that very identity is also the name of a potential prison-house. It is very hard to imagine and appreciate the complicated entanglement of our togetherness-in-difference from within the prison-house of identity.

Deconstructing diaspora

I explored the ambiguous ramifications of identity politics for the first time in the opening chapter, 'On not speaking Chinese'. This chapter examines the ambivalences of my being interpellated, increasingly frequently, as 'Chinese' (even though I was born in Indonesia, a very different place in Asia than China). There is of course an excitement in the self-affirmation and self-assertion that is inextricably linked to the rise of identity politics since the 1960s: there is a pleasure in the sheer realization of a distinctive shared identity and the empowered sense of belonging it imparts. Identity politics, in this regard, is a logical offshoot of the decline of assimilationism and its illusory promise of equality on the basis of a strived-for but never achieved sameness: the politics of identity relies quintessentially on the recognition and mobilization of difference once the ideal of sameness has proved unreachable. Claiming one's *difference* (from the mainstream or dominant national culture) and turning it into symbolic capital has become a powerful and attractive

11

strategy among those who have never quite belonged, or have been made to feel that they do not quite belong in the West.

The wildly preferred name for that symbolic capital, in recent years, has been *diaspora*. In this era of globalization, it is diasporic identity politics in which millions of migrants throughout the West (and beyond) have invested their passion and their fealty. In light of global power relations, the significance of diasporic identity resides in its force as a symbolic declaration of liberation from the abject position of 'ethnic minority' in 'an oppressive national hegemony' (Clifford 1997: 255). As James Clifford (ibid.) has remarked, 'diasporic identifications reach beyond ethnic status within the composite, liberal state', imparting a 'sense of being a "people" with historical roots and destinies outside the time/space of the host nation'. In this sense, diasporic identity holds the promise of being part of a world-historical political/cultural formation, such as 'China', 'Asia' or 'Africa', which may be able to turn the tables on the West, at least in the imagination. It is undeniable, then, that the idea of diaspora is an occasion for positive identification for many, providing a sense of grandiose transnational belonging and connection with dispersed others of similar historical origins. In my own experience, this reaching back to one's ancestral 'roots' can be a powerful, almost utopian emotive pull. But notwithstanding the benefits, what are the costs of diasporic identity?

In the course of writing the chapters of Part I of this book, I have become increasingly reluctant to join the chorus of celebrating the idea of diaspora. Indeed, it is important, I would argue, to recognize the double-edgedness of diasporic identity: it can be the site of both support and oppression, emancipation and confinement. The Chinese diaspora, especially, has by virtue of its sheer critical mass, global range and mythical might evinced an enormous power to operate as a magnet for anyone who can somehow be identified as 'Chinese' – no matter how remote the ancestral links. The contradictory politics of this global diasporic pulling power – as embodied in Tu Wei-ming's famed but controversial 'cultural China' project – is the subject of Chapter 2, 'Can one say no to Chineseness?' I argue that as 'China' and 'Chineseness' are increasingly becoming signs for global political and economic power in the early twenty-first century, there is no necessary political rightousness in Chinese diasporic identity, the long-standing Chinese tradition of feeling victimized and traumatized notwithstanding. Indeed, there could well be circumstances and predicaments in which it would be politically more pertinent to say *no* to a particularist Chinese identity, at least if our commitment is a universalist and cosmopolitan one, encompassing all people of the world, not just 'our own'. In the Asian context, in South-East Asia especially, the stakes are quite clear: it is well known that so-called overseas Chinese entrepreneurs – card-carrying members of the Chinese diaspora – are the key operators behind the region's economic growth, which is reflected in their relative wealth and affluence but also in the tradition of suspicion which historically has grown against them since colonial times. In this context, to this day, Chinese identity is never a simple issue: it is both an expression of political marginalization in the postcolonial nation–state and an indication of (real and imagined) economic privilege.

In this sense, being Chinese in (South-East) Asia is often an even more precarious predicament than being Asian in the West! But to respond to this situation by retreating into an essentialized Chinese identity – the diasporic solution – would be tantamount to overlooking the complex, historically determined relations of power in which 'Chinese' identities have come to be constructed in relation to non-Chinese, 'native' identities, on the one hand, and European identities, on the other. I reflect on these complex interrelationships in Chapter 3, 'Indonesia on my mind', the writing of which was prompted by the anti-Chinese riots in Indonesia in 1998 and its aftermath, as played out on the Internet – with its electronic immediacy and accessibility one of the most spectacular, potent amplifiers of the expansion of global diasporas in the late twentieth century. It is in this chapter, especially, that I confront some of the more painful contradictions and ambiguities of diasporic identity. In my own case, the question can be asked, do I belong to the Chinese diaspora, as all too often spontaneously assumed, or to a notional Indonesian diaspora? And why is it that the latter option has so much less currency than the former? This leads me, in Chapter 4, 'Undoing diaspora', to problematize – though not completely discard – the value of diasporic identity politics, indeed, the importance of Chineseness itself as the symbolic anchor of such a politics. I not only question the boundaries of the (Chinese) diaspora itself, but also point to the implicit local/global power relations established in the very construction of the imagined community of 'the Chinese diaspora'. Thus, while the transnationalism of diasporas is often taken as an implicit point of critique of the territorial boundedness and the internally homogenizing perspective of the nation–state, the limits of diaspora lie precisely in its own assumed boundedness, its inevitable tendency to stress its internal coherence and unity, logically set apart from 'others'.[6] Ultimately, diaspora is a concept of sameness-in-dispersal, not of togetherness-in-difference.

Negotiating multiculturalism

If the liberating prospect of diasporic identity is generally sought in its transnational, even global reach and scope, this very deterritorializing move (out of the place of location) may also be seen as one of its drawbacks. As Clifford (1997: 258) has rightly noted, 'theories and discourses that diasporize or internationalize "minorities" can deflect attention from long-standing, structured inequalities of class and race'. That is, by projecting its political and cultural faith onto the imagined community with others *elsewhere* (based on primordialist assumptions of racial and ethnic kinship), diaspora, as a concept, tends to de-emphasize, if not diminish the import of living *here*. In Clifford's (ibid.: 255) apt phrase, diaspora communities are 'not-here to stay'.

In practice, of course, this cannot be the case. All migrants ultimately have to forge an accommodation with where they find themselves relocated, and to reconcile with their situation *here*, whether this be the United States, the Netherlands, Australia, or anywhere else. For Asians who have migrated to the West, this means coming to terms somehow with racial minority status, and acting upon it. Identity politics *within* the nation–state, then, especially in Western liberal states, has taken on the form predominantly of what Charles Taylor (1992) famously calls a 'politics of recognition'. The demand for – and granting of – recognition (of one's minority rights, one's culture, one's identity) are central to the idea of *multiculturalism* – a political response to that demand which has had a particularly strong and controversial influence in the past few decades. Multiculturalism can be defined, in very simple terms, as the official and informal recognition that racial and ethnic minorities in a particular nation–state have their own distinct cultures and communities, and that these have to recognized and appreciated as such. Thus, the idea of multiculturalism implies, in its bare bones, an acknowledgement of the co-existence of multiple cultures and peoples within one space, generally the space of the nation–state. In contrast with diaspora, multiculturalism emphasizes the fact that a constellation of racial/ethnic groups have to make do with sharing the space here. In this sense, multiculturalism takes the challenge of togetherness in difference seriously. It is multiculturalism's assumed *mode* of sharing, however, which is problematic.

In its most significant usage – and the one I engage with in this book – multiculturalism is a government policy to manage cultural diversity within a pluralist nation–state. If the nation–state can no longer maintain its homogeneity, so goes the pluralist train of thought, then the best solution would be to allow for the preservation of a diversity of cultures, but within certain, well-demarcated limits, so as not to disturb or threaten the national unity. This is what Homi Bhabha (1990), the postcolonial diasporic intellectual *par excellence*, describes ironically as the simultaneous encouragement and containment of cultural diversity. Thus we have the 'multicultural nation' or the 'multicultural state', in which differences are carefully classified and organized into a neat, virtual grid of distinct 'ethnic communities', each with their own 'culture'. The problem with this conception of the multicultural society is that it does not respond to the dynamism that occurs when different groups come to live and interact together, 'tumbled into endless connection' as Geertz put it. It is an all too ordered and well-organized image of society as a unity-in-diversity – a convenient image from a bureaucratic-managerial point of view, but problematic because it does not take account of forces, rampant in any complex, postmodern society, which are in excess of or subvert the preferred multicultural order. In other words, multiculturalism is based on the fantasy that the social challenge of togetherness-in-difference can be addressed by reducing it to an image of living-apart-together. Acknowledging this is one way to understand why multiculturalism has not been able to do away with racism: as a concept, it depends on the fixing of mutually exclusive identities, and therefore also on the reproduction of potentially antagonistic, dominant and subordinate others.

The chapters in Part II have been written in my struggle to come to terms with multiculturalism in Australia, one of the few countries in the world which has declared itself officially multicultural. In particular, as Australian multiculturalism lurched into a severe crisis after 1996, when anti-multiculturalist, populist-nationalist forces gained spectacular momentum, I was interested in tracking the troublesome place of Asia and Asians in this supposedly so tolerant and cosmopolitan, multicultural Australia. Chapter 5 provides a genealogy of this multiculturalism in crisis, which is a crisis of legitimacy associated closely with the way in which multiculturalist discourse, in the Australian context at least, tends to present itself as having overcome the language of race, and therefore that of rac*ism*. But the discourse of race cannot be so easily repressed, especially not as it has been one of the master discourses of the very (self-)constitution of the Australian nation as a nation of the West. One of the classic defining characteristics of the West has been its whiteness, so the very entry of increasing numbers of non-whites is all too easily read as a crisis in the making – a crisis of the very unmaking of the West. In this ideological context, as I argue in Chapter 6, 'Asians in Australia' is a logical contradiction in terms, as amply expressed by the constant fear of 'too many' Asians: a fear which reveals an Orientalist anxiety of being overtaken, in numbers as well as in status. Western fears of 'the yellow peril' are all too well known, of course, but there is a distinct Australian version of this fear, which has to do with the peculiarities of Australian history and geography. The Australian island-continent, the most recent European settler colony, was both very empty – in relative terms – and relatively accessible to the teeming masses of Asia, whose imagined 'invasion' from the North has always animated important strands of the Australian imagination. I characterize this imagination in Chapter 7 as 'racial/spatial anxiety'.

But times change, of course, and by the time I made my own entry as a migrant into Australia, in the early 1990s, fear of Asia was complexly supplemented by a desire for Asia. I describe the ambivalences of this fear/desire complex in Chapter 8, especially as it articulates itself in a gendering of Asia, a feminization of the Asian other. In this framework, being an Asian *woman* places one in a contradictory and ironic position of acceptance/submission, hence, 'the curse of the smile'! The harmonious multicultural society, then, is a myth – a utopian fantasy rather than social reality. Moreover, as a cultural fantasy, it creates power hierarchies of its own. An oft-expressed view is that multiculturalism – with its emphasis on the celebration of cultural diversity – advances and privileges the way of life of so-called cosmo-politan elites (who relish the consumption of diversity) at the expense of those who are both economically disadvantaged and culturally marginalized in an increasingly fluid, globalized and postmodern world, where no 'identity' is secure any longer. These considerations matter to the migrant or diasporic intellectual because she is, to all intents and purposes, a representative of those 'cosmopolitan elites'!

In Chapter 9, 'Identity blues', I reflect on my own relative empowerment as an economically secure, well-educated migrant, and its implications for the politics of identity. In a context where the cultural capital of the diasporic intellectual provides her with undeniable social advantage, it makes no longer sense simply to reproduce the serviceably self-victimizing image of Asian identity. Indeed, while racism has by no means disappeared and while many Asians remain severely marginalized, it is clear that being Asian in the West today no longer necessarily or only means being the object of discrimination or exclusion; after all, great numbers of people of Asian backgrounds in Australia and elsewhere have successfully gone on the path of upward mobility (which is the partial rationale of the designation of 'model minority' to Asian Americans).[7] There is no homogeneous Asianness which can comprise the experiences of all who might fit in that category in some reductionist, 'racial' terms. In other words, in today's multicultural societies race and class (as well as gender, religion, location, and so on) form complex and dynamic articulations which thoroughly disturb the neat and static categories of managerial multiculturalism. Togetherness-in-difference, then, cannot be reduced to some notion of living-apart-together, but must be understood in terms of the complicated entanglement of living hybridities.

Living hybridities

Both diaspora and multiculturalism are concepts ultimately limited by their implied boundedness. While each ostensibly points to a transgression of particular boundaries, a going beyond, each also ultimately produces a closure. In the case of diaspora, there is a transgression of the boundaries of the nation–state on behalf of a globally dispersed 'people', for example, 'the Chinese', but paradoxically this transgression can only be achieved through the drawing of a boundary around the diaspora, 'the Chinese people' themselves. In the case of multiculturalism, it is the ideal of national homogeneity – in racial/cultural terms – which is being transgressed in favour of an idea of cultural diversity, but more often than not multiculturalism is understood to maintain the boundaries between the diverse cultures it encompasses, on the one hand, and the overall boundary circumscribing the nation–state as a whole, on the other. That is why the Australian government, for example, is so at pains to sing the praises not just of multiculturalism, which on its own is feared to have fragmenting, centrifugal effects, but of *Australian* multiculturalism, which affirms the ultimate importance, despite the diversity within, of overall national cohesion (*A New Agenda* 1999). In this sense, multiculturalism is nothing more and nothing less than a more complex form of nationalism, aimed at securing national boundaries in an increasingly borderless world.

Hybridity is a concept which confronts and problematizes all these boundaries, although it does not erase them. As a concept, hybridity belongs to the space of the frontier, the border, the contact zone. As such, hybridity always implies a blurring or at least a problematizing of boundaries, and as a result, an unsettling of identities. This unsettling of identity is the focus of Part III. In Chapter 10, 'Local/global negotiations', the very notions of crossroads and borderlands – popular within cultural studies – are critically examined in the context of our desire to be able to communicate globally, cross-culturally, across all disciplinary boundaries. It turns out, of course, that such borders are not easily crossed or transgressed, on the contrary. Precisely our encounters at the border – where self and other, the local and the global, Asia and the West meet – make us realize how riven with potential miscommunication and intercultural conflict those encounters can be. This tells us that hybridity, the very condition of in-betweenness, can never be a question of simple shaking hands, of happy, harmonious merger and fusion. Hybridity is not the solution, but alerts us to the incommensurability of differences, their ultimately irreducible resistance to complete dissolution. In other words, hybridity is a heuristic device for analysing complicated entanglement. I illuminate an instance of this complicated entanglement, which, I would argue, is how we should conceive the condition of togetherness-in-difference, in Chapter 11, 'I'm a feminist, but . . .'. Encapsulated here is the very paradox of hybridity: any identity can only be a temporary, partial closure, for there is always a 'but' nagging behind it, upsetting and interfering with the very construction of that identity. This chapter takes as its bone of contention one of the West's most important and influential recent political movements: feminism. Western feminism's desire to have a 'politically correct' politics of difference through a strategy of inclusion will always be subverted, at least partially, by the perspective of the included other, who, like the diasporic intellectual, can never be completely assimilated nor fully recognized: she will always be 'inside' and 'outside' at the same time. In this sense, the world of feminism can stand for the West as a whole, as it is being infiltrated by increasing numbers of 'others', including 'Asians'. One consequence of this, as we all know, is the slow but undeniable hybridization and creolization of 'Western culture' – especially the culture of the metropolis, the global city, which Iris Marion Young (1990: 318) forcefully describes as 'the "being-together" of strangers'. This does not mean that there are no longer any differences and hierarchies, but that they are no longer easily separated out. Hybridity, as I conclude in the last chapter, best describes this world, in which the complicated entanglement of togetherness in difference has become a 'normal' state of affairs.

In such a thoroughly postmodern context, what it means to be 'Asian' can no longer be defined or described in clear-cut, unambiguous terms despite the increased salience of the very term 'Asian' as a self-conscious marker of identity in the wake of identity politics. Speaking about Asians in the United States, author Elaine Kim (1993) suggests that while Asian American communities and cultures were shaped by legal exclusion and containment until quite recently, contemporary experiences are being shaped by intensified globalization. The contrast is huge:

> Yesterday's young Asian immigrant might have worked beside his parents on a pineapple plantation in Hawaii or in a fruit orchard on the Pacific Coast, segregated from the mainstream of American life. Today's Asian immigrant teenager might have only Asian friends, but she probably deals daily with a not necessarily anguishing confusion of divergent influences, a collision of elements she needs to negotiate in her search to define herself.
> (Kim 1993: xx–xi)

Arguably such hybrid multiplicity increasingly characterizes the lives of 'Asians' everywhere, in Asia and in the West: we are all, symbolically speaking, situated 'between Asia and the West'.

Part I

BEYOND ASIA
Deconstructing Diaspora

1

ON NOT SPEAKING CHINESE
Diasporic identifications and
postmodern ethnicity

No ancestors, no identity.

(Chinese saying)

The world is what it is; men [*sic*] who are nothing, who allow
themselves to become nothing, have no place in it.

(V.S. Naipaul, *A Bend in the River*, 1979)

The first time I went to China, I went for one day only. I crossed the border by
speedboat from Hong Kong, where I had booked for a daytrip to Shenszhen and
Guangzhou – the so-called New Economic Zone – with a local tourist company.
'This is the most well-off part of China. Further north and inland it is much
worse,' the arrogant Hong Kong guide warned. It was, of course, the arrogance
of advanced capitalism. Our group of twelve consisted mainly of white, Western
tourists – and me. I didn't have the courage to go on my own since I don't speak
any Chinese, not even one of the dialects. But I had to go, I had no choice. It was
(like) an imposed pilgrimage.

'China', of course, usually refers to the People's Republic of China, or more
generically, 'mainland China'. This China continues to speak to the world's
imagination – for its sheer vastness, its huge population, its relative inaccessibility,
its fascinating history and culture, its idiosyncratic embrace of communism, all
of which amounts to its awesome difference. This China also irritates, precisely
because its stubborn difference cannot be disregarded, if only because the forces
of transnational capitalism are only too keen to finally exploit this enormous market
of more than a billion people. Arguably this was one of the more cynical reasons
for the moral high ground from which the West displayed its outrage at the
crushing of the students' protests at Tiananmen Square in June 1989, discourses
of democracy and human rights notwithstanding.

My one-day visit occurred nine months after those dramatic events in Beijing.
At the border we were joined by a new guide, a 27-year-old woman from Beijing,
Lan-lan, who spoke English in a way that revealed a 'typically Chinese' commitment
to learn: eager, diligent, studious. It was clear that English is her entry to the world

at large (that is, the world outside China), just as being a tourist guide means access to communication and exchange with foreigners. It shouldn't come as a surprise, therefore, as Lan-lan told us, that it is very difficult for young Chinese people to become tourist guides (they must pass a huge number of exams and other selection procedures): after all, these guides are the ones given the responsibility of presenting and explaining China to foreign visitors. International tourism emphasizes and reinforces the porousness of borders and is thus potentially dangerous for a closed society like China which nevertheless, paradoxically, needs and promotes tourism as an important economic resource in the age of globalization.

How Lan-lan presented and explained China to us, however, was undoubtedly not meant for the ears of government officials. Obviously aware that we all had the political events of the previous year in mind, she spontaneously started to intersperse the usual touristic information with criticism of the current communist government. 'The people *know* what happened last year at Tiananmen Square,' she said as if to reassure us, 'and they don't approve. They are behind the students. They want more freedom and democracy. We don't talk about this in public, but we do among friends.' She told us these things so insistently, apparently convinced that it was what we *wanted* to hear. In other words, in her own way she did what she was officially supposed to do: serving up what she deemed to be the most favourable image of China to significant others – that is, Westerners.[1]

But at the same time it was clear that she spoke *as a Chinese*. She would typically begin her sentences with 'We Chinese . . .' or 'Here in China we . . .' Despite her political criticism, then, her identification with China and Chineseness was by no means in doubt. On the contrary, voicing criticism of the system through a discourse that she knew would appeal to Western interlocutors, seemed only to strengthen her sense of Chinese identity. It was almost painful for me to see how Lan-lan's attempt to promote 'China' could only be accomplished by surrendering to the rhetorical perspective of the Western other. It was not the content of the criticism she expounded that I was concerned about. What upset me was the way in which it seemed necessary for Lan-lan to take up a *defensive* position, a position in need of constant self-explanation, in relation to a West that can luxuriate in its own taken-for-granted superiority. My pain stemmed from my ambivalence: I refused to be lumped together with the (other) Westerners, but I couldn't fully identify with Lan-lan either.

We were served a lunch in a huge, rather expensive-looking restaurant, complete with fake Chinese temple and a pond with lotus flowers in the garden, undoubtedly designed with pleasing international visitors in mind, but paradoxically only preposterous in its stereotypicality. All twelve of us, members of the tourist group, were seated around a typically Chinese round table. Lan-lan did not join us, and I think I know why. The food we were served was obviously the kind of Chinese food that was adapted to European taste: familiar, rather bland dishes (except for the delicious crispy duck skin), not the 'authentic' Cantonese delicacies I was subconsciously looking forward to now that I was in China. (Wrong assumption, of course: you have to be in rich, decadent, colonial capitalist Hong Kong for that, so I found out. These were the last years before the impending 'handover' in 1997.) And we did not get bowl and chopsticks, but a plate with spoon and fork. I was shocked, even though my chopstick competence is not very great. An instant sense of alienation took hold of me. Part of me wanted to leave immediately, wanted to scream out loud that I didn't belong to the group I was with, but another part of me felt compelled to take Lan-lan's place as tourist guide while she was not with us, to explain, as best as I could, to my fellow tourists what the food was all about. I realized how mistaken I was to assume, since there seems to be a Chinese restaurant in virtually every corner of the world, that 'everybody knows Chinese food'. For my table companions the unfamiliarity of the experience prevailed, the anxious excitement of trying out something new (although they predictably found the duck skin 'too greasy', of course, the kind of complaint about Chinese food that I have heard so often from Europeans). Their pleasure in undertaking this one day of 'China' was the pleasure of the exotic.

But it was my first time in China too, and while I did not quite have the freedom to see this country as exotic because I have always had to see it as somehow *my* country, even if only in my imagination, I repeatedly found myself looking at this minute piece of 'China' through the tourists' eyes: reacting with a mixture of shame and disgust at the 'thirdworldiness' of what we saw, and with amazement and humane wonder at the peculiarities of Chinese resilience that we encountered. I felt captured in-between: I felt like wanting to protect China from too harsh judgements which I imagined my fellow travellers would pass on it, but at the same time I felt a rather irrational anger towards China itself – at its 'backwardness', its unworldliness, the seemingly naïve way in which it tried to woo Western tourists. I said goodbye to Lan-lan and was hoping that she would say something personal to me, an acknowledgement of affinity of some sort, but she didn't.

Identity politics

I am recounting this story for a number of reasons. First of all, it is my way of apologizing to you that this text you are reading is written in English, not in Chinese. Perhaps the very fact that I feel like apologizing is interesting in itself. Throughout my life, I have been implicitly or explicitly categorized, willy-nilly, as an 'overseas Chinese' (*hua qiao*). I look Chinese. Why, then, don't I speak Chinese? I have had to explain this embarrassment countless times, so I might just as well do it here too, even though I might run the risk, in being 'autobiographical', of coming over as self-indulgent or narcissistic, of resorting to personal experience as a privileged source of authority, uncontrollable and therefore unamendable to others. However, let me just use this occasion to shelter myself under the authority of Stuart Hall (1992: 277): 'Autobiography is usually thought of as seizing the authority of authenticity. But in order not to be authoritative, I've got to speak autobiographically.' If, as Janet Gunn (1982: 8) has put it, autobiography is not conceived as 'the private act of a self writing' but as 'the cultural act of a self reading', then what is at stake in autobiographical discourse is not a question of the subject's authentic 'me', but one of the subject's location in a world through an active interpretation of experiences that one calls one's own in particular, 'worldly' contexts, that is to say, a reflexive positioning of oneself in history and culture. In this respect, I would like to consider autobiography as a more or less deliberate, rhetorical construction of a 'self' for public, not private purposes: the displayed self is a strategically fabricated performance, one which stages a *useful* identity, an identity which can be put to work. It is the quality of that usefulness which determines the politics of autobiographical discourse. In other words, what is the identity being put forward *for*?

So I am aware that in speaking about how it is that I don't speak Chinese, while still for the occasion identifying with being, and presenting myself as, an 'Overseas Chinese', I am committing a political act. I care to say, however, that it is not my intention to just carve out a new niche in what Elspeth Probyn (1992: 502) somewhat ironically calls 'the star-coded politics of identity', although I should confess that there is considerable, almost malicious pleasure in the flaunting of my own 'difference' for critical intellectual purposes. But I hope to get away with this self-empowering indulgence, this exploitation of my ethnic privilege, by moving beyond the particulars of my mundane individual existence. Stuart Hall (1990: 236–7) has proposed a theorization of identity as 'a form of representation which is able to constitute us as new kinds of subjects, and thereby enable us to discover places from which to speak'. To put it differently, the politics of self-(re)presentation as Hall sees it resides not in the establishment of an identity *per se*, full fledged and definitive, but in its use as a strategy to open up avenues for new speaking trajectories, the articulation of new lines of theorizing. Thus, what I hope to substantiate in staging my 'Chineseness' here – or better, my (troubled) relationship to Chineseness – is precisely the notion of *precariousness* of identity which has preoccupied cultural studies for some time now. As Gayatri Chakravorty Spivak (1990: 60) has noted, the practice of 'speaking as' (e.g. as a woman, an Indian, a Chinese) always involves a distancing from oneself, as one's subjectivity is never fully steeped in the modality of the speaking position one inhabits at any one moment. My autobiographic tales of Chineseness are meant to illuminate the very *difficulty* of constructing a position from which I can speak *as* an (Overseas) Chinese, and therefore the *indeterminacy* of Chineseness as a signifier for identity.

At the same time, however, I want to mobilize the autobiographic – i.e. the narrating of life as lived, thereby rescuing notions of 'experience' and 'emotion' for cultural theorizing[2] – in order to critique the formalist, post-structuralist tendency to overgeneralize the global currency of so-called nomadic, fragmented and deterritorialized subjectivity. Such, what James Clifford (1992) has dubbed 'nomadology', only serves to decontextualize and flatten out 'difference', as if 'we' were all in fundamentally similar ways always-already travellers in the same postmodern universe, the only difference residing in the different itineraries we undertake. Epistemologically, such a gross universalization of the metaphor of 'travel' runs the danger of reifying, at a conveniently abstract level, the infinite and permanent flux in subject formation, thereby privileging an abstract, depoliticized, and internally undifferentiated notion of 'difference' (Mani 1992). Against this tendency, which paradoxically only leads to a complacent *in*difference toward real differences, I would like to stress the importance for cultural studies to keep paying attention to the particular historical conditions and the specific trajectories through which actual social subjects become incommensurably different *and* similar. That is to say, in the midst of the postmodern flux of nomadic subjectivities we need to recognize the continuing and continuous operation of 'fixing' performed by the categories of race and ethnicity, as well as class, gender, geography, etc. on the formation of 'identity', although it is never possible, as determinist theories would have it, to decide ahead of time how such markers of difference will inscribe their salience and effectivity in the course of concrete histories, in the context of specific social, cultural and political conjunctures. To be more specific, it is some of the peculiarities of the operative dynamics of 'Chineseness' as a racial and ethnic category which I would like to highlight here. What I would like to propose is that Chineseness is a category whose meanings are not fixed and pregiven, but constantly renegotiated and rearticulated, both inside and outside China.

But this brings me also to the *limits* of the polysemy of Chineseness. These limits are contained in the idea of diaspora, the condition of a 'people' dispersed throughout the world, by force or by choice. Diasporas are transnational, spatially and temporally sprawling sociocultural formations of people, creating imagined communities whose blurred and fluctuating boundaries are sustained by real and/or symbolic ties to some original 'homeland'. As the editors of *Public Culture* have put it, 'diasporas always leave a trail of collective memory about another place and time and create new maps of desire and of attachment' (1989: 1). It is the myth of the (lost or idealized) homeland, the object of both collective memory and of desire and attachment, which is constitutive to diasporas, and which ultimately confines and constrains the nomadism of the diasporic subject. In the rest of this chapter, I will describe some moments of how this pressure toward diasporic identification with the mythic homeland took place in my own life. A curious example occurred to me when I first travelled to Taiwan – a country with which I do not have any biographical or familial connection. However, as a result of the Chinese *ius sanguinis* which is still in force in Taiwan, I found myself being automatically positioned, rather absurdly, as a potential national citizen of this country, that is to say, as a Chinese national subject.

In the end, what I hope to unravel is some of the possibilities and problems of the cultural politics of diaspora. But this, too, cannot be done in general terms: not only is the situation different for different diasporas (Jewish, African, Indian, Chinese, and so on), there are also multiple differences within each diasporic group. For the moment, therefore, I can only speak from my own perspective; in the chapters that follow I will elaborate in more general terms on the complexities of Chinese diaspora politics.

Colonial entanglements

colonial Indonesia into a middle-class, *peranakan* Chinese family.
re people of Chinese descent who are born and bred in South-
trast to the *totok* Chinese, who arrived from China much later
d much closer personal and cultural ties with the ancestral
atus of the *peranakans* as 'Chinese' has always been somewhat
...oiguous. Having settled as traders and craftsmen in South-East Asia long
before the Europeans did – specifically the Dutch in the case of the Indonesian
archipelago – they tended to have lost many of the cultural features usually
attributed to the Chinese, including everyday practices related to food, dress and
language. Most *peranakans* lost their command over the Chinese language a long
time ago and actually spoke their own brand of Malay, a sign of their intensive
mixing, at least partially, with the locals. This orientation toward the newly adopted
place of residence was partly induced by their exclusion from the homeland by an
Imperial Decree of China, dating from the early eighteenth century, which formally
prohibited Chinese from leaving and re-entering China: after 1726 Chinese subjects
who settled abroad would face the death penalty if they returned (FitzGerald
1975: 5; Suryadinata 1975: 86). This policy only changed with the weakening of
the Qing dynasty at the end of the nineteenth century, which prompted a mass
emigration from China, and signalled the arrival of the *totoks* in Indonesia.

However, so the history books tell me, even among the *peranakans* a sense
of separateness prevailed throughout the centuries. A sense of 'ethnic naturalism'
seems to have been at work here, for which I have not found a satisfactory explanation so far: why is it that these early Chinese traders and merchants still maintained
their sense of Chineseness? This is something that the history books do *not* tell me.
But it does seem clear that the construction of the *peranakan* Chinese as a separate
ethnic group was reinforced considerably by the divide-and-rule policies of Dutch
colonialism. Dubbed 'foreign Orientals' by the Dutch colonizers, Chinese people
in Indonesia – both *peranakans* and *totoks* – were subject to forms of surveillance
and control which set them apart from both the Europeans and Eurasians in
the colony, on the one hand, and from the indigenous locals, on the other. For
example, the Dutch enforced increasingly strict pass and zoning systems on the
Chinese in the last decades of the nineteenth century, requiring them to apply for
visas whenever they wanted to travel outside their neighbourhoods. At the same
time, those neighbourhoods could only be established in strict districts, separate
residential areas for Chinese (Williams 1960: 27–33).[5] Arguably, the widespread
resentment caused by such policies of apartheid accounted for the initial success of
the pan-Chinese nationalist movement which emerged in the early decades of the
twentieth century. In this period diverse and dispersed Chinese groups (Hokkiens,
Hakkas, Cantonese, as well as ethnic Chinese from different class and religious
backgrounds) were mobilized to transform their self-consciousness into one of
membership in the greater 'imagined community' of a unified pan-Chinese nation
– a politicization which was also a response to the imperialist assault on China, the

homeland, in the late 1800s. According to Lea Williams (1960), Overseas Chinese Nationalism was the only possible way for Chinese at that time to better their collective conditions as a minority population in the Netherlands Indies.[6] However, animosities and cultural differences continued to divide *totoks* and *peranakans*. The *peranakans* only partly responded to calls for their resinification, predominantly in the form of education in Chinese language, values and customs. This made the *totoks* regard the *peranakan* Chinese as 'unpatriotic' and their behaviour as 'non-Chinese' (Suryadinata 1975: 94).

Peranakan identity then is a thoroughly hybrid identity. In the period before World War Two Chinese Malay (*bahasa Melayu Tionghoa*) was Malay in its basic structure, but Hokkien and Dutch terms were extensively used. My grandmother was sent to a Dutch-Chinese school in Batavia, but her diary, while mainly written in Dutch, is interspersed with Malay words and Chinese characters I can't read. In the late 1920s, encouraged by the Chinese nationalist mood of the day, my grandfather decided to go 'back' to the homeland and set up shop there, only to realize that the mainland Chinese no longer saw him as 'one of them'. Upon his return to Indonesia, he sent his daughters (my mother and her sister) to study in the Netherlands. At the same time other *peranakans* were of the opinion that 'it was in the interests of *peranakan* Chinese to side with Indonesians rather than with the Dutch' (Suryadinata 1975: 57).[7] It is not uncommon for observers to describe the *peranakan* Chinese situation in the pre-World War Two period as one caught 'between three worlds'. Some more wealthy *peranakan* families invested in the uncertain future by sending one child to a Dutch school, another to a Chinese one, and a third to a Malay school (Blussé 1989: 172).

However, all this changed when Dutch colonialism was finally defeated after World War Two. Those who were previously the ruled in the power structure, the indigenous Indonesians, were now the rulers. Under these new circumstances, most *peranakans*, including my parents, chose to become Indonesian citizens, although they remained ethnic Chinese. But it was a Chineseness which for political reasons was not allowed to be cultivated. Indonesian nationalism has always tended to define the Indonesian nation as comprising only the indigenous peoples of the archipelago, excluding the Chinese – and other 'non-natives' such as the Arabs – who were considered an 'alien minority'. To this day, as I will discuss in greater detail in Chapter 3, the pressure on the Chinese minority to assimilate, to erase as many traces of Chineseness as possible, has been very strong in Indonesia. For example, in the late 1960s my uncle, who had chosen to stay and live in Indonesia, Indonesianized his surname into Angka.

It would be too easy, however, to condemn such assimilation policies simply as the result of ordinary racism on the Indonesians' part. This is a difficult point as I am implicated in the politics of memory here. How can I know 'what happened' in the past except through the stories I hear and read? And the stories don't cohere: they are a mixture of stories of oppression and opportunism. I was told stories about discrimination, about how the Indonesians didn't like 'us' Chinese because 'we' were more well-off (and often by implication: because 'we' worked harder).

But I also heard stories about how the Chinese exploited the indigenous Indonesians: how, under the rule of the Dutch, the Chinese felt safe because the Dutch would protect them from the ire of the 'natives'. In retrospect, I am not interested in reconstructing or fabricating a 'truth' which would necessarily put the Chinese in an unambiguously favourable light – or in the position of victim (see Ang 2001). But nor am I interested in accusations such as the one made by a morally superior, self-declared anti-racist in the Netherlands a few years ago: 'Your parents were collaborators.' History, of course, is always ambiguous, always messy, and people remember – and therefore construct – the past in ways that reflect their present need for meaning. I am not exempt from this process. So, burdened with my intellectual capital, I resort to Benedict Anderson's (1991) explanation of the origins of Indonesian nationalism: it was by the separating out of the 'foreign Orientals' and the 'natives' in the colonial administration that a space was opened up for the latter, treated as lowest of the low by the Dutch, to develop a national consciousness which excluded the former.

My mother, who spent part of her youth in China (as a result of my grandfather's brief romance with the homeland) and speaks and writes Chinese fluently, carefully avoided passing this knowledge on to me. So I was cut off from this immense source of cultural capital; instead, I learned to express myself in *bahasa Indonesia*. Still, it was in my early youth in Indonesia that I was first yelled at, 'Why don't you go back to your own country?' – a remark all too familiar to members of immigrant minorities anywhere in the world. Trouble was, to my own best knowledge as a 10 year old Indonesia *was* my own country. In Sukarno's Indonesia (1945–65) all schoolchildren were heavily exposed to the discourses and rituals of Indonesian nationalism – as is the case in all newly independent nations – and during that time the singing of *Indonesia Merdeka* (the national anthem) did make me feel intensely and proudly Indonesian. Therefore, to be told, mostly by local kids, that I actually didn't belong there but in a faraway, abstract, and somewhat frightening place called China, was terribly confusing, disturbing, and utterly unacceptable. I silently rebelled, I didn't *want* to be Chinese. To be sure, this is the kind of denial which is the inner drive underpinning the urge toward assimilation. That is to say, cultural assimilation is not only and not always an official policy forced and imposed by host countries upon their non-native minorities; there is also among many members of minority populations themselves a certain *desire* to assimilate, a longing for fitting in rather than standing out, even though this desire is often at the same time contradicted by an incapability or refusal to adjust and adapt.

Chineseness then, at that time, to me was an imposed identity, one that I desperately wanted to get rid of. It is therefore rather ironic that it was precisely our Chinese ethnicity which made my parents decide to leave Indonesia for the Netherlands in 1966, as a result of the rising ethnic tensions in the country. This experience in itself then was a sign of the inescapability of my notional Chineseness, inscribed as it was on the very surface of my body, much like what Frantz Fanon (1970) has called the 'corporeal malediction' of the fact of his blackness. The 'corporeal malediction' of Chineseness, of course, relates to the 'fact of yellowness', identifiable among others by those famous 'slanted eyes'. During the Los Angeles uprising in 1992 my father's brother, who lived there, felt threatened because, as he said, he could be mistaken for a Korean – a dangerous quandary because the Koreans were the target of African-American anger and violence in that racial conflict. But the odd trajectories of labelling can also have some surprising twist and turns. Thus, when I was in Hong Kong my (Hong Kong Chinese) host assured me that people wouldn't expect me to be able to speak Chinese because I would surely be mistaken for a Filipina. That is to say, racial categories obviously do not exist outside particular social and cultural contexts, but are thoroughly framed by and within them.

Anyway, in the new country, the former colonizer's country, a new cycle of forced and voluntary assimilation started all over again. My cherished Indonesian identity got lost in translation, as it were, as I started a life in a new language (Hoffman 1989). In the Netherlands I quickly learned to speak Dutch, went to a Dutch school and a Dutch university, and for more than two decades long underwent a thorough process of 'Dutchification'. However, the artificiality of national identity – and therefore the relativeness of any sense of historical truth – was brought home to me forever when my Dutch history book taught me that Indonesia became independent in 1949. In Indonesia I had always been led to commemorate 17 August 1945 as Independence Day. The disparity was political: Sukarno *declared* Indonesia's independence in 1945, but the Dutch only *recognized* it in 1949, after four years of bloody war. But it is not the nuances of the facts that matter; what is significant is the way in which nations choose to construct their collective memories, how they narrate themselves into pride and glory (Bhabha 1990). The collision of the two versions of history in my educational experience may have paved the way for my permanent suspicion of any self-confident and self-evident 'truth' in my later intellectual life. As Salman Rushdie (1991: 12) has remarked, those who have experienced cultural displacement are *forced* to accept the provisional nature of all truths, all certainties.

At the level of everyday experience, the 'fact' of my Chineseness confronted me only occasionally in the Netherlands, for example, when passing 10-year-old red-haired boys triumphantly would shout behind my back, while holding the outer ends of their eyes upwards with their forefingers: 'Ching Chong China China', or when, on holiday in Spain or Italy or Poland, people would not believe that I was 'Dutch'. The typical conversation would run like this, as many non-whites in Europe would be able to testify:

> 'Where are you from?'
> 'From Holland.'
> 'No, where are you *really* from?'

To this usually insistent, repetitive and annoying inquiry into origins, my standard story has become, 'I was born in Indonesia but my ancestors were from China' – a shorthand (re)presentation of self for convenience's sake. Such incidents were disturbing signals for the impossibility of complete integration (or perhaps 'naturalization' is a better term), no matter how much I (pragmatically) strived for it. To put it in another way, it is the very question 'where are you from?' – a question so easily thrown up as the bottom line of cultural identity (thereby equating cultural identity with national identity) – which is a problem for people like me, as it lacks transparency. Of course, this is a problem shared by millions of people throughout the world today, where migration has become an increasingly common phenomenon. The experience of migration brings with it a shift in perspective: to paraphrase Paul Gilroy (1990/1), for the migrant it is no longer 'where you're from', but 'where you're at' which forms the point of anchorage. However, so long as the question 'where you're from' prevails over 'where you're at' in dominant culture, the compulsion to explain, the inevitable positioning of yourself as deviant *vis-à-vis* the normal, remains. In other words, the relation between 'where you're from' and 'where you're at' is a deeply problematic one. To be sure, it is this very problem which is constitutive to the idea of diaspora, and for which the idea of diaspora attempts to be a solution. As William Safran (1991: 87) put it, 'diaspora consciousness is an intellectualization of an existential condition', an existential condition that becomes understood and reconciled through the myth of a homeland from which one is removed but to which one actually belongs. But I would argue that this solution, at least at the cultural level, is by no means sufficient or unambiguously effective: in fact, the diasporic imagination itself creates and articulates a number of new problems.

Take, for example, the position of ethnic minorities in Western advanced capitalist societies today. In Western Europe, including the Netherlands, issues of race and ethnicity, now so familiar and almost obligatory to us working within cultural studies, only became a matter of public debate and concern in the late 1970s or so. Discourses of ethnicity started to proliferate as minority communities began to assert themselves in their stated desire to 'maintain their cultural identity'. However, such (self-)ethnicization, which is in itself a confirmation of minority status in white, Western culture, can paradoxically serve as an alibi for what Rey Chow (1991: xvi) has called 'prescribed "otherness"'. Thus, 'Chinese' identity becomes confined to essentialist and absolute notions of 'Chineseness', the source of which can only originate from 'China', to which the ethnicized 'Chinese' subject must adhere to acquire the stamp of 'authenticity'. So it was one day that a self-assured, Dutch, white, middle-class, Marxist leftist, asked me, 'Do you speak Chinese?' I said no. 'What a fake Chinese you are!', was his only mildly kidding response, thereby unwittingly but aggressively adopting the disdainful position of judge to sift 'real' from 'fake' Chinese. In other words, in being defined and categorized diasporically, I was found wanting.

'Not speaking Chinese', therefore, has become a personal political issue to me, an existential condition which goes beyond the particularities of an arbitrary personal history. It is a condition that has been hegemonically constructed as a lack, a sign of loss of authenticity. This, then, is the reason why I felt compelled to apologize that I have written this text in English – the global *lingua franca*

30

which is one of the clearest expressions of the pervasiveness of Western hegemony. Yet it is precisely this urge to apologize which I would now like to question and counter as well. In order to do this, however, I need to come to terms with my relationship to 'Chineseness', the complexities and contradictions of which were dramatized in the story about my one-day visit to China and my encounter with Lan-lan. It was, of course, a drama born out precisely of a diaspora problematic.

Haunted by Chineseness

If the 'Indonesian Chinese' can be described as a distinctive 'people' – one which, as I have sketched above, has its historical birth in colonial Dutch East Indies – then they in turn have become diasporized, especially after the military coup in 1965. While my parents, among many thousands, chose the relative wealth and comfort of a life in the Netherlands ('for the sake of the education of the children'), I was recently informed by an aunt that I have some distant relatives in Brazil, where some two hundred Indonesian Chinese families live in São Paulo. There is also a large Indonesian Chinese community in Hong Kong, many of whom ended up there after a brief 'return' to 'the homeland', Mao's China, where they found, just like my grandfather earlier in the century, that their very 'Chineseness' was cast in doubt: the mainlanders did not consider them Chinese at all (Godley and Coppel 1990). Nevertheless, this Chineseness has never ceased to be a major identity preoccupation in this unlikely diaspora.

The small *peranakan* Chinese-Indonesian community in the Netherlands, while generally well integrated in Dutch society, has re-ethnicized itself tremendously in the last decade or so. Interestingly, it is Chineseness, not Indonesianness which forms the primary focal point of ethnic identitification, especially among the older generation – that of my parents. There are now *peranakan* Chinese associations, sports and entertainment clubs, discussion evenings; lessons in Chinese language and culture, and special trips to China are being organized. Since the 1980s, my parents have built up a large video collection of films and documentaries about China and China-related subjects, all taped from television – and it is amazing how often European public television features programmes about China! Whenever I visit them these days (which is not often as I now live in Australia), I am assured of a new dose of audiovisual education in Chineseness, as it were, as we watch films together about the Yellow River, the Silk Route, on Taoism, Chinese village life, the Great Wall, the Chinese Red Army, the history of Chinese communism, the Tiananmen Square massacre, or whatever is available, or otherwise any Chinese feature film that was recently televised (the Fifth Generation films of Zhang Yimou and others loom large here), and so on and so on. So my familiarization with the imputed 'homeland', and therefore my emotional subjection to the homeland myth, has been effected rather informally, through intimate and special family rituals and practices and through media and popular culture. In other words, I felt I already 'knew' China, albeit a mythic China, a fetishized China, when I went there for that one-day visit.

But this symbolic orientation toward the 'homeland' tends to complicate the problem of identity, as 'China' is presented as the cultural/geographical core in relation to which the westernized overseas Chinese is forced to take up a humble position, even a position of shame and inadequacy over her own 'impurity'. In this situation the overseas Chinese is in a no-win situation: she is either 'too Chinese' or 'not Chinese enough'. As Chow (1991: 28/9) has observed, 'Chinese from the mainland are [often felt to be] more "authentic" than those who are from, say, Taiwan or Hong Kong, because the latter have been "Westernized".' But the problem is exacerbated for more remote members of the Chinese diaspora, say, for the Indonesian *peranakan* Chinese or for second-generation Chinese Americans, whose 'Chineseness' is even more diluted and impure.

Of course, this double-bind problem is not unique to migrants of Chinese descent. In a sense, it enters into the experience of all diasporic peoples living in the West. What is particular to the Chinese diaspora, however, is the extraordinarily strong originary pull of the 'homeland' as a result of the prominent place of 'China' in the Western imagination. The West's fascination with China as a great, 'other' civilization began with Marco Polo and remains to this day (see e.g. MacKerras 1991). In the Western imagination China cannot be an ordinary country, as a consequence, everything happening in that country is invested with more than 'normal' significance, as testified by the intense and extreme dramatization of events such as the 'Tiananmen massacre' and the 'Hong Kong handover' in the Western media (Chow 1993; 1998a). There is, in other words, an excess of meaningfulness accorded to 'China'; 'China' has often been useful for Western thinkers as a symbol, negative or positive, for that which the West was not. As Zhang Longxi (1988: 127) has noted, even Jacques Derrida, the great debunker of binary oppositions, was seduced into treating the non-phonetic character of the Chinese language as 'testimony of a powerful movement of civilization developing outside of all logocentrism', that is, as the sign of a culture totally different from what he conceives as Western culture. Worse still, this powerful othering is mirrored by an equally strong and persistent tendency within Chinese culture itself to consider itself as central to the world, what Song Xianlin and Gary Sigley (2000) call China's 'Middle Kingdom mentality', exemplified by the age-old Chinese habit to designate all non-Chinese as 'barbarians', 'foreign devils' or 'ghosts'. This is a form of self-Orientalization expressed in the famous inward-looking aloofness of Chinese culture criticized, within China itself, in the controversial television series *River Elegy*, and which I also sensed in Lan-lan's ultimate insistence, through a para-doxical, assertive defensiveness in relation to the West, on China's pure otherness.

In the interlocking of this mutual discursive exclusionism overseas Chinese people often find themselves inevitably entangled in China's elevated status as privileged Other to the West, depriving them of an autonomous space to determine their own trajectories for constructing cultural identity. I recognize Rey Chow's (1991) observation that there is, among many Chinese people, an 'obsession with China'. What connects the diaspora with the 'homeland' is ultimately an emotional, almost visceral attachment. The relationship is, to use Amitav Ghosh's (1989) term, an *epic* one. It is precisely this epic relationship which invests the homeland myth with its power: it is this epic relationship to 'China', for example, which made millions of overseas Chinese all over the world feel so inescapably and 'irrationally' sick and nauseous when the tanks crushed the students' movement at Tiananmen Square on 4 June 1989, as if they felt the humiliation on their own bodies, despite the fact that many, if not most of them would never think of actually 'returning' to this distant 'motherland'. The desires, fantasies and sentimentalities that go into this 'obsession with China', says Chow (1991: 25), should be seen at least in part as 'a *response* to the solicitous calls, dispersed internationally in multiple ways, to such a [collective, "Chinese"] identity'. In other words, the subjective processes of diasporic ethnic identification are often externally instigated, articulating and confirming a position of subordination in relation to Western hegemony. To be sure, I think that it is this structure of dominance and subjection which I internalized when I found myself caught between my Western co-tourists and Lan-lan – an *impossible* position, a position with no means of its own to assert itself.

The contradictions and complexities in subject positioning that I have tried to explicate are neatly summed up in the memoirs of Ruth Ho, a Malaysian *peranakan* Chinese woman who grew up in Malacca before World War Two. In the chapter of her book, called 'On learning Chinese', she complains about the compulsory lessons in Chinese that she had to undergo as a young girl:

> Mother always felt exceedingly guilty about our language deficiency and tried to make us study Chinese, that is Mandarin, the national dialect. . . . [But] I suppose that when I was young there was no motivation to study Chinese. . . .
>
> 'But China was once the greatest and most cultured nation in the world! Weren't you proud to be Chinese? Wasn't that reason enough to study Chinese?' Many people felt this way but unfortunately we just didn't feel very Chinese! Today we are described by one English writer as belonging to 'the sad band of English-educated who cannot speak their own language'. This seems rather unfair to me. Must we know the language of our forefathers when we have lived in another country (Malaysia) for many years? Are the descendants of German, Norwegian and Swedish emigrants to the USA, for instance, expected to know German or Norwegian or Swedish? Are the descendants of Italian and Greek emigrants to Australia expected to study Italian and Greek? Of course not, and yet overseas Chinese are always expected to know Chinese or else they are despised not only by their fellow Chinese but also by non-Chinese! Perhaps this is due to the great esteem with which Chinese history, language and culture are universally regarded. But the European emigrants to the USA and Australia also have a not insignificant history, language and culture, and they are not criticized when they become English speaking.
>
> (Ho 1975: 97–99)

33

Ho's comparison with the European immigrants in the USA and Australia is well taken. Perhaps the double standard she refers to is an expression of a desire to keep Western culture white? Wouldn't this explain why an English-speaking Chinese is still seen, from a Western perspective, as so much more 'unnatural' than an English-speaking Norwegian or Italian? From such a perspective, the idea of diaspora serves as a ploy to keep non-white, non-Western elements from fully entering and therefore contaminating the centre of white, Western culture. Ho's heartfelt indignation then should be read as a protest against exclusion through an imposed diasporic identification in the name of a fetishized and overly idealized 'China'. It exemplifies the fact that when the question of 'where you're from' threatens to overwhelm the reality of 'where you're at', the idea of diaspora becomes a dispowering rather than an empowering one, a hindrance to 'identity' rather than an enabling principle.

Hybridity and postmodern ethnicity

I am not saying here that diasporic identifications are intrinsically oppressive, on the contrary. It is clear that many members of ethnic minorities derive a sense of joy and dignity, as well as a sense of (vicarious) belonging from their identification with a 'homeland' which is elsewhere. But this very identification with an imagined 'where you're from' is also often a sign of, and surrender to, a condition of actual marginalization in the place 'where you're at'. Khachig Tölölyan (1991) is right to define diasporas as transnational formations which interrogate the privileged homogeneity of the nation–state. At the same time, however, the very fact that ethnic minorities within nation–states are defining themselves increasingly in diasporic terms, as Tölölyan indicates, raises some troubling questions about the state of intercultural relations in the world today. The rise of militant, separatist neo-nationalisms in Eastern Europe and elsewhere in the world signals an intensification of the appeal of ethnic absolutism and exclusionism which underpin the homeland myth, and which is based on the fantasy of a complete juncture of 'where you're from' and 'where you're at' so that, ideally, all diasporized peoples should return 'home'.[8]

It is not only that such a fantasy is at odds with the forces of increasing transnationalization and 'globalization' in world economy, politics and communications.[9] At a more fundamental, cultural level, the fantasmatic vision of a new world *order* consisting of hundreds of self-contained, self-identical nations – which is the ultimate dream of the principle of nationalist universalism – strikes me as a rather disturbing duplication of the divide-and-rule politics deployed by the colonial powers to ascertain control and mastery over the subjected. It is against such visions that the idea of diaspora can play a critical cultural role.

Since diasporas are fundamentally and inevitably transnational in their scope, always linking the local and the global, the here and the there, past and present, they have the potential to unsettle static, essentialist and totalitarian conceptions of 'national culture' or 'national identity' which are firmly rooted in geography and history. But in order to seize on that potential, diasporas should make *the most of* their 'complex and flexible positioning . . . between host countries and homelands' (Safran 1991: 95), as it is precisely that complexity and flexibility which enable the vitality of diaspora cultures. In other words, a critical diasporic cultural politics should privilege neither host country nor (real or imaginary) homeland, but precisely keep a creative tension between 'where you're from' and 'where you're at'. I emphasize *creative* here to foreground the multiperspectival *productivity* of that position of in-between-ness (Gilroy 1993b). The notion of 'biculturality', often used to describe this position, hardly does justice to this hybrid productivity. Such a notion tends to construct the space of that in-between-ness as an *empty* space, the space in which one gets lost in the cultural translation from one side to the other in the bipolar dichotomy of 'where you're from' and 'where you're at'. But the productivity I am referring to precisely fills that space up with *new* forms of culture at the collision of the two: *hybrid* cultural forms born out of a productive, creative syncretism. This is a practice and spirit of turning necessity into opportunity, the promise of which is perhaps most eloquently expressed by Salman Rushdie (1991: 17): 'It is normally supposed that something always gets lost in translation; I cling, obstinately, to the notion that something can also be gained.'

What the recognition of the third space of hybridity enables us to come to terms with is not only that the diasporic subject can never return to her/his 'origins', but also, more importantly, that the cultural context of 'where you're at' always informs and articulates the meaning of 'where you're from'. This is, to speak with Rushdie, what the diasporic subject gains. In this sense, hybridity marks the emancipation of the diaspora from 'China' as the transparent master-signified of 'Chineseness': instead, 'Chineseness' becomes an open signifier invested with resource potential, the raw material for the construction of syncretic identities suitable for living 'where you're at'.

It is by recognizing the irreducible productivity of the syncretic practices of diaspora cultures that 'not speaking Chinese' will stop being a problem for overseas Chinese people. 'China', the mythic homeland, will then stop being the absolute norm for 'Chineseness' against which all other Chinese cultures of the diaspora are measured. Instead, Chineseness becomes an open signifier, which acquires its peculiar form and content in dialectical junction with the diverse local conditions in which ethnic Chinese people, wherever they are, construct new, hybrid identities and communities. Nowhere is this more vigorously evident than in everyday popular culture. Thus, we have the fortune cookie, a uniquely Chinese-American invention quite unknown elsewhere in the Chinese diaspora or, for that matter, in China itself. In Malaysia one of the culinary attractions is *nyonya* food, a cuisine developed by the *peranakan* Chinese out of their encounter with local, Malay spices and ingredients. Some time ago I was at a Caribbean party in Amsterdam full of immigrants from the Dutch West Indies; to my surprise the best salsa dancer of the party was a young man of Chinese descent who grew up in Surinam. There I was, facing up to my previously held prejudice that a Chinese can never become a Latino!

These examples make it clear that the peculiar meanings of diasporic Chineseness are the result of the irreducible *specificity* of diverse and heterogeneous hybridizations in dispersed temporal and spatial contexts. This in turn means that the unevenly scattered imagined community of the diaspora itself cannot be envisioned in any unified or homogeneous way.[10] Chinese ethnicity, as a common reference point for this imagined community, cannot presume the erasure of internal differences and particularities, as well as disjunctures, as the basis of unity and collective identity. What then is still its use? Why still identify ourselves as 'Chinese' at all?

The answer depends on context: sometimes it is and sometimes it is *not* useful to stress our Chineseness, however defined. In other words, the answer is political. In this thoroughy mixed-up, interdependent, mobile and volatile postmodern world clinging to a traditional notion of ethnic identity is ultimately self-defeating. Inasmuch as the stress on ethnicity provides a counterpoint to the most facile forms of postmodernist nomadology, however, we might have to develop a postmodern notion of ethnicity. But this postmodern ethnicity can no longer be experienced as naturally based upon tradition and ancestry. Rather, it is experienced as a provisional and partial 'identity' which must be constantly (re)invented and (re)negotiated. In this context, diasporic identifications with a specific ethnicity (such as 'Chineseness') can best be seen as forms of 'strategic essentialism' (Spivak 1987: 205): 'strategic' in the sense of using the signifier 'Chinese' for the purpose of contesting and disrupting hegemonic majoritarian definitions of 'where you're at'; and 'essentialist' in a way which enables diasporic subjects, not to 'return home', but, in the words of Stuart Hall, to 'insist that others recognize that what they have to say comes out of particular histories and cultures and that *everyone* speaks from positions within the global distribution of power' (1989: 133).

In short, if I am inescapably Chinese by *descent*, I am only sometimes Chinese by *consent*.[11] When and how is a matter of politics.

2

CAN ONE SAY NO
TO CHINESENESS?

Pushing the limits of the diasporic paradigm

William Yang was born in 1943 and grew up in Dimbulah, a small mining town in Northern Queensland, Australia. Today a celebrated photographer working and living in Sydney, he is presented – classified – as 'a third-generation Australian-Chinese'. In an autobiographical account of his life he recounts:

> One day, when I was about six years old, one of the kids at school called at me 'Ching Chong Chinaman, Born in a jar, Christened in a teapot, Ha ha ha.' I had no idea what he meant although I knew from his expression that he was being horrible.
>
> I went home to my mother and I said to her, 'Mum, I'm not Chinese, am I?' My mother looked at me very sternly and said, 'Yes, you are'.
>
> Her tone was hard and I knew in that moment that being Chinese was some terrible curse and I could not rely on my mother for help. Or my brother, who was four years older than me, and much more experienced in the world. He said, 'And you'd better get used to it.'
>
> (Yang 1996: 65)

This is a classic tale of revelation that can undoubtedly be told in countless variations and versions by many people throughout the world, articulating the all-too-familiar experience of a subject's harsh coming into awareness of his own, unchosen, minority status. 'Chineseness' here is the marker of that status, imparting an externally imposed identity given meaning, literally, by a practice of discrimination. It is the dominant culture's classificatory practice, operating as a territorializing power highly effective in marginalizing the other, which shapes the meaning of Chineseness here as a curse, as something to 'get used to'. Yang reveals that for most of his life he has had negative feelings about 'being Chinese'. But what does his Chineseness consist of?

> We were brought up in the western way. None of us learned to speak Chinese. This was partly because my father, a Hukka [*sic*], spoke Mandarin, whereas my mother, a See Yup [*sic*], spoke Cantonese, and

they spoke English at home. My mother could have taught us Cantonese
but she never did – frankly, she couldn't see the point.

(ibid.: 63/4)

This glimpse into one ordinary family's history indicates the apparent lack of interest
Yang's parents had in transmitting their Chinese roots or cultural traditions to their
children. This would have been a difficult thing to do anyway in 1940s and 1950s
Australia, when the official ideology was still one of 'white Australia' and required
the few non-white people in the country to assimilate. But at the same time Yang's
family obviously never lost a sense of certainty about the self-declared *fact* of their
Chineseness. But are they indeed 'Chinese'? What makes them so? And how do they
know?

The diasporic paradigm

Scholars have always been bewildered about China. The intricate empirical
multifariousness and historical complexity of this enormous country are hardly
containable in the sophisticated (inter)disciplinary apparatus and theoretical
armoury of Western researchers. Language, culture, civilization, people, nation,
polity – how does one describe, interpret, and understand 'China', that awesome
other country which has never ceased to both fascinate and infuriate its dedicated
scholar? The difficulty has grown exponentially with the emergence of a so-called
diasporic paradigm in the study of 'Chineseness'. The booming interest in what is
loosely termed the Chinese diaspora has unsettled the very demarcation of 'China'
as an immensely complex yet ontologically stable object of study. The diasporic
paradigm has shattered the convenient certainty with which Chinese Studies has
been equated, quite simply, with the study of China. 'China' can no longer be
limited to the more or less fixed area of its official spatial and cultural boundaries,
nor can it be held up as providing the authentic, authoritative, and uncontested
standard for all things Chinese. Instead, how to determine what is and what is not
Chinese has become the necessary preliminary question to ask, and an increasingly
urgent one at that. This, at least, is one of the key outcomes of the emergent
diasporic paradigm.

As I have already argued in Chapter 1, central to the diasporic paradigm is the
theoretical axiom that Chineseness is not a category with a fixed content – be it
racial, cultural or geographical – but operates as an open and indeterminate signifier
whose meanings are constantly renegotiated and rearticulated in different sections
of the Chinese diaspora. Being Chinese outside China cannot possibly mean the
same thing as inside. It varies from place to place, moulded by the local circumstances in different parts of the world where people of Chinese ancestry have settled
and constructed new ways of living. There are, in this paradigm, many different
Chinese identities, not one. This proposition entails a criticism of Chinese
essentialism, a departure from the mode of demarcating Chineseness through an
absolutist oppositioning of authentic and inauthentic, pure and impure, real and
fake. The anti-essentialism of the diasporic paradigm opens up a symbolic space for

people such as William Yang, arguably a distant member of the diaspora, to be Chinese in his own way, living a de-centred Chineseness that does not have to live up to the norm of 'the essential Chinese subject'.[1]

One of the distinctive characteristics of cultural studies is its recognition of the positionality of any mode of intellectual practice or style of knowledge production. Such a recognition implies a de-universalization of knowledge and an emphasis on the particular historical and cultural coordinates which inform the enunciation of discourse and the formation of knowledge. For cultural studies, as Lawrence Grossberg (1996a: 153) puts it, 'There can be no separation between theory, at whatever level of abstraction, and the concrete social historical context which provides both its object of study and its conditions of existence.' Importantly, this is both a political and an epistemological statement. Thus, any intellectual investment in an object of study, say, Chineseness, is not the innocent reflection of a natural reality that is passively waiting to be discovered; rather, the very quest for knowledge actively brings into being, in the knower's experience and under-standing of the world, slices of reality he or she then calls and classifies as 'Chinese'. Furthermore, there are stakes involved in the ongoing ontological confirmation of Chineseness, just as nineteenth-century Western science had a stake, beyond the noble one of scientific progress, in producing the existence of distinct, and hierarchically ordered, human 'races'. This analogy should provoke us to inter-rogate the political and ideological significance of the ongoing currency, as well as shifting currents, of discourses, claims and disclaims to Chineseness in the modern world. How Chineseness is made to mean in different contexts, and who gets to decide what it means or should mean, are the object of intense contestation, a struggle over meaning with wide-ranging cultural and political implications.

I also have a personal investment in this interrogation of Chineseness. Like William Yang, though along a rather different historical trajectory, I am intimately familiar with the injunction to 'get used to being Chinese'. I was born into a so-called *peranakan* Chinese family in Indonesia, a country that has always had a problem with its long-standing and economically significant Chinese minority (as, of course, is the case throughout South-East Asia except Singapore, where ethnic Chinese are in a comfortable majority) (Suryadinata 1997). In Chapter 3, I will go at length into the predicament and the contradictions of Chinese identi-fication in the context of contemporary Indonesia. Suffice it to say at this point that while growing up in Indonesia in the 1960s, I found 'being Chinese' a profoundly ambivalent experience, fraught with feelings of rejection (by the majority of non-Chinese Indonesians) and alienation (from an identity that was first and foremost an imposed one). The need to come to terms with the 'fact' of my Chineseness remained a constant after I relocated – in a peculiar diasporic itinerary informed by the historical connections established by European colonialism – to the Netherlands, where I spent my teenage and young adult years, and later after I relocated to Australia (where I have lived for the past ten years). In these divergent geocultural spaces the meaning of being Chinese was both the same and different, framed by the fateful condition that I could not take my Chineseness (or lack of it) for granted: just like Yang, I was regularly made to be painfully aware that being Chinese in these countries was, to all intents and purposes, a curse. In short, the status of Chineseness as a discursive construct, rather than something natural, is a matter of subjective experience to me, not just a question of theory.

Conceiving Chineseness as a discursive construct entails a disruption of the ontological stability and certainty of Chinese identity; it does not, however, negate its operative power as a cultural principle in the social constitution of identities *as* Chinese. In other words, the point is not to dispute the fact that Chineseness exists (which, in any case, would be a futile assertion in a world where more than a billion people would, to all intents and purposes, identify themselves as Chinese in one way or another, either voluntarily or by force), but to investigate how this category operates in practice, in different historical, geographical, political and cultural contexts. As Stuart Hall (1996b) has remarked, the fact that 'race' is not a valid scientific category does not undermine its symbolic and social effectuality. The same could be said about Chineseness. What highlighting the constructed nature of categories and classificatory systems does, however, is 'shifting the focus of theoretical attention from the categories "in themselves" as repositories of cultural [meaning] to the process of cultural classification itself' (ibid.: 302). In other words, how and why is it that the category of 'Chineseness' acquires its persistence and solidity? And with what political and cultural effects?

What I would like to illuminate in this chapter is that the diasporic paradigm is necessarily unstable. After all, the very spirit of the idea of diaspora, motivated as it is by notions of dispersal, mobility and disappearance, works against its consolidation as a 'paradigm' proper. Contained in the diasporic perspective itself, therefore, are the seeds of its own deconstruction, which provides us with an opportunity to interrogate, not just the different meanings Chineseness takes on in different local contexts – a limited anti-essentialism which still takes the category of Chinese itself for granted – but, more radically, the very significance and validity of Chineseness as such as a category of identification and analysis.

Cultural China?

The process of decentring the centre, which is so pivotal to diasporic theory, has been forcefully articulated recently in the influential collection *The Living Tree: The Changing Meaning of Being Chinese Today*, edited by Tu Wei-ming (1994a), Professor of Chinese History and Philosophy at Harvard University.[2] In this collection, Tu elaborates the contours of a symbolic universe he calls 'cultural China', a newly constructed cultural space 'that both encompasses and transcends the ethnic, territorial, linguistic, and religious boundaries that normally define Chineseness' (Tu 1994b: v). For Tu, the project of cultural China is one designed to decentre the cultural authority of geopolitical China (that is, the People's Republic), an intellectual effort to redefine 'the periphery as the center' in current engagements with what it means to be Chinese (Tu 1994c). This project is critical insofar as it aims to break with static and rigid, stereotypical and conventional definitions of Chinese as 'belonging to the Han race, being born in China proper, speaking Mandarin, and observing the "patriotic" code of ethics' (Tu 1994b: vii). Instead, Tu wants to

> explore the fluidity of Chineseness as a layered and contested discourse, to open new possibilities and avenues of inquiry, and to challenge the claims of political leadership (in Beijing, Taipei, Hong Kong or Singapore) to be the ultimate authority in a matter as significant as 'Chineseness'.
>
> (ibid.: viii)

The impetus for this intervention is a certain disillusion, if not despair, about the political reality of the People's Republic of China. As Tu observes,

> Although realistically those who are on the periphery . . . are seemingly helpless to effect any fundamental transformation of China proper, the center no longer has the ability, insight, or legitimate authority to dictate the agenda for cultural China. On the contrary, the transformative potential of the periphery is so great that it seems inevitable that it will significantly shape the intellectual discourse on cultural China for years to come.
>
> (Tu 1994c: 33–4)[3]

It is important to note the political implications of Tu's project. His position is known to be explicitly neo-confucianist and largely anti-communist, which we need to keep in mind in assessing his critiques of 'the center'. Placed in the context of Chinese *cultural* history, however, the assertion of the (diasporic) periphery as the centre is a radical one. The notion of a single centre, or cultural core, from which Chinese civilization has emanated – the so-called Central Country complex – has been so deeply entrenched in the Chinese historical imagination that it is difficult to disentangle our understandings of Chineseness from it. Yet the very emergence of a powerful discourse of cultural China enunciated from the periphery and formulated to assert the periphery's influence at the expense of the centre is a clear indication of the increasingly self-confident voice of some diasporic Chinese intellectuals, such as Tu Wei-ming himself. This growing self-confidence has much to do with the historical and economic state of affairs in global modernity at the end of the twentieth century. As Tu put it, 'while the periphery of the Sinic world was proudly marching toward an Asian-Pacific century, the homeland seemed mired in perpetual underdevelopment' (1994c: 12). Indeed, it is precisely the homeland's seeming inability to transform itself according to the ideal image of a truly modern society – an image still hegemonically determined by the West – which has led to the perceived crisis of Chineseness which the project of cultural China aims to address.

Central to the intellectual problematic of cultural China is what has been seen as the urgent need to reconcile Chineseness and modernity as the twentieth century was drawing to a close. There are two interrelated sides to this challenge. On the one hand the question is how to modernize Chineseness itself in a way that would correct and overcome the arguably abject course taken by the existing political regime in the PRC – a course almost universally perceived as morally wrong and, provocatively, as somehow having a debilitating effect on the fate of Chineseness.[4] According to Tu, the Chinese diaspora will have to take the lead in the modernization of Chineseness. He writes in an implicit attack on the 'center': 'While the overseas Chinese may seem forever peripheral to the meaning of being Chinese',

> they [can] assume an effective role in creatively constructing a new vision of Chineseness that is more in tune with Chinese history and in sympathetic resonance with Chinese culture.
>
> (ibid.: 34)

On the other hand, there is also the reverse question of how to sinicize modernity; how, that is, to create a modern world that is truly Chinese and not simply an imitation of the West. The radical iconoclasm of the 1919 May Fourth Movement, which was based on the assumption that China's modernization could only be realized through a wholesale process of Westernization and a simultaneous renunciation of Chinese culture, is now regarded as completely outdated. Instead, inspiration is drawn from the economic rise of East Asia in the 1970s and 1980s to look for models of modernity – Chinese modernity – which pose challenging cultural alternatives to the Western model (Ong 1999). Tu refers specifically to Taiwan, Hong Kong, Singapore and the Chinese communities in South-East Asia. The experiences of these countries suggest for Tu that 'active participation in the economic, political, social, and cultural life of a throroughly modernized community does not necessarily conflict with being authentically Chinese', signalling the possibility that 'modernization may enhance rather than weaken Chineseness' (1994c: 8).

The privileging of the periphery – the diaspora – as the new cultural centre of Chineseness in Tu's discourse is an important challenge to traditional, centrist and essentialist conceptions of Chinese culture and identity. Yet I want to suggest that the very postulation of a 'cultural China' as the name for a transnational intellectual community held together not just by a 'common awareness' but also by 'a common ancestry and a shared cultural background', 'a transnational network to explore the meaning of being Chinese in a global context' (Tu 1994c: 25), is a move that is driven by a desire for, and motivated by, another kind of centrism, this time along notionally cultural lines.

An important element here is the continued orientation of, if not obsession with, the self-declared periphery as centre in the discourse of cultural China in relation to the old centre, even if this centre is so passionately denied its traditional authority and legitimacy. 'What mainland China eventually will become remains an overriding concern for all intellectuals in cultural China,' writes Tu (1994c: 33), and in this ongoing preoccupation with the centre the periphery not only reproduces unintentionally its own profound entanglement with the former; it also, by this very preoccupation, effects its own unwarranted internal homogenization and limits the much more radical potential that a diasporic paradigm allows. In other words, while the aim would seem to be to rescue Chineseness from China, to de-hegemonize geopolitical China (the PRC) which is found wanting in its own, heavy-handed politics of modernizing Chineseness/sinicizing modernity, the rescue operation implies the projection of a new, alternative centre, a decentred centre whose name is *cultural* China, but China nevertheless. It is clear, then, that the all-too-familiar 'obsession with China' which has been a key disposition in the work of Chinese intellectuals in the twentieth century remains at work here with undiminished intensity (Hsia 1971). This obsession, which is so profoundly inscribed in the psychic structure of a wounded Chinese civilizationalism, 'privileges China's problems as uniquely Chinese, which lays absolute claim to the loyalty of Chinese in all parts of the world' (Lee 1994: 232).

According to Leo Ou-fan Lee (1994), who came from Taiwan to the United States as a graduate student more than thirty years ago and who describes himself as 'a voluntary exile situated forever on the fringes of China', the 'excessive obsession with their homeland has deprived Chinese writers abroad of their rare privilege of being truly on the periphery'. For Lee, it is only by being truly on the periphery that one can create a distance 'sufficiently removed from the center of the obsession', allowing one to 'subject the obsession itself to artistic treatment' (1994: 226). From this point of view, cultural China definitely does *not* occupy a truly peripheral position at all. On the contrary. An overwhelming desire – bordering, indeed, on obsession – to somehow maintain, redeem, and revitalize the notion of Chineseness as a marker of common culture and identity in a rapidly postmodernizing world is the driving force behind Tu's conception of cultural China. While the meaning of Chineseness is defined explicitly as fluid and changeable, the category of Chineseness itself is emphatically not in question here: indeed, the notion of cultural China seems to be devised precisely to exalt and enlarge the global significance of Chineseness, raising its importance by imbuing it with new, modernized meanings, and heightening its relevance by expanding its field of application far beyond the given spatial boundaries of geopolitical China.

The Chinese diaspora, as we have seen, is posited as one of the key pillars of the imagined community of cultural China. It is noteworthy that Tu persistently accentuates the quest for Chineseness as a central motif in his wide-ranging discussion of variant diaspora narratives. In the case of South-East Asian families of Chinese descent remigrating from Malaysia or Vietnam to North America, Western Europe, or Australia, he sees the 'irony of their not returning to their ancestral homeland but moving farther away from China with the explicit intention of preserving their cultural identity' (Tu 1994c: 24). In mainland Chinese intellectuals' decision not to return to China after the Tiananmen event in 1989, he reads a 'conscious and, for some, impulsive choice to realize one's Chineseness by moving far away from one's homeland' (ibid.). But isn't Tu being too insistent in foregrounding the salience of Chineseness in the configuration of these diasporic flows and movements? Doesn't this emphasis unduly strait-jacket diverse strands of the diaspora into the narrow and claustrophobic shaft of a projected, if highly abstract 'obsession with Chineseness'?

The organic metaphor of 'the living tree' to describe cultural China provides us with a clear insight into the problem I am hinting at here. A living tree grows and changes over time; it constantly develops new branches and stems that shoot outward, in different directions, from the solid core of the tree trunk, which in turn feeds itself on an invisible but life-sustaining set of roots. Without roots, there would be no life, no new leaves. The metaphor of the living tree dramatically imparts the ultimate existential dependence of the periphery on the centre, the diaspora on the homeland. Furthermore, what this metaphor emphasizes is continuity over discontinuity: in the end, it all flows back to the roots.

In thus imputing an essential continuity and constancy in the diaspora's quest for Chineseness, the discourse of cultural China risks homogenizing what is otherwise a complex range of dispersed, heterogeneous, and not necessarily commensurable diaspora narratives – a homogeneity for which the sign of 'Chineseness' provides the *a priori* and taken-for-granted guarantee. But in this way the hegemony of 'China' (cultural if not geopolitical China) is surreptitiously reinforced, not undercut. As Tu rightly notes, 'hegemonic discourse, charged with an air of arrogance, discriminates not only by excluding but also by including. Often it is in the act of inclusion that the art of symbolic control is more insidiously excercised' (1994b: vii). Tu refers here to the coercive manner in which the People's Republic includes a variety of others (such as the non-Han minorities inside the borders of China) within the orbit of its official political control. But a wholesale incorporation of the diaspora under the inclusive rubric of cultural China can be an equally hegemonic move, which works to truncate and suppress complex realities and experiences that cannot possibly be fully and meaningfully contained within the singular category 'Chinese'.

Ironically, Tu recognizes the fact that not all members of the diaspora would feel comfortable with their inclusion in the grand design of cultural China. Indeed, he writes, 'Learning to be truly Chinese may prove to be too heavy a psychological burden for minorities, foreign-born, non-Mandarin speakers, or nonconformists; for such people, remaining outside or on the periphery may seem preferable' (1994b: vii–viii). Let's ignore the surprising return to cultural essentialism – the ghost of the 'truly Chinese' – here. What we must start to question is the very validity and usefulness of the spatial matrix of centre and periphery that is so constitutive of the conventional thinking about the Chinese diaspora; we must give the living tree a good shake.

The prison-house of Chineseness

The condition of diaspora, literally 'the scattering of seeds', produces subjects for whom notions of identity and belonging are radically unsettled. As James Clifford puts it in his very useful discussion of contemporary theorizing on diasporas:

'Diasporic subjects are distinct versions of modern, transnational, intercultural experience' (1997: 266). In this sense, diasporic subjects are exemplary cases of the multiple and hybrid subjectivities so favoured by postmodern and poststructuralist theory. Interestingly, however, as I have discussed above, a dominant tendency in thinking about the Chinese diaspora is to suppress what Clifford calls 'the lateral axes of diaspora', the ways in which diasporic identities are produced through creolization and hybridization, through both conflictive and collaborative co-existence and intermixture with other cultures, in favour of a hierarchical centring and a linear rerouting back to the imagined ancestral home. Such a conceptual focus on the centre, Clifford notes, inhibits an understanding of the significance of diaspora cultures in the late twentieth century. As he puts it:

> The centering of diasporas around an axis of origin and return overrides the specific local interactions (identifications and ruptures, both constructive and defensive) necessary for the maintenance of diasporic social forms. The empowering paradox of diaspora is that dwelling *here* assumes solidarity and connection *there*. But *there* is not necessarily a single place or an exclusivist nation.
>
> (Clifford 1997: 269, italics in original)

Indeed, for Clifford the most important aspect of diasporic formations is the multiplicity of 'here's' and 'there's' which together make up 'decentered, partially overlapping networks of communication, travel, trade, and kinship [that] connect the several communities of a transnational "people"' (ibid.). The metaphor of the living tree is not at all suited to capture the features of such dispersed, discontinuous, fractal cultural formations. Interestingly, Paul Gilroy (1993a) has chosen the image of ships as a starting point for his ground-breaking work on the African diaspora: 'ships in motion across the spaces between Europe, America, Africa, and the Caribbean as a central organizing symbol' for the particular diasporic formation that has developed historically as a result of the transatlantic slave trade, a formation he calls the 'Black Atlantic' (Gilroy 1993a: 4). What is highlighted in this image is a virtual space of continuous mobility, of criss-crossing flows and multiple horizontal exchanges between different sites of black diasporic concentration, in which there is no centre. I am not suggesting here that a similar image should be adopted for the Chinese diaspora – indeed, the image of the ship is particularly appropriate in Gilroy's context for its evocation of the African diaspora's founding moment of the Middle Passage – but this comparative note might serve to illuminate the fact that the metaphor of the living tree is by no means ideologically innocent. It could encourage us to problematize the predominance of centrist and organicist conceptions of Chineseness, Chinese culture and Chinese identity in diaspora.[5]

Leo Lee, with his claimed desire to be 'truly on the periphery', comes close to embodying the diasporic Chinese subject who has renounced the debilitating obsession with the centre. 'By virtue of my self-chosen marginality I can never fully identify myself with any center', he writes (1994: 231). He defines his marginality in relation to two centres, China and America: 'On the peripheries of both countries, I feel compelled to engage actively in a dialogue with both cultures' (ibid.: 229). Freed from the usual obsession with China, Lee declares himself 'unbounded' by his homeland. Instead, he advocates what he calls a 'Chinese cosmopolitalism': 'one that embraces both a fundamental intellectual commitment to Chinese culture and a multicultural receptivity, which effectively cuts across all conventional national boundaries' (ibid.). Cosmopolitanism, of course, is an idea warranting a discussion of its own which I cannot provide here (see e.g. Cheah and Robbins 1998), but what is the surplus gained in the addition of *Chinese* to cosmopolitanism here? And what does Lee mean by a fundamental (that is to say, *a priori*, fundamentalist) intellectual commitment to *Chinese* culture? What makes Lee's vantage point so interestingly contradictory is that while he places himself on the margins of both 'China' and 'America', he does this from a position of unquestioned certainty about his own ontological Chineseness and his (inherited?) proprietorship of 'Chinese culture'. Once a Chinese, always a Chinese?

Ouyang Yu, a poet and a specialist in English and Chinese literature who moved from mainland China to Australia many years ago, actively resists such, what could be called, ethnic determinism. 'Where is the way out for people such as me?' he asks. 'Is our future predetermined to be Chinese no matter how long we reside overseas?' (Ouyang 1997: 10). Ouyang expresses a desire to contribute to his present culture – Australian culture – 'more than as just a Chinese' (ibid.: 35). But, so he tells us, he has been prevented from doing so:

> My effort to 'English' myself has met with strong resistance from all sorts of people ever since I came here. Even if I wanted to be English, they wouldn't let me be. I would find my frequent criticism of China was not appreciated. On many occasions, I found people preaching that I should be proud of being a Chinese. . . . I was made to feel uneasy with my disloyalty.
>
> (ibid.: 10)

This story highlights how difficult it can be for people like Ouyang to embrace a truly diasporized, hybrid identity, because the dominant Western culture is just as prone to the rigid assumptions and attitudes of cultural essentialism as is Chinese culture. In other words, there seems to be a cultural prohibition of de-sinicization, at least for intellectuals from mainland China or Taiwan, such as Ouyang Yu and Leo Lee, who have moved to the West. It would be interesting to speculate why this should be so. It would be easy – and perhaps too simplistic – to suggest the antagonizing work of racism or orientalism here; their capacity as forces that perpetuate and reinforce essentialist notions of Chinese otherness should not be underestimated. However, the important point to make here is that Lee's ideal of 'being truly on the periphery' is inherently contradictory, if not a virtual impossibility, because his notion of periphery is still grounded in the recognition of a centre of sorts, the deterritorialized centre of Chinese culture or, perhaps, Chineseness itself.

While Lee and Ouyang now live in different parts of the (Western) world, their diasporic Chineseness is still clearly linked to their obvious biographical rootedness in the cultural formations of the territorial centre of the ancestral 'homeland'. Moreover, even though they no longer live in this centre, their subjectivities are still steeped in Chineseness, as it were: being first generation migrants, they possess the linguistic and cultural capital that is generally recognized as authentically Chinese. Lee and Ouyang *know* that they are Chinese, and they are known by others as such. While both express a desire to go beyond their Chinese identities – Lee by staking a claim to a Chinese cosmopolitanism, and Ouyang in wanting to be more than *just* Chinese – their bottom-line Chineseness is not in doubt. Theirs, in other words, is a relatively straightforward narrative of (self-)exile from 'the homeland', and as such they are still easily incorporated in Tu's cultural China and firmly attached to one of the branches of the living tree.

Without wanting to devalue the decentring discourses articulated by intellectuals such as Lee and Ouyang, I would nevertheless argue that there are other narratives that tell of much more radical, complicated and chequered routes of diasporic dispersal. In these narratives, the very validity of the category of 'Chineseness' is in question, its status as signifier of identity thrown into radical doubt. It is in these narratives that the diasporic paradigm is pushed to its limits, to the extent that any residual attachment to the 'centre' tends to fade.

The *peranakan* Chinese in South-East Asia are often mentioned as one distinct group of Chinese people who have lost their Chinese cultural heritage and have gone 'native'. The *peranakans* are an old diaspora: from the tenth century onwards traders, mostly from South China, visited various South-East Asian ports. At first they remained temporarily and rarely established permanent Chinese communities, but between the sixteenth and nineteenth centuries Chinese trading quarters in cities such as Bangkok, Manila, and Batavia became large and permanent, aided by the ascendancy of European colonialism in the region. Over the course of centuries they (who were mostly men) intermarried with local women, began to speak the local languages, and adapted to local lifestyles (while selectively holding on to some Chinese traditions). This is not the place to enter into a detailed discussion of this important history of Chinese migration; the question to ask here is: why are they still called 'Chinese?' As David Yen-ho Wu (1994: 161) observes: 'While the "pure" Chinese may question the legitimacy of the *peranakans*' claim to being authentic Chinese, the *peranakans* themselves are quite confident about the authenticity of their Chineseness. They are often heard referring to themselves as "we Chinese".'

Having been born into a *peranakan* family myself, I can testify to the correctness of this observation: there is an instinctiveness to our (sometimes reluctant) identification as 'Chinese' which eludes any rationalization and defies any doubt. Yet it is a fraught and ambivalent Chineseness, one that is to all intents and purposes completely severed from the nominal centre, China. In Suharto's Indonesia (1966–98), for example, where the state deployed a strict assimilation policy to eradicate Chinese difference within the national culture (for example, by banning the use of Chinese characters from public display), *peranakan* Chinese were said

47

to 'see themselves as Indonesian rather than Chinese, [but] recognize their Chinese origin, albeit knowing very little of Chinese culture and tradition' (Tan 1997: 51). And as for many *peranakans* China has no relevance at all in their lives, what meaning does the notion of 'Chinese origin' still carry?[6]

Wu (1994) argues that two sentiments identify those who see themselves as 'Chinese'. The first, a culturalist sentiment, is a feeling of connectedness with the fate of China as a nation, a patriotism associated with 'a sense of fulfillment, a sense of being the bearers of a cultural heritage handed down from their ancestors, of being essentially separate from non-Chinese' (Wu 1994: 149). But it is clear that this sentiment does not apply to those in the diaspora who not only have 'lost' most of their cultural heritage, language being chief among them, but also do not have a great attachment to the ancestral homeland at all, while still identifying themselves (and being identified) in one way or another as 'Chinese'. The *peranakans* in Indonesia are a case in point, but so, for that matter, is William Yang, the 'Australian-Chinese' photographer with whose story I began this chapter.

Yang's story illuminates the precarious meaning of Chineseness at the outer edge of the diaspora. If Yang, brought up the Western way in small-town Australia, can be described as Chinese at all, then his is a Chineseness stripped of any substantial cultural content. This, of course, is the case with millions of 'ethnic Chinese' throughout the West, those who have settled in all corners of the world in a chequered history of several centuries of dispersal from the original 'homeland'. To understand Yang's Chineseness in terms of his imaginary and subjective relationship to this imputed homeland, which can only be an extremely tenuous relationship anyway, would be missing the point altogether. As his own account of the formative event shows, he came to know about his Chinese identity only because someone else, arguably a non-Chinese, labelled him as such, to Yang's own initial surprise and to his later chagrin, when his mother confirmed that he *was* indeed Chinese. In other words, Yang's identification as Chinese took place in a context of co-existence and interaction with others, others who were identifiably *different* from him. Yang's Chineseness then is fundamentally relational and externally defined, as much as it is partial. Its boundaries are fuzzy. Its meaning is uncertain. Yang both is and is not Chinese, depending on how he is perceived by himself and by others. But what is it, we might ask, that still ultimately determines the possibility of Yang's categorization as Chinese in the first place?

This bring us to the second sentiment which, according to Wu, is common to those identifying themselves as Chinese. This is the sentiment that Chinese share of seeing themselves as being members of 'the Chinese race' or 'the Chinese people' (Wu 1994: 150). We return here to a concept that, as I remarked earlier, refuses to go away from social discourse despite its repudiation as a scientific concept in the West: 'race'. So when Yang's mother affirmed sternly that he *was* Chinese, his brother adding insult to injury by informing him that 'he'd better get used to it', the only tangible markers of distinction could only have been those associated with 'race'. The glee with which the schoolkid, most probably white, could yell 'Ching Chong Chinaman' at Yang was based on the former's dominant positioning within the prevailing social network, which gave him the *power* to offend in this way. But it also depended on the availability of some clues which enabled him to single out the guileless, young William Yang as an appropriate object of such an attack. What else could it have been but his 'yellow skin' and 'slanty eyes', the key 'racial' markers for Chineseness in the West?

While scientific racism has long been discarded, then, it is in situations like these that the notion of race continues to thrive in everyday life. Here, race theories operate in practice as popular epistemologies of ethnic distinction, discrimination and identification, which are often matched by more or less passionate modes of self-identification. As Balibar (1991) has remarked, the idea of being part of a race produces a sense of belonging based on naturalized and fictive notions of kinship and heredity. In Chinese discourse, of course, this is eminently represented by the enduring myth of the unity of the Chinese people as children of the Yellow Emperor.[7] What Rey Chow (1993: 24) calls the 'myth of consanguinity' has very real effects on the self-conception of diasporic subjects, as it provides them with a magical solution to the sense of dislocation and rootlessness that many of them experience in their lives. William Yang describes it this way:

> I've been back to China and I've had the experience that the ex-patriot (*sic*) American writer Amy Tan describes; when she first set foot in China, she immediately became Chinese. Although it didn't quite happen like that for me I know what Amy's talking about. The experience is very powerful and specific, it has to do with land, with standing on the soil of the ancestors and feeling the blood of China run through your veins.
>
> (1996: 23)

In this extraordinary narrative of 'return' to the imposing 'centre', Yang constructs himself as a prodigal son who had almost lost his way, a fallen leaf that has blown back to the soil where the living tree has its roots. In this narrative, race – blood – operates as the degree zero of Chineseness to which the diasporic subject can resort to recover his imaginary connectedness with China, and to substantiate, through the fiction of race, what otherwise would be a culturally empty identity.

But, as Chow (1993: 24) has rightly pointed out, 'the submission to consanguinity means the surrender of agency'. The fiction of racial belonging would imply a reductionist interpellation (in the Althusserian sense of the term) which constructs the subject as passively and lineally (pre)determined by 'blood', not as an active historical agent whose subjectivity is ongoingly shaped through his/her engagements within multiple, complex and contradictory social relations which are over-determined by political, economic and cultural circumstances in highly particular spatio-temporal contexts. Race, in other words, provides a reductionist, essentializing discursive shortcut, in which, to paraphrase Stuart Hall, the signifier 'Chinese' is 'torn from its historical, cultural and political embedding and lodged in a biologically constituted racial category' (Hall 1996e: 472). In the imagining of 'the Chinese race', differences which have been constructed by heterogeneous diasporic conditions and experiences are suppressed in favour of illusory modes of bonding and belonging. Recently I had a taxi ride in Sydney with a driver who was from mainland China. We mutually recognized each other as 'Chinese', but I had to tell him that, unfortunately, I couldn't speak Chinese. 'Well,' he said, 'it will be easy for you to learn. After all, you have Chinese blood.' As if my imputed racial identity would automatically and naturally give me access to some enormous reservoir of cultural capital!

As Balibar (1991: 100) has remarked, 'The racial community has a tendency to represent itself as one big family or as the common envelope of family relations.' Indeed, there is an equivalence between the organicist metaphor of the living tree and the lineal notion of race-as-family which is profoundly problematic if we are to interrogate Chineseness effectively from the diasporic point of view. In his work on the African diaspora Gilroy has criticized 'the dubious appeal to family as the connective tissue of black experience and history' (1993b: 203), as it disables black intellectuals from developing alternative perspectives on black lives in diaspora. In Gilroy's view, the diasporic formation must be grounded in explicitly disorganic, hybrid and synthetic notions of identity and community, not in some cosy, familial notion of blackness. Similarly, Hall (1996e: 474) has argued against 'reaching for an essentialized racial identity of which we think we can be certain' as guarantee for political solidarity or cultural unity. Instead, the very category 'black' needs to be interrogated. In black British film-maker Isaac Julian's words:

> blackness as a sign is never enough. What does that black subject do, how does it act, how does it think politically . . . being black isn't really good enough for me: I want to know what your cultural politics are.
>
> (in Hall 1996e: 474)

In the same vein, if we are to work on the multiple, complex, over-determined politics of 'being Chinese' in today's complicated and mixed-up world, and if we are to push the theoretical promise of the diasporic perspective to its radical conclusion, we must not only resist the convenient and comforting reduction of Chineseness as a seemingly natural and certain racial essence; we must also be prepared to interrogate the very significance of the category of Chineseness *per se* as a predominant marker of identification and distinction. Not only does the moment of pure Chineseness never strike, there are also moments – occurring regularly in the lives of those 'truly on the periphery', in Leo Ou-fan Lee's words – in which the attribution of Chineseness does not make sense in the first place. The liberating productivity of the diasporic perspective lies, according to Rey Chow (1993: 25), in the means it provides 'to *unlearn* that submission to one's ethnicity such as "Chineseness" as the ultimate signified' (italics in original). This will allow diasporic subjects to break out of the prison of Chineseness and embrace lives – personal, social, political – 'more than just as a Chinese' (Ouyang 1997); to construct open-ended and plural 'post-Chinese' identities, if you like, through investments in continuing cross-influences of diverse, lateral, unanticipated

50

intercultural encounters in the world at large. As it happens, William Yang, who now calls himself 'bicultural', does occupy such a position in his public life. His celebrated photographs of friends suffering from AIDS testify to his identification with Western gay culture, which he represents as entangled with, but also distinct from, the cultural identifications derived from his ethnicity, and articulate a hybrid, disaggregated, multiple identity that is uncontainable, in any meaningful sense, by the category 'Chinese'.[8]

To reiterate my conclusion in the previous chapter, 'if I am inescapably Chinese by *descent*, I am only sometimes Chinese by *consent*. When and how is a matter of politics.' The politics involved here reaches far beyond the identity politics of individual subjects, in diaspora or otherwise. What is at stake are the possibilities and responsibilities of these subjects to participate, as citizens of the world, in the ongoing political construction of world futures. As we enter the twenty first century, the world faces ever greater challenges in light of growing global economic disparity, continuing environmental degradation, rapid technological change, increasingly massive transnational migrations and shifting geopolitical (im)balances of power. There is no necessary advantage in a 'Chinese' identification here; indeed, depending on context and necessity it may be politically mandatory to *refuse* the primordial interpellation of belonging to the largest 'race' of the world, the 'family' of 'the Chinese people'. In such situations the significant question is not only: Can one say no to China? (Chow 1997), but also: Can one, when called for, say no to Chineseness?

3

INDONESIA ON MY MIND

Diaspora, the Internet and
the struggle for hybridity

I was twelve when my parents decided to relocate their family of seven from Indonesia to the Netherlands. It was 1966. As soon as the plane touched down at Amsterdam airport, my father said, 'From now on I don't want you to speak Indonesian anymore. You must learn to speak Dutch as quickly as possible.' Probably because I was a good Asian daughter, I did. As our family chose the immigrant strategy of rapid assimilation into the 'host society', I stepped into a new world – a Western Europe in ferment. In my desire to create a meaningful identity for myself in this advanced white world, I embroiled myself in the new political and intellectual movements that swept across the West in the 'radical' decades of the 1960s and 1970s and, for better or worse, became what I am today – a cultural studies intellectual. Indonesia, the place we left behind, gradually disappeared from my dreams and worries, although never completely: my childhood years spent in the heat and dust of Surabaya have always remained somewhere in the back of my mind.

I have not, to date, explicitly 'returned' to the country of my youth as a site of active intellectual engagement. However, as Italian-American writer Marianna Torgovnick (1994: ix) has remarked, 'There are always crossings between personal history and intellectual life.' So it was that a few years ago I suddenly found myself irrevocably absorbed in Indonesian affairs, from the safe solitude of my computer screen, through the Internet. This chapter tells the story of this electronic involvement, but it will also give me an opportunity to reflect on some of the dilemmas facing the so-called diasporic intellectual, a rather controversial topic today (see e.g. Ahmad 1992; Chow 1993; Dirlik 1994a; Hall 1996a; Radhakrishnan 1996; Friedman 1997; Robbins 1999). The terms 'diaspora' and 'hybridity' are often conflated in contemporary cultural and postcolonial studies, as if the two refer to the same field of experience and practice, and necessarily go hand in hand. Here, I wish to argue for a clear distinction between the two. Perhaps somewhat surprisingly, I will caution against 'diaspora' and come out strongly for 'hybridity'.

In the previous two chapters, I have elaborated my own perspective on the Chinese diaspora. The Indonesian focus of this chapter will throw light on the political biases attendant on the current global valorization of the Chinese diaspora, both at the macro level of international relations and at the micro level of identity politics and the politics of everyday life. Let me put it clearly at the outset: coming from a family of Chinese descent, my relationship to Indonesia is necessarily a profoundly troubled one. Not having forgotten my early years of growing up in that mind-boggling country, it is still an ambivalent site of identification and disidentification for me. It is precisely this ambivalence that will point me towards the necessity for an intellectual and cultural politics of hybridity.

Indonesia is a non-Western nation–state that arose out of the legacy of Dutch colonialism, and is now the fourth most populous country in the world. Its territory encompasses an archipelago of thousands of islands, scattered over a vast area of sea between the South China Sea and the Indian Ocean. As an imagined community, Indonesia is a new nation: Indonesian nationalists, under the leadership of Bung Sukarno who would become the country's founding President, declared national independence on 17 August 1945, which was only formally recognized in 1949 after four years of bloody struggle against the Dutch colonizers. The Indonesian nation–state is not only postcolonial but also multi-ethnic – an ambitiously synthetic and syncretic, irrevocably modern and modernist project. Being constructed out of a complex and conflictive colonial history, Indonesia has to negotiate massive economic, political and cultural challenges and immense internal and external contradictions to keep the nation together. This is testified by recent troubles across the country such as in Aceh, West Papua and Timor, where forces of separatism and demands for local autonomy – against the central power of Jakarta – have been particularly strong. (The situation of the Chinese, as I will illuminate below, is qualitatively different.)

As for many other 'Third World' countries, the 1960s were tumultuous times for Indonesia. I remember clearly how we, as postcolonial Indonesian children, were deeply infused with a desire to become a strong and respectable, modern nation. Children are a captive and impressionable audience to appeals of national feeling. Our sentiments of national pride were cultivated not only by the many schoolbook stories about national heroes and heroines who struggled against the Dutch colonizers, but also by seemingly mundane cultural practices such as the regular singing of the national anthem and the raising of the Indonesian flag – solemn rituals which, certainly in my own case, never failed to bind me ever more strongly to the Indonesian nation. The fact that we were a poor, newly decolonized nation was deeply ingrained in our young minds, and it was an incentive – inculcated into us and internalized by many of us – to work and learn hard for the modern future of the nation, what I felt to be *our* nation.

But this march forward was disrupted dramatically by the failed *coup d'état* of 1965. Official history would have it that this coup was masterminded by the Indonesian Communist Party (PKI) and supported by the communist regime in Beijing. I remember vividly when it happened, as the whole nation was inescapably thrown into turmoil in the months after that fated September night, when six generals were killed and the government of then President Sukarno, beloved leader of the struggle for national independence, was thrown into disarray. Schools closed down indefinitely. The economy collapsed, with prices rocketing sky-high as the value of the rupiah plummeted. As popular anger and frustration burst out on the streets, at least half a million people were killed in riots and mass attacks on communists and people who were otherwise targeted as culprits. Many of these were Chinese.[1] As a young girl, I was unaware of the full seriousness of the situation, although I have always known that 'we Chinese' were often the object of discrimination by the majority Indonesians, but my parents now tell me that everyone in their circles lived in fear then. Stories abounded that the rivers were red with blood and full of floating dead bodies. It was during this period that my parents decided finally to get out.

According to Stuart Hall, diasporic intellectuals – usually, born in the 'Third' World but educated and working in the 'First' – occupy a 'double space', and 'are deeply embedded in both worlds, both universes' (1996c: 399). It is just as important, however, to stress the diasporic intellectual's profound *dis*embeddedness from the worlds in which she finds herself biographically enmeshed. It is the articulation of embeddedness and disembeddedness, the 'lived tension' between 'the experiences of separation and entanglement' that marks the construction of diasporic subjectivities (Clifford 1997: 255). The current popularity of the notion of diaspora is an index of the sense of alienation many migrants feel in their present land of residence. While in the so-called host country they are condemned always to be positioned as 'different' or 'foreign', (re)defining themselves as 'diasporic' – as belonging to an idealized home elsewhere – affords them the promise of symbolic escape from the pains and frustrations of marginalization. But this belonging to a 'there' while being 'here' remains a vicarious, virtual one; never to be conflated with the 'real' thing.

For diasporic subjects are not only spatially disembedded, 'out of place'; they are also temporally disembedded, that is, displaced from the 'normal' passing of historical time. It is frequently noted that migrants who go back to their homeland after, say, thirty years away, find themselves disorientated because they have to realize that the place they have left behind is no longer the same. It has moved on, too. This disjuncture of memory and history leaves many diasporic subjects in limbo, as it were: they have to come to terms with being foreigners in their own homeland because they are 'out of time'. By migrating, they break the flow of continuous historical time as lived when one stays in one place. Not only are notions of past, present and future no longer anchored in a sense of evolving continuity, they also become doubled, as it were, as the migrant steps into the temporality of a different historical trajectory. As I entered the Western 'sixties' and began to insert myself into a world evolving out of *that* particular historical moment, I lost touch with the everyday process of history-making in Indonesia, in which I was so deeply immersed until we left.

So I cannot speak for the 'real' Indonesia now: my relationship to it is extremely tenuous, based more on memory than on present enmeshment. The Indonesian pop stars whose names I still remember – Lilis Suryani, Rachmat Kartolo – are relics from the 1960s long forgotten in the Indonesia of 2000. I no longer share, with Indonesians of my generation, common histories and experiences of growing up in a 'Third World' postcolonial nation. I have not gone through the turbulent social, political and economic changes brought about after the upheaval of 1965. I have no sense of what it was like to live through the so-called 'New Order' installed by Sukarno's successor, Suharto – generally represented as a time of brisk economic growth, increasing affluence and rapid modernization as Indonesia launched itself as one of the tigers of South-East Asia, but marred by Suharto's autocratic rule, rampant nepotism and corruption and a growing disparity between rich and poor.

My disconnection from my Indonesian past was highlighted dramatically when news broke about the devastating effects of the economic crisis which ravaged through Asia in 1997. Indonesia was among the hardest hit by the crisis. Again, the value of the rupiah tumbled, massive social chaos set in as millions lost their jobs and livelihoods, and mass riots erupted which targeted Chinese retailers and shopkeepers, who were scapegoated for the rising prices of basic staples such as rice. Student demonstrations against the Suharto regime became increasingly militant. The unrest led ultimately to Suharto's surprisingly swift stepping down on 21 May 1998, but not before four students from Trisakti University in Jakarta had been killed by security forces and mass violence broke out in the following days throughout the city, leaving more than 1200 people dead. As thousands of frightened ethnic Chinese were reported fleeing the country, I kept being reminded of my parents' ever so casual remark about rivers red with blood – a haunting image that somehow failed to arouse in me any deep feeling, whether it was rage, resentment or fear. The most tangible feeling I had was one of confusion, of detached ambivalence, of no longer knowing how to relate to the place I used to be so committed to call 'home'.

'The problematic of "home" and belonging', Avtar Brah (1996: 193) remarks in her book *Cartographies of Diaspora*, 'may be integral to the diasporic condition, but how, when, and in what form questions surface, or how they are addressed, is specific to the history of a particular diaspora.' But an even more basic question to ask is how, when, and in what form particular groups begin to define themselves *as* a diaspora in the first place. Against the current tendency to objectify and dehistoricize diasporas as if they were given, always-already existing formations, it is useful to suggest, paraphrasing Raymond Williams (1961), that there are no diasporas, only ways of thinking about groups of people as diasporas.[2] In the present global historical conjuncture, the notion of an 'Indonesian diaspora' has very little public currency. While many Indonesians have migrated elsewhere (for example, as labour migrants across the Asia-Pacific region), they have not generally represented and organized themselves collectively in terms of their long-term dispersal from 'the homeland'. There is, however, a hugely powerful and increasingly expansive discourse of the 'Chinese diaspora', and it is within this discourse that people of my family background routinely tend to be included and include themselves. Indeed, most Indonesians who have migrated out of the country are people who identify themselves as 'Chinese', and they often cite this very fact as the reason why they have moved out.

My parents' dogged determination to assimilate their family into Dutch society after leaving Indonesia behind was, I believe, a reaction to their disappointment at their failure, as citizens of Chinese background, to assimilate into, and to be accepted as full members of post-war Indonesian society. In retrospect, I know that my own childhood dedication to the nation, my deep and heartfelt investment in national belonging and nationalist commitment, was doomed from the start: modern Indonesian nationalism has never managed to accommodate successfully the presence of the Chinese minority in its construction of an imagined community.[3] While the Indonesian nation was from its inception imagined as a multi-ethnic entity – something which was necessary to unify the hundreds of ethnic and linguistic groupings making up the country whose spatial boundaries were determined by the imposition of Dutch colonialism – the place of those marked as 'Chinese' in this 'unity-in-diversity' has always been resolutely ambiguous and uncertain.[4] In an attempt to control what came to be called 'the Chinese problem' in postcolonial Indonesia, the Suharto regime demanded that ethnic Chinese assimilate into mainstream Indonesian society through name-changing policies, bans on the public display of Chinese cultural expression such as the use of Chinese language and Chinese New Year celebrations, and so on. At the same time, those of Chinese descent were prevented from forgetting their categorical difference as the government continued to differentiate between indigenous and non-indigenous groups, for example, by using special identity cards for ethnic Chinese. Thus, if I had stayed, my Chineseness – itself, as I have explained in Chapter 1, a doubtful marker of identity – would have prevented me, politically and culturally, from ever being able to consider Indonesia 'home' in any comfortable, unproblematic sense (Tan 1997; Thung 1998).

In this context, the recourse to *Chinese* identification among many Indonesians of Chinese descent, especially among those who no longer live in Indonesia, is more than understandable: it is a symbolic attempt to claim a vicarious 'home' where a sense of belonging to Indonesia has been thwarted. But staking a claim to a belonging to the 'Chinese diaspora' poses its own problems, given that most Indonesian Chinese do not speak, read or write any Chinese, no longer have connections with China, the imputed ancestral motherland, and have very little active knowledge of Chinese cultural traditions, rituals and practices. In other words, from a 'pure' Chinese point of view, the standards of which are generally determined within the inner circle of Greater China, and Mainland China in particular, most Indonesian Chinese are just not Chinese enough, lacking in 'authenticity'. Our residual Chineseness is always inevitably diluted, hybridized and creolized precisely because of our long-term history of living outside of China proper and of intermingling with a wide range of non-Chinese others. Thus, for those who call themselves 'Chinese Indonesian' or 'Indonesian Chinese': the interchangeable use of the two reveals the uncertainty and ambivalence many have in identifying themselves – the imaginary belonging to a vast and powerful 'Chinese diaspora' can never provide a satisfactory solution to the question of 'home'. Imagining oneself to be a member of the Chinese diaspora aligns one with a powerful deterritorialized community notionally bound together by an abstract sense of racial sameness and an equally abstract sense of civilizational pride, but it does not relieve one from the difficulties involved in the very concrete, historically specific condition of occupying a minority status in the social and political context of the Indonesian nation–state. For a twice-migrated subject such as myself the quandary is clear: do I indeed belong to the Chinese diaspora, or to a notional Indonesian diaspora?

Electronic diasporic mobilization

As what came to be known as the 'anti-Chinese riots' erupted throughout Indonesia in the first months of 1998,[5] my distance from the site of turbulence and trauma was put to a test when one day in February, out of the blue, I received an email from the initiators of a new website, http://www.huaren.org. The website was set up, so I was informed, specifically in response to the plight of the Chinese in Indonesia. 'Since every crisis in Indonesia would almost always turned out to be anti-Chinese, we all felt enough is enough and let's use the internet technology to broadcast our concerns,' so I was told.[6] I checked out the site immediately and kept logging in for several months. 'Huaren', the standard pinyin transliteration of the term 'Chinese people', was chosen as the name for the site for its brevity. Huaren was initiated by a number of diasporic Chinese living in the West, most importantly Joe Tan, a Malaysian-born, New Zealand-based R&D chemist, and Dan Tse, a research engineer from Hong Kong who now lives in Vancouver, Canada. Together they sought the assistance of a Chinese Malaysian computer specialist in California, W.W. Looi, who set up the Huaren website, and a Chinese American lawyer, Edward Liu, to establish the World Huaren Federation, a non-profit organization based in San Francisco (Arnold 1998). The specifically Chinese character of this new mode of electronic diasporic mobilization was emphasized lightheartedly by Liu, who said in an interview: 'Computers and the global huaren are like soy sauce and rice. Combined together, they taste delicious and give sustenance, packing energy and carbohydrates. At least four million of us around the world are Internet users, computer geeks and techies' (*The Straits Times*, 20 August 1998). It is no accident that Huaren has its base near Silicon Valley!

Huaren's mission is 'to serve as a conduit for Chinese around the world to discuss issues that are relevant to the Chinese Diaspora with the goal of promoting understanding within and among its numerous geographical groups' (www.huaren.org/mission/). Although this Internet organization identifies itself as one by, about and for all diasporic Chinese, what propelled the establishment of the site was news about the crisis in South-East Asia, Indonesia in particular. In the course of 1998, it became an intense, politically charged space for many self-identified Chinese people from all over the world to express and share, mostly in English but sometimes in Indonesian and occasionally in Chinese, their responses to the evolving crisis in Indonesia. The use of English, explicitly encouraged by the site keepers, signals a desire to have a global reach, an international hearing, even as it also means that access to the site would be limited to those who are relatively well educated and economically privileged. (I will return to the more general significance of Huaren in the global production of the Chinese diaspora in Chapter 4.)

Reading through the Bulletin Board of the site, I was made aware of a growing sense of collective militancy and indignation I was not exposed to before.[7] After riots in the town of Medan in early May 1998, where according to news reports at least six people were killed and hundreds of Chinese-owned shops were looted, hostility towards non-Chinese Indonesians, generally referred to as 'natives' by Huaren users or, to use the official Indonesian term, *pribumi*,[8] hardened. In a posting titled 'Indonesia, curse?' one contributor set the tone:

> After reading so many postings and responses in this Bulletin Board, Do you know that the pribumi in Indonesia are useless? Looting, robbing, stealing, killing, scape goating are all they know. I can't believe seeing some Indonesian Chinese . . . still saying good things about the Indonesians! Sad, so sad! (I wish I was in Medan, together with my huaren friends fighting those bastards!) Hate ya, pribumi suckers!
>
> (7 May 1998)

And another:

> What makes me so sick is that those so-called 'good' pribumi did nothing much to raise their concern for their Chinese friends, ignoring riots, atrocities on Chinese. This type of outrageous racial violence has been allowed to carry on for decades. How on earth can other people just listen and watch the situation on TV? In the past Chinese tried the diplomatic way to get the Indonesian authorities to put effort in eliminating such criminal acts of violence. . . . We have tried the soft approach, it has not worked. We simply cannot keep waiting for them to change their attitude, other action plans must be implemented. Those mobs must be laughing away knowing they still can get away with murders.
>
> (7 May 1998)

I cite these examples here because they are particularly explicit in their expression of ethnic resentment, and I would not like to suggest that all the contributors spoke with one voice. But what was generally enunciated on the site, and what the site itself made possible through the interactive immediacy of Internet technology, was an assertive politicization of Chinese ethnicity determined to defend and fight against its enemies in Indonesia. Furthermore, there was clearly a transnational dimension to this electronic community as people wrote in from Germany, the USA, Australia, Canada, Hong Kong, Malaysia, Singapore and so on, as well as from Indonesia. One author explicitly called for 'Huaren outside Indonesia [to] play a leading role in the organization [of support] because we Indonesian Huaren cannot afford such visibility' (7 May 1998).

Clearly, what was being articulated here were claims to a new diasporic solidarity under the common signifier of 'Huaren'. In the website guestbook we can read announcements from non-Indonesians such as, 'To all Chinese in Indonesia, we are with you all the way! Chinese world over, unite now!' Whereas Indonesians write things like, 'It's nice to know that there are a lot of people like us out there who care about us.' The transnational sense of Chinese togetherness established by the site allowed Indonesian Chinese to feel embraced, recognized, vindicated. This electronic diasporic Chinese solidarity, in turn, propelled calls for political mobilization. One posting, entitled, 'Indonesian-Chinese intellectuals must unite!', made the interesting suggestion that being part of the largest race of the world would help the cause of Chinese Indonesians:

> Persecution of the Chinese minority in Indonesia will never end if the Indonesian Chinese intellectuals do not rise up to voice their aspirations and claims for equal rights and equal opportunities in Indonesia. . . . You will have the economic clout of the Indonesian-Chinese community behind you. You will have the sympathy and support of Human Rights Organizations. You are members of 20% of the world's population.
>
> (16 May 1998)

In their email personally addressed to me the website initiators asked me to give them permission to reproduce some of my essays on Chineseness on the site, and more generally to support the site and to contribute to it. The appeal was inescapable: I felt interpellated directly and straightforwardly as a diasporic Chinese intellectual, and was asked to speak up as a member of this group, to speak on behalf of it and for it. In this age of global diasporas, there is a powerful pressure on diasporic intellectuals to operate as representatives of their scattered 'people'. But I'm afraid I could not respond in unambiguously positive terms to this call for co-ethnic diasporic solidarity.

Instead, my ambivalent, if engaged, detachment prevented me from becoming an organic intellectual for the Chinese cause in Indonesia. This did not mean, of course, that I did not sympathize, at a personal level, with the victims of rioting, plundering and killing that had once again swept through Indonesia, although it must be emphasized that not all victims were Chinese. It was also easy enough to pledge my support for the passionate calls against racial prejudice and discrimination and for social equality and justice, although precisely my formation as a cultural studies intellectual had made me all too aware that such seemingly simple demands cannot ever do justice to the complex political struggles and contradictions emanating from them. And yes, I do worry, even agonize about the fact that popular violence in times of crisis in Indonesia tends so predictably to be directed at the ethnic Chinese minority. But I have been unable to translate this agony into a singular political and intellectual partisanship in favour of 'the Chinese' against 'the Indonesians'.

Critics might argue that it was my being physically removed from the site of violence itself, living comfortably in the West, that has allowed me to maintain this stance of ambivalence – a stance that one may not have the luxury to sustain in the heat of the violence and in the face of personal assault. Such ambivalence is often dismissed by self-appointed radical First World theorists as leading to political passivity and intellectual quietism (e.g. Hutnyk 1997). However, I believe that my diasporic ambivalence can serve the elaboration of a more positive, even necessary political discourse: it enables me to maintain the detachment needed to resist the drift towards ethnic absolutism that many contributions to the Huaren website seemed to exhibit and to argue for a less antagonistic articulation of 'Chinese' and 'Indonesian' – in short, to argue for a politics of hybridity. But such an argument can only meaningfully be made with a nuancedly situated and historically informed sense of the stakes involved.

Chinese/Indonesian negotiations

As I read through the plethora of international, mostly Western newspaper reports on the crisis in Indonesia, I was numbed by a narrative that is monotonous in its constant reiteration of the following refrain: 'The six million Chinese make up only 3% of the total population of 200 million in Indonesia, but they account for 70% of the country's wealth.' Repeated with some minor variations in all the articles I have read about the crisis, this 'fact', constructed through objectivist statistical discourse, just sits there like a solid, silent rock, apparently defying any further unpacking and specification. The apparent obviousness of the 'fact' provides the illusion of a simple, parsimonious 'explanation' for the whole crisis, a sense of immediate understanding that does not warrant any further questioning. This does not mean that the 'fact' is not 'true' in some general empirical sense, but we all know that any 'truth' is not only constructed, but also produces a sense of reality that compresses and represses the intersecting power relations and complex historical contradictions that have worked to generate it. What is particularly disturbing about the constant reiteration of this 'fact' is that its seductive simplicity will only serve to reinforce the way in which 'the Chinese' are permanently locked into an antagonistic relationship with the *pribumi*, and with 'Indonesia' more generally.

To be sure, the 'fact' reflects a common-sense truth shared and accepted throughout all layers of Indonesian society: that the Chinese are richer and better off than the *pribumi*. Personally, I have always known this truth for a fact: it was the taken-for-granted experiential reality which my family lived by when we were still living in Indonesia, and a statement I have heard repeated countless times after we left. Chinese-Indonesian common sense would have it that anti-Chinese sentiment among the majority Indonesians is to be blamed on 'jealousy', whereas many non-Chinese Indonesians routinely accuse the Chinese of 'arrogance' and 'exclusiveness'. The depth of feeling that keeps the two categories apart cannot be overestimated: it pervades daily life and colours everyday social interaction and experience.

As I read through all press accounts I could find on the Indonesian crisis, I came across a short article by Yenni Kwok, a 25-year-old journalist with *Asiaweek*. Born and bred in Jakarta, she confirms that she feels 'as Indonesian as any indigenous pribumi', but that she is also 'ethnically Chinese'. 'Some people think I can't be both. Not completely, anyway.' She is acutely aware of the social separation between most Chinese and *pribumi* in daily life and the mutual distrust that governs relations between them:

> But now a confession. For all my 'Indonesian-ness', I was brought up almost in a different world from the pribumi. Chinese schools are banned in Indonesia . . . so most Chinese go to private Christian schools. At the one I attended, the only other children were Chinese. There were pribumi living on my street, but I can't honestly say I knew much about them. . . . It wasn't until I returned from studying in the U.S. and took a job in journalism that I got to know any pribumi. Now I count a number of them among my closest friends. But I am an exception. For most Chinese, the only pribumi they ever get to know is their household maid, their pembantu. Once they reach adulthood, there is almost no further social contact. Even in professional life, the two groups rarely mingle.
>
> (Kwok 1998)

She also testifies to the tacit sense of superiority that many Chinese have in relation to their non-Chinese fellow Indonesians:

> I remember, when I was a youngster, asking my father why they [*pribumis*] were referred to as fangui (literally 'rice devils', but meaning inferior). 'We eat rice too,' I said. 'So we're also fangui, right?' My father just smiled. It was too difficult – and probably too embarrassing – to explain.
>
> (ibid.)

Kwok's description resonates painfully with my own experiences of more than thirty years ago,[9] and it was confirmed during a short return visit I made to Indonesia in 1996. During this trip I was made to feel uncomfortable immediately when one of the first things the taxi driver did was complain about how the Chinese conspired to keep 'us', the real Indonesians, poor. He also made the improbable comment that 'they' wanted to take over the country and multiplied themselves much more quickly than 'us'. My companion, an Indonesia specialist from Australia, kept quiet, while I decided that it was better not to reveal that I was a Chinese-Indonesian myself – I let him believe I was a Japanese tourist. A few days later in Jakarta, I was appalled by the strict social division in the rather nice restaurant I was having lunch: all the servants were Javanese *pribumi*, while almost all the guests, well-dressed and at ease with their middle-class life-style, were visibly Chinese. The proprietor, predictably, could also be identified as Chinese. It was the obliviousness of all involved with the ethnic inequality so materially enacted here that disturbed me most. As an outsider, I could of course afford not only to notice, but also to morally reject the uneasy hierarchy in the arrangement – and it was an unease fed by the egalitarian structure of feeling I had internalized so thoroughly in the West – and it made me want to disidentify with the Chinese, even though I know all too well that it is impossible to homogenize all Chinese-Indonesians and I do understand, ethnomethodologically, that those living *within* the arrangement cannot constantly question the assumptive world they live in: being Chinese in Indonesia does signify, on the whole, being positioned on the winning side of economic well-being – a reality one cannot easily extract oneself from.

According to Leo Suryadinata (1998), a Singapore-based expert on the situation of the Chinese in South-East Asia, 'Some of Indonesia's wealthiest citizens are Chinese, but most Chinese are not rich.' Indeed, the experiences I have described above – Kwok's and my own – cannot really be considered representative, though they are certainly not untypical. As an urban-based minority, the Chinese are a major component of the Indonesian middle class. Throughout the country they have always dominated commercial life and the retail trade. It misses the point here to suggest, as more Marxist-inclined analysts would do, that the 'Chinese problem' in Indonesia is not one of 'race', but one of 'class'. The problem is that in this context, 'class' is lived in the modality of 'race': Indonesia is an intensely racialized social formation, in which the Chinese/*pribumi* distinction is generally read in terms of economic advantage/disadvantage. In other words, 'Chineseness' in contemporary Indonesia does not connote primarily cultural identities, but *economic* identities. It is this real and perceived economic divide that determines, in the first instance, the manner in which real and perceived cultural differences are transformed into social incompatibilities and antagonisms, both ideologically and in practice.[10]

We are dealing with an extremely complex set of historically formed relations here. Chinese merchants and traders in South-East Asia have often been dubbed 'the Jews of the Orient', an antipathetic term of abuse first used by King Vajiravudth of Thailand in 1920s (Tejapira 1997). This designation refers to the crucial role the Chinese 'enterpreneurial minority' has for centuries played in the commercial practices throughout the region. In colonial times, the Chinese were brokers between the European colonizers and the indigenous population, particularly in the system of tax farming for the collection of state revenues. Revenue farming brought great wealth to Chinese farmers, but it contributed in the long term to the hostility towards them because the position of revenue farmer was 'at the cutting edge of colonial oppression' (Cribb 2000: 185). They were the ones who had to extract tax money (plus some profit) from the natives and thus were perceived as greedy and exploitative. Thus, in Cribb's words:

> Although differences between Islam and Chinese religious practices, as well as Chinese cultural chauvinism, may have contributed to the hostility towards the Chinese, there is no factor as likely to have created an anti-Chinese racism as Chinese dominance of the revenue farms.
>
> (ibid.: 185–6)

More generally, the colonial economy has played a crucial role in producing a profound and enduring racial bias in socio-economic relations. As Anthony Reid puts it: 'Colonial policies encouraged a division of function, a dual economy, between the "native" majority of peasants, under their own, often anticommercial, aristocratic-bureaucratic hierarchy, and the commercial sector of Europeans, Chinese and other minorities' (1997: 45). The legacy of this dual colonial economy resonates deep into postcolonial times, as it reinforced the competitive advantage of Chinese capitalists *vis-à-vis* indigenous merchants, who lacked the capitalist know-how, experience and networks that the Chinese had built up over the decades. To this day, ethnic Chinese throughout South-East Asia have been able to seize this advantage, an advantage that has been historically inscribed in their very habitus, cultural orientation and mode of subjectivity. Such conditions are still a fertile breeding ground for anti-Chinese populist sentiment today, but it is important to keep in mind that this antagonism has a long and deep-seated history, going back to colonialism's divide and rule policies (see further Ang 2001).

The tragic paradox is that the relative economic advantage of the Chinese is matched by their political powerlessness in the wake of decolonization and the advent of the postcolonial nation–state. The ideological force of nationalism, imported from Europe, was a key factor in the anti-colonial struggle of the Indonesians; indeed, the very creation of the Indonesian nation as an imagined community was both a precondition and an outcome of the protracted struggle for independence from the Dutch colonizers (Anderson 1991). In this new imagined community, the place of the Chinese minority, who during the colonial period were called 'foreign Orientals', was problematic. While anti-colonial Indonesian nationalism was not in general directed against the Chinese but against foreign European rule, in the postcolonial period the presence of the Chinese posed a problem in the process of nation-building. As Daniel Chirot puts it:

> the rise of modern nationalism hardened attitudes toward those newly viewed as outsiders. Entrepreneurial minorities, previously seen as just one more among many specialized ethnic and religious groups that existed in most complex, premodern agrarian societies, now became, in the eyes of the new nationalists, something considerably more threatening.
>
> (1997: 8)

It should be pointed out, however, that the Chinese themselves were not simply passive pawns in this historical drama. In an ironic twist, nationalist awakening occurred earlier among the Chinese than among the indigenous Indonesians. But, as I will discuss in greater detail in Chapter 4, most overseas Chinese across South-East Asia and elsewhere rallied behind a *Chinese* nationalism, one oriented towards China, the putative homeland, and not the countries in which they reside – encouraged as such by nationalist activists from China (Williams 1960; Duara 1997). The Chinese revolution of 1911 strongly emboldened Chinese pride and faith in China's power to challenge European hegemony. Charles Coppel

(1983: 15) remarks in his historiographical study of the Chinese in Indonesia that 'the dominant theme of Chinese political activity in the late colonial period was to press for equality of status for the Chinese with the Europeans'. In no way did the Chinese in this period see any benefit in forging alliances with the 'natives', who were at the bottom of the oppressive colonial hierarchy.[11] Is it surprising then that at a later stage, when the 'natives' mobilized themselves, they didn't rush to invite the Chinese to join their ranks? Post-independence efforts by Indonesia-oriented Chinese leaders to be integrated into the syncretic national community of 'Indonesia' have always had to struggle against the legacy of separateness reinforced by the competing force of Chinese nationalism. As Suryadinata (1979: xv) puts it, 'the Indonesian nationalist movement, having emerged after overseas Chinese nationalism in Java, understandably tended to exclude the Chinese from the movement'. In short, the emergence of modern nationalism in colonial Indonesia has solidified the distinction between the 'indigenous' and the 'non-indigenous' – a distinction that continues to frame ethnic relations in Indonesia today. As Takashi Shiraishi (1997: 205) has remarked, 'the rise of modern politics . . . signified the "awakening" of the Chinese as Chinese and of "natives" as natives.' Postcolonial Indonesia inherited this state of affairs, and is living with its legacy to this day.

As modern nationalism is in principle a practice of constructing a unified peoplehood, the question of who does and who does not belong to the Indonesian people is central to the operation of the Indonesian nation–state. Thus, while ethnic Chinese people during colonial rule were not in general concerned about the formality of their national belonging – such a concern being a feature of fully fledged political modernity which simply didn't apply on colonial territory[12] – after decolonization those who chose or were forced to stay in Indonesia were faced with the necessity to declare formal loyalty to the new nation–state, now under control of 'the natives'. In other words, ethnic Chinese subjects were placed in the quandary of having to take on, formally, a singular, bounded and exclusive national identity, but at the same time always remaining under suspicion that their loyalty might not be undivided – the trace of their Chineseness, no matter how residual, always read as a sign of imperfect national belonging.

I know that my father suffered deeply from this ambivalent positioning. Having grown up in the last decades of colonialism, he actively chose Indonesian citizenship and made a conscious decision to help build the new nation directly after independence. But in social terms, he experienced directly how his Chineseness impeded a harmonious and productive working together with *pribumi* colleagues. The truth is inescapable: his life as an ethnic Chinese was easier and more secure during Dutch rule! My father, by virtue of his generation, can be described as a colonial subject, for whom the creation of the new nation–state of Indonesia and its imposition of a fixed, state-related, national identity was a restriction on his earlier, more fluid and blurred sense of communal Chinese identity under colonial rule. When the discrimination became too confining he decided to sever all his ties with the country that he could no longer consider as his 'homeland'. Indonesia, for him, or rather the postcolonial nationalist project of 'Indonesia', was the very reason for his diasporization to the West.

By contrast, I grew up as a postcolonial subject in the 1950s and 1960s, and I internalized the desire to be a full national subject. I identified deeply with the Indonesian people as a whole, as they emerged from three centuries of colonial oppression. Then, I experienced my Chineseness primarily as a frustrating stumbling block in my smooth insertion into this national narrative; now, I know that it was the sign of a structural contradiction that refused to be erased. As a discursive category, Chineseness in the Indonesian context will always be uneasily articulated with conflicts around class, nation and race. As a visible marker of ethnic difference, it affects the lives of individuals who can be read as being of Chinese ancestry irrespective of their personal political commitments and their degree of assimilation, their efforts to be accepted as 'just as Indonesian as anybody else' (Kwok 1999). Indeed, as Ariel Heryanto has argued, the very emphasis on the need to assimilate the Chinese tends to reinforce 'the active and conscious othering of the Chinese' in 'the reproduction of the native Self' (1998a: 101).

I left Indonesia because my parents decided to, and I will never know what I would have done had I been forced to make my own decision either in 1966 or, indeed, in 1998, when so many Chinese Indonesians again diasporized themselves as we did more than thirty years ago. However, if there is anything from my childhood that remains a central affect in my diasporic intellectual engagement – an affect strengthened, not weakened, by my adult formation as a non-Western but Westernized intellectual living and working in the West – it is my 'third worldist' attachment to the hopes and aspirations of the postcolonial nation, even as I am deeply disturbed by the pernicious antagonism between Chinese and *pribumi* that so profoundly fractures the Indonesian nation. In other words, I care about both the plight of the millions of ethnic Chinese people in Indonesia who are condemned to live in fear for their safety whenever an economic or political crisis strikes, *and* for the well-being of the Indonesian people as a whole. This expression of dual care may sound naïvely utopian, articulated by a distant diasporic subject who can no longer claim to be an Indonesian today. However, precisely my position as a diasporic intellectual leads me here to resist, both theoretically and politically, the common diasporic temptation: that of an increasingly absolutist ethnic identification.

Globalizing diasporic rage

As the riots worsened and the death toll rose in Jakarta and other cities from 12 May onwards, messages on the Huaren website Bulletin Board became more desperate and exasperated. There were calls for help, rumours about new riots, eyewitness accounts, stories of pain and suffering, tips on how to defend oneself, encouragements to fight back or advice on how and where to flee, calls for all *huaren* in the world to protest and express solidarity, further indignation about the *pribumi*. This went on for weeks after the rioting had subsided, and after Suharto had stepped down: the sense of confusion and bewilderment, of not knowing what to do or where to turn, was palpable. In the midst of the fear, despair and anger, imaginary strategies to deal with the whole situation were thrown up which signalled a desire to solve the problem once and for all – a desire for a 'final solution'. Some suggested organizing the exodus of all ethnic Chinese out of Indonesia to whatever country would be prepared to take them in. Others proposed the creation of a separate state for Indonesian Chinese, to create another 'Singapore' – a majority overseas Chinese state. Some cast their hope on China to become the strongest nation in the world, which, so it was implied, would gain respect for all Chinese around the world. Still others indulged in blind revenge fantasies and wanted to see Indonesia completely bankrupt. In such imagined futures, any connection with 'Indonesia', and the possibility of living together with non-Chinese Indonesians, were given up. Even more moderate voices, those who still allowed some discursive space for the prospect of co-existence, tended to reproduce and feed on the dichotomy, as in this posting entitled 'Decent pribumi should control those mobs before they drive Indonesia deeper into ground':

> To those responsible pribumi and Indonesian politicians and pribumi business people, you cannot afford to sit and wait for the current atrocities against Chinese to blow over and expect Chinese will forget about it. This time you are wrong. . . . The lack of positive and responsible actions in Indonesia despite continual urging and cry for help from the victims will only make the global Chinese communities more angry and united to intensify the campaign.
>
> (27 May 1998)

In response, one particularly angry participant flatly denied that there were any 'decent pribumi' in a posting entitled 'Decent pribumi? Where are they?':

> I have yet to find ONE decent pribumi. If they are decent, they would have stopped their blood brothers from killing Huarens. The fact that they didn't do so, after so many anti-Huaren pogroms, only shows that those 'decent' pribumis are as IN-decent as their parang welding cousins.
>
> (27 May 1998)

Of course such strong language was not appreciated by everyone, and this particular contributor, who called himself Chin, was urged by many others to 'calm down' in his outbursts of anger and hatred, only to be bullied back by Chin and others that the Chinese should stop being so meek and finally be ready to fight back. Whenever a more moderate contributor put forward that there were *pribumi* Indonesians who have condemned the anti-Chinese riots, the retort would be: 'So what? They're not to be trusted.' There was an exasperated demand for action: 'I'm tired of all this talk. What are we going to DO?' In the ongoing conversation, more conciliatory calls for justice and respect for human rights were overshadowed by the more extremist, emotive demands for retaliation and retribution. In the process, a dominant discourse was consolidated in which the scapegoating of Chinese Indonesians was described in terms of genocide and holocaust. As one Huaren editorial put it, 'Unlike the Jews of World War II, we global Huarens will not stand back and wait for the Holocaust to happen. We will fight back! And we will fight back with impunity!' This is excessive language which is indicative of the extent of anger and frustration being ventilated.[13] In the course of this consternation, the diasporic electronic community was solidified, a community constructed through the relegation of Indonesia and the so-called *pribumi* to the realm of the Bad Other. The Good Chinese Self has to defend himself against this Other – a Chinese Self defined in absolutist terms of innocent victimhood, at the passive receiving end of aggression and violence.

I lurked on the site with increasing dismay. What I was witnessing was the escalating mobilizing effect made possible by the immediacy of deterritorialized Internet interaction: the accumulative production of an imagined community that constructs itself through a massive sense of beleagueredness, a paranoid closure of its discursive boundaries, and the absolutization of a singular normative truth that could be summarized as, 'All Chinese in the world unite: stop the killings of our people in Indonesia.' I understand, of course, that the sudden surge of anti-Chinese violence in crisis-ridden Indonesia has been an extremely traumatic experience, especially as it was widely believed that ethnic tension had been softening in 1990s' Indonesia (Heryanto 1998a). I also know that the voices expressed on www.huaren.org cannot be read as representative: the electronic diasporic community is a tiny, self-selecting group.[14] Still, in an increasingly networked, globalized world the very existence of the website is of novel significance, providing the infrastructure for the reinforcement of a self-absorbed and self-rightous transnational Chineseness, one with which I did not wish to identify.

To be fair, the Huaren editors have tried to do their best, in their own words, to counter the excesses of Chinese chauvinism: 'Global Huarens are not against the Indonesian people. We support the voices of conscience. We feel for the Pribumis who are equally victimized by the extremists, racists, and the fanatics inside Indonesia' (Huaren, 14 August 1998). Nevertheless, the very logic of Huaren cyber-politics reinforces the cultivation of an exclusive diasporic community – that of 'global Huarens' – which homogenizes the meaning of being Chinese throughout the world. Presenting itself as 'on the cutting edge of the global digital revolution' (Huaren, 31 July 1998), Huaren has played a crucial role in mobilizing thousands of ethnic Chinese people across the globe to condemn and protest the 'atrocities' against the Chinese in Indonesia. When news broke that dozens of Chinese Indonesian women were gang-raped during the May riots, shocking photographs of alleged victims – one was of the body of a young, horribly tortured and raped Asian-looking woman lying naked in a shower stall – were circulated over the Internet, multiplying rapidly across cyberspace and, understandably, occasioning an even larger crescendo of outrage. (It turned out later that some of these photographs were fake) (Heryanto 1999). Anger was turned into action by the on-line activists through an email chain-letter, the 'Yellow Ribbon Campaign', which was an urgent call to action to all global Huaren who received the message. Thus it was with the help of the rapid and expansive communication channels of the Internet that anti-Indonesian demonstrations were held in many North American, European and Asian cities including San Francisco, New York, Toronto, Washington, Hong Kong, Bangkok, Sydney and Beijing. This was an unprecedented instance of global activism in the Chinese diaspora, and it had the immediate effect of gaining the attention of world leaders all over. In this sense, the Indonesian crisis was a defining moment in the coming into visibility of the Chinese diaspora on the global political stage, with the Internet as a unifying force. So successful was the creation of this, what Arjun Appadurai (1996a) calls 'diasporic public sphere' that Huaren became, as one newspaper report put it, 'a one-stop meeting place for Chinese worldwide' (*The Straits Times*, 20 August 1998).

With much confidence one editorial put it this way:

> Huaren knows the power of the internet, Huaren knows that there is a need out there to create a Third Space for ethnic Chinese overseas. We know the potential and potency of projecting a global Third Force against racism, fascism, and ethnic stigmatization and oppression.
>
> (Huaren, 31 July 1998)

Indeed, in the months after the May riots of 1998 the number of visits to the site and the number of people wanting to help the movement snowballed so exponentially that the initiators had every reason to be euphoric about their achievement and their new-found political power. *The Straits Times* even called the phenomenon a 'revolution of sorts' and described it in superlative terms: 'It changed dramatically the way governments, societies and communities conducted themselves by tearing down national boundaries and making their deeds transparent to the entire world' (20 August 1998). We should not forget, however, that similar revolutionary rhetoric was used about ten years ago to describe the role of fax machines and satellite television – in the form of CNN – in disseminating information and galvanizing global solidarity for protesting students at Tiananmen Square in Beijing. The impact of any new communication technology, from the invention of the telegraph in the nineteenth century onwards, has always been subject to exaggerated predictions and announcements and the Internet is no exception (see e.g. Ebo 1998). But Huaren's momentum as a self-appointed 'Third Force' for the global Chinese diaspora was short-lived. It was only a matter of months before the editorial board noticed 'the onset of compassion fatigue among many of us' (Huaren, 4 September 1998) and by 2000, the Huaren website still had a sizable discussion group dedicated to the Chinese Indonesian case – now relegated to a specialist section in the Bulletin Board called 'Indo-huaren crisis', but it no longer seemed to attract worldwide attention and most participants were clearly engrossed in discussing the intricate details of the stormy developments in Indonesia.

There are, then, clear limits to the electronic politics of global diasporic mobilization. For one thing, there is an intrinsic contradiction, in Huaren's global call for justice, between the universalism of the cause, on the one hand, and the explicitly Chinese signature of this electronic 'Third Force', on the other. Of course, political mobilization to protest against human rights abuses is laudable, but why should the basis of such mobilization be one of presumed ethnic sameness with the victims? The immediacy of the Internet promoted a readiness to buy into highly emotive evocations of victimization which work to disregard the historical complexity and specificity of the situation *within* Indonesia, in favour of a reductionist discourse of pan-ethnic solidarity cemented by an abstract, dehistoricized and absolutist sense of 'Chineseness'. Here the idea of diaspora – Chinese diaspora – enables the projection of a vast, dispersed, transnational, borderless, technologically savvy yet ultimately bounded imagined community. This may produce a strong sense of collective power, but it is in the nature of such ethnic absolutist identity politics – founded as they are on the militant oppositioning of self and other – that they evoke equally militant counter-identities by the other. It was not surprising, therefore, that a 'native Indonesian' Internet mailing list was soon launched by a Komite Gerakan Anti Cina di Indonesia (Anti-Chinese movement in Indonesia), by its own description with the aim to be a 'native Indonesian' antidote to the Huaren website. The logic of diaspora, in this context, ironically reinforces the antagonism which the 'Third Force' was purported to fight against!

But this violent antagonism is not only ideologically problematic and politically counter-productive at the level of global politics. More importantly, it is practically unlivable for those for whom separatism is simply not an option. A contributor living in the city of Bandung, Mrk, wrote this cry from the heart when the rage was spiralling to uncommon heights on the Huaren website:

> OK, let's just say all pribumi are bad, whether they're educated or uneducated, you've convinced me, they're all evil, none of them are good, none of them are trustworthy, they were born bad and they'll die bad, they don't deserve anything. I hate all pribumi too. I'm on your side now, I'm a true huaren-lover now, I'm not a pribumi lover annymore. There. Happy? Now what should I do? Is my change of heart from neutralism to hate going to save me? Strange, I don't feel better. As a matter of fact I feel worse now that I've suddenly realized that I've spent 13 years of my life surrounded by crooks whom I thought were my friends and neighbours. Tell me when I'm supposed to feel good about hating them, ok? . . . And I DON'T KNOW what we huaren in Indonesia should do, sorry again, I appreciate all the suggestions but PLEASE stop telling us huaren who are inside to fight fight fight back, that's impossible, we can't fight them, we can't fight Rambo-style the way you want us to, sorry, and PLEASE stop calling all pribumis bad, PLEASE stop trying to make all of us in Indonesia hate all pribumi, it won't make anything better, it can't fix anything, it'll only make things worse.
>
> (16 May 1998)

This message, entitled 'I am going to keep my mouth (partially) shut from now on', was by no means representative of what was going on in the discussion. On the contrary, it represented a voice that, in the drift towards ethnic absolutism and diasporic Chinese tribalism, tended to be silenced on the site. Here we have a dramatic case of the imposition of the global dynamic of diaspora on local understanding: it illuminates, as Arjun Appadurai puts it, how 'large-scale identities forcibly enter the local imagination and become dominant voice-overs in the traffic of ordinary life' (1996a:152–3). But it is precisely the expression of this local imagination – enunciated from *within* Indonesia – that brings me to the importance of hybridity.

The necessity of hybridity

Hybridity is a fashionable term in contemporary cultural theory, and its use is often associated with the celebration of transgressive triumph, innovative creativity and audacious cultural fusion. Indeed, it is this celebratory stance that has irked many anti-hybridity critics (e.g. Dirlik 1994b; Friedman 1997; Hutnyk 1997; Cheah 1998). In their view the celebration of hybridity is an elitist posture promoted by privileged diasporic and postcolonial intellectuals located in the West (such as Stuart Hall, Paul Gilroy and Homi Bhabha) who can afford the postmodern cosmopolitan ideology of mixture, transcultural exchange, etc. Friedman (1997: 75) dismisses 'hybridisation ⌊as⌋ a politically correct solution for this group', while for Hutnyk (1997: 122) hybridity is 'a rhetorical cul-de-sac which trivialises . . . political activity'. As he asks, 'Why talk hybridity now rather than a more explicitly radical language?' My answer would be that hybridity matters because it is precisely the more explicitly radical language that may be the rhetorical cul-de-sac!

Tejaswini Niranjana (1992: 46) has made the astute remark that '[t]o restrict 'hybridity' . . . to a post-colonial elite is to deny the pervasiveness, however hetero- geneous, of the transformations wrought across class boundaries by colonial and neocolonial domination'. In other words, the history of colonization has left indelible marks on the social, cultural and symbolic worlds of the colonized, which no formal process of decolonization can ever fully erase. In this context, conflating hybridity with the privileged celebration of first-world postmodern flux and cosmopolitan freedom – as many critics tend to do – is particularly misleading. Instead, I will argue here that a critical validation of hybridity is an urgent *necessity* in a postcolonial context such as Indonesia.

According to James Clifford (1998: 367), one does not 'have to leave home to be confronted with the concrete challenges of hybrid agency'. In other words, not only the diasporic migrant in the 'First World' is faced with the necessity of hybridity, but also those who have no choice but to stay put in the 'Third World'. Indeed, despite the exodus reported in the media, particularly of more well-off Chinese Indonesians who took their capital with them to safer places such as Singapore, most Indonesians of Chinese descent are likely to remain in Indonesia, no matter how uncomfortable, and they cannot wait until a 'final solution' to the 'Chinese problem' has been found. They cannot dissociate themselves from Indonesia, the country in which their lives are profoundly embedded. Much less would a dis-embedding gesture of virtual belonging to a deterritorialized Chinese diaspora provide them with useful resources of power in their day-to-day efforts to make a living within the territory that is Indonesia. As one news report notes somewhat dramatically, quoting an ethnic Chinese businessman during the riots in Medan: 'If you're rich, you leave the country. If you're comparatively well off, you go to a hotel. If you are poor, you stay and fight' (Gopalakrishnan 1998). But given the precariousness of racial and ethnic relations in Indonesia, this 'fight' is not likely to be of a confrontational kind. Instead, an ongoing politics of hybridity, of cultural collaboration, mixings and cross-overs, is desperately needed, a tactical politics 'associated more with survival and the ability to articulate locally meaningful, relational futures than with transformation at a systemic level' (Clifford 1998: 367).

This doesn't mean of course that systemic, structural change – articulated in, as Hutnyk would have it, 'a more explicitly radical language' – should not be fought for, on the contrary. Indeed, in the wake of the May 1998 violence and the fall of Suharto political activism against the discrimination of Chinese Indonesians has surged (Kwok 1999). Importantly, much of this activism was a collaborative affair, undertaken by Indonesians of mixed ethnicities, genders and religions and involving many intellectuals, artists, religious leaders and politicians (Heryanto 1999). At the official level, steps have been taken to abolish the distinction between *pribumi* and non-*pribumi* – a distinction that tends to essentialize differences and to sharpen the dichotomy between 'real' Indonesians and 'Chinese' – and more generally, to remove the ban on Chinese cultural expression.[15] In other words, it would be mistaken to believe, as one would were one to rely uncritically on the impression produced by Huaren and other similar global information providers, that there are no political forces within Indonesia who work in solidarity with Chinese Indonesians to improve their situation.

It would be unrealistic, however, to expect that change in official politics and representation would automatically lead to change in everyday attitudes and popular common sense. The undoing of a divide that has been so entrenched in the Indonesian national imaginary since colonial times, and that has only been further solidified in postcolonial Indonesia, can only be slow process, involving the *longue durée* of cultural change and gradual reconciliation in ordinary social relationships. In short, it is a matter of the micro-politics of everyday life as much as the macro-politics of structural change.

Hybridity is crucial to such micro-politics. A politics of hybridity which empha-sizes an accommodation of cultures and peoples at the local level is a *necessary condition* for the very possibility of larger social and political transformation. After all, the latter can only be based on a belief in the continued viability of Chinese-Indonesian interconnections and mutual entanglements in the face of pressures which stress the mounting incommensurability between 'Chinese', on the one hand, and 'Indonesian', on the other. What is at stake in a politics of hybridity is neither a submission to the misguided and impossible idea of assimilation, nor a retreat into Chinese tribalism – a misguided strategic essentialism which would only help perpetuate the master dichotomy – but the implementation of contingent cultural practices which disrupt, in ever so modest ways, the fixity of the dichotomy itself. Such practices of hybridization are in the orbit of what ordinary people, Chinese and non-Chinese, think, believe and do in their local situations, and they are undoubtedly much more pervasive than is commonly recognized. But their significance remains unaccounted for precisely because the discursive force of global diaspora – and its loud assertion of globally applicable ethnic boundaries – tend to submerge what Appadurai (1996a: 153) describes as 'the incessant murmur of urban political discourse and its constant, undramatic cadences', the everyday terrain where, I would argue, ordinary hybridity is practised. Mrk from Bandung obviously felt he had to make a case for the importance of hybridity as a survival strategy when he wrote to the Huaren Bulletin Board:

> My grandma was the one who taught all of us to treat pribumi as equals, if we did then they'd treat us right. She always thought of all the tukang becak and everyone else who lived near our house in Solo as her friends. . . . Grandma was and still is a very wise person . . . I was just trying to share her views with other huaren over here [on the list], but I'm not as wise nor as persuasive as Grandma is.
>
> (16 May 1998)

In an important sense, hybridity is the politics of those 'who do not have claims to territorial propriety or cultural centrality' (Chow 1993: 25). This is particularly pertinent for groups such as Chinese Indonesians, who are 'stuck' in a country they have not been allowed to call their own despite the fact that they have lived there for generations. The difference between Chinese Indonesians and other ethnic groupings in Indonesia such as the Acehnese, the Bataks, the Balinese, and so on – the diverse local ethnicities that make up the imagined community of the Indonesian nation – is of cardinal significance here. The latter, 'natives' all, can claim to be the rightful inhabitants of particular territorial parts of the country. Their 'territorial propriety' is undisputed, and they could, in principle, though not in practice as long the concept of the Indonesian nation still holds, decide to secede and construct their own nation (state).[16] No such option is open to the Chinese Indonesians: dispersed as they are throughout the archipelago, they literally have no space of their own. In other words, they have no choice but to live among and side by side with the (other) Indonesians and in this sense, paradoxically, their fate is intimately connected with the national project of 'Indonesia' – itself, one could argue, a formidable hybrid construction. The entangled histories of colonialism, competing nationalisms and the postcolonial consolidation of the Indonesian nation–state have left a legacy which present generations cannot wish away – whether they like it or not, they have to negotiate its consequences from a position of marginalization, of what I have described elsewhere as being 'trapped in ambivalence' (Ang 2001). This is why hybridity is not a luxury, but a necessity.

In the context I have described here, then, hybridity is not the extravagant privilege of diasporic intellectuals and First World postmodernists. Here, the power of hybridity is of a much more modest and mundane, but also a more vital kind. It has to do with securing the very possibility for Chinese Indonesians to continue to live in Indonesia in a situation of unchosen co-existence and entanglement with (other) Indonesians. Indeed, it is only *through* hybridization that Chinese Indonesians can stake a claim on the validity and, yes, 'authenticity' of their Indonesianness. There is nothing to be exalted about this situation, nor to be naïvely utopian about the promise of hybridity. As Garcia Canclini (2000: 48) rightly remarks, 'hybridisation is not synonymous with reconciliation among ethnicities and nations, nor does it guarantee democratic interactions'. Hybridity is not a superior form of transformative resistance, nor the only mode of politics available, but, rather more humbly, a limited but crucial, life-sustaining tactic of everyday survival and practice in a world overwhelmingly dominated by large-scale historical forces whose effects are beyond the control of those affected by them.

Let me return, finally, to my own speaking position as a diasporic intellectual. Rey Chow's (1993) unorthodox conception of 'writing diaspora' is of particular pertinence here. For Chow, the intellectualization of the diasporic condition is not an occasion for the affirmation of 'roots', but on the contrary, a process which enables a critical questioning of the powerful discourse of roots. Chow writes specifically about the situation of Hong Kong around the time of its handover to China, where, she observes, 'one has the feeling that the actual social antagonisms separating China and Hong Kong . . . are often overwritten with the myth of consanguinity' (ibid.: 24), the myth of a shared, primordial Chineseness. In this respect, as I have already argued in Chapter 2, claims to Chineseness as the *a priori* reason for loyalty and solidarity can act as a form of symbolic violence which narrows the basis for political agency to that of blood and race. A similar reductionism can be observed in the global Huaren embrace of the Indonesian Chinese cause as integral to their own. The diasporic intellectual's task would be to work against such reductionism and, in Chow's words, 'to set up a discourse that cuts across some of our new "solidarities" by juxtaposing a range of cultural contradictions that make us rethink the currently dominant conceptualizations of the solidarities themselves' (ibid.). It is such an 'ambivalent' discourse that I have tried to develop in this chapter.

At stake here then is what R. Radhakrishnan (1987: 203) refers to as 'the representative and representational connection between theory and constituency.' Problematizing the positionality of what he calls the 'ethnic theorist', he points to 'the paradox' that 'whereas the intellectual perceives theory to be an effective intervention on behalf of ethnicity, the people/masses that are the constituency are deeply skeptical and even hostile to the agency of the theorist' (ibid.: 202). This hostility amounts to the same anti-hybridity stance adopted by critics such as Hutnyk and Friedman who, claiming rather superciliously to speak on behalf of the people/masses, argue that hybridity is both elitist and politically toothless. But as I have indicated above, hybridity is not only crucial for the conduct of ordinary everyday life in situations of complicated entanglement, it is also widely practised by the people/masses – against the grain of imposed fixed identities. The diasporic intellectual needs to hold on to her detached ambivalence, too often dismissed as a failure of solidarity, as a necessary stance to go beyond the primordialist truisms and passions of diasporic ethnicity as it is promoted in dominant discourse – a discourse which, as this chapter has shown, is being globalized in a dramatic fashion through the new networks of cyberspace.

Which leads me to conclude that if I *am* a diasporic intellectual – and I am certainly not always one – then my diasporic reference point, my imaginary 'home', cannot be 'China'; it has to be 'Indonesia'. But my position as an Indonesian diasporic intellectual is necessarily ambivalent and double-edged, always already steeped in hybridity. In pointing to the social and political contradictions condensed within the valorization of diaspora, we can be guided by Zygmunt Bauman's (1993: 245) 'postmodern wisdom' that 'there are problems in human and social life with no good solutions, twisted trajectories that cannot be straightened up, . . . moral agonies which no reason-dictated recipes can soothe, let alone cure'. Acting on this wisdom is the wisdom of hybridity.

4

UNDOING DIASPORA

Questioning global Chineseness
in the era of globalization

If, as Armenian-American scholar Khachig Tölölyan has claimed, 'diasporas are the exemplary communities of the transnational moment' (1991: 3), then what can diasporas say about the social and cultural processes of globalization we are experiencing today? Globalization, as we know, is pre-eminently characterized by the increasing interconnectedness of disparate parts of the world through the intensification of transnational networks, relationships and flows. In this sense, the growing visibility of diasporas – formations of people bound together, at least nominally, by a common ethnic identity despite their physical dispersal across the globe – makes them without doubt one of the key instances *and* symptoms of today's globalizing world. As such, they are also suitable sites for a reflection on the ramifications of globalization for social relations in contemporary societies, societies which we still tend to define predominantly in national terms, even though the eroding effects of globalization itself are felt by all national societies as their borders are transgressed and worn down by ever-increasing transnational social and cultural traffic.

Tölölyan made his claim that diasporas are the exemplary communities of the transnational moment in the editorial of the first issue of the journal *Diaspora: A Journal for Transnational Studies*, which he set up in 1991.[1] Since then, he has continued to edit this increasingly influential journal, an influence which resonates with the increasing popularity of the term diaspora itself. While this term was once reserved as a descriptor for the historical dispersion of Jewish, Greek and Armenian peoples, today the term tends to be used much more generically to refer to almost any group living outside of their country of origin, be it Italians outside Italy, Africans in the Caribbean, North America or Western Europe, Cubans in Miami and Madrid, or Chinese all over the world. Indeed, as Tölölyan remarks:

> the significant transformation of the last few decades is the move towards re-naming as diasporas . . . communities of dispersion . . . which were known by other names until the late 1960s: as exile groups, overseas communities, ethnic and racial minorities, and so forth.
>
> (1996: 3)

To put it differently, the burgeoning language and consciousness of diaspora are a manifestation and effect of intensifying cultural globalization. While migrations of people have taken place for centuries and have been a major force in the creation of the modern world of nation–states since the nineteenth century, it is only in the past few decades, with the increased possibilities of keeping in touch with the old homeland and with co-ethnics in other parts of the world through faster and cheaper jet transport, mass media and electronic telecommunications, that migrant groups are collectively more inclined to see themselves not as minorities within nation–states, but as members of global diasporas which span national boundaries.

It is clear, then, that the discourse of diaspora owes much of its contemporary currency to the economic, political and cultural erosion of the modern nation–state as a result of postmodern capitalist globalization – what Tölölyan calls 'the transnational moment'. Tölölyan even nominates diasporas as the paradigmatic Others of the nation–state: the increasing assertiveness of diasporic groups in representing and organizing themselves *as* transnational communities forces nation–states to 'confront the extent to which their boundaries are porous and their ostensible homogeneity a multicultural heterogeneity' (1991: 5). Seen this way, diasporas not only are placed in direct opposition to the nation–state, but are also implicitly designated as key socio-cultural formations capable of *overcoming* the constrictions of national boundaries, the means through which people can imagine and align themselves *beyond* 'an oppressive national hegemony' (Clifford 1997: 255). Much contemporary work on diaspora, both scholarly and popular, represents this transnational diasporic imaginary as a liberating force: simply put, the nation–state is cast as the limiting, homogenizing, assimilating power structure, which is now, finally, being deconstructed from within by those groups who used to be marginalized within its borders but are now bursting out of them through their diasporic transnational connections.

This diametrical oppositioning of nation–state as site of oppression and diaspora as site of liberation is obviously an exaggeratedly simplified depiction of current theorizing on these issues. Yet it serves to elucidate what I wish to problematize in this chapter, namely the privileged status of 'diaspora' as a metaphor for transnational formations characteristic of the globalized, presumably post-national world (Appadurai 1996a; Cohen 1997). At the end of this chapter, I will contrast the metaphor of diaspora with that of the multicultural global city, to sketch an alternative, more open-ended model for analysing social relations in the age of globalization. The global city, as various authors have pointed out (Sassen 1991), is a key physical manifestation of contemporary globalization, and migrations are an important factor in the formation and make-up of global cities. Global cities are points of destination for large numbers of migrants from many different parts of the world, and as such they are spaces where disparate diasporic groups settle and operate from, rubbing shoulders with each other and with locals on a daily basis. As a result, intense processes of cultural hybridization are rife in the global city, leaving no coherent identity and community untouched and putting all of them under erasure, so to speak. Interestingly, the very notion of diaspora as a

coherent transnational community is unsettled when placed within the re
hybridizing framework of the global city.

Continuing on from the argument I have developed in the previous c
will in this chapter question all too uncritical celebrations of diaspora in li‿
processes of globalization the world is undergoing today. I will explore the limiting
conceptual and political implications of diaspora discourse, suggesting that a narrow
focus on diaspora will hinder a more truly transnational, if you like, cosmopolitan
imagination of what it means to live in the world 'as a single place' (Robertson
1992). I will return to the Chinese diaspora, not only because it is one of the oldest
and largest diasporic formations in the world, but also because it has – and,
considering its strength in numbers, can afford to have – global aspirations. I
will do some conceptual ground-clearing, and reflect on the concept of 'Chinese
diaspora' itself: how it is currently used, how this relates to older conceptions of
diasporic Chinese, and its intellectual and political implications. In doing this, my
theoretical starting point will be that just like nations, diasporas are not natural,
always-already existing entities but 'imagined communities' (Anderson 1991). As
such, I will conclude that the transnationalism of the Chinese diaspora is actually
nationalist in its outlook, because no matter how global in its reach, its imaginary
orbit is demarcated ultimately by the closure effected by the category of Chineseness
itself.

The global production of Chinese diaspora

The modern nation–state has classically, in its nineteenth-century European
conception, operated as a territorially bounded sovereign polity, imagining itself
as an internally homogeneous community, unified by a common language, culture
and people. To be sure, this very ideal of the nation as (having to be) racially and
culturally homogeneous was one of the main ideological justifications for the
various policies of Chinese exclusion introduced in new-world nation–states such
as the USA, Canada and Australia in the late nineteenth century (Markus 1979;
Stratton and Ang 1998). In South-East Asia, where most of so-called 'overseas
Chinese' live, they have long been an integral part of colonial society and economy.
After World War Two, they were subjected to rule of the newly independent
postcolonial nation–states with strong nationalist aspirations of their own. In
many cases, as in Malaysia and Indonesia, the Chinese found themselves relegated
to being second-class citizens, economically well-off but socially and politically
discriminated against. 'Being Chinese', under all these circumstances, has meant
being locked into an unenviable, paralysingly disempowered position *vis-à-vis* the
dominant national culture and the state undergirding it.

While 'overseas Chinese' used to be the common English term to describe
the dispersed migrant Chinese communities around the world, in the past decade
or so they are increasingly frequently described collectively as 'Chinese diaspora'.
A key marker of this shift was the publication of Lynn Pan's hugely popular book
Sons of the Yellow Emperor, a sprawling history of the Chinese diaspora (Pan 1990).

This was followed in a more scholarly vein by the two volumes of essays edited by Wang Gungwu and Wang Ling-chi, *The Chinese Diaspora: Selected Essays* (1998). Pan was also the general editor of a massive encyclopedia of the Chinese diaspora, published under the aegis of the Chinese Heritage Centre in Singapore, which was established in 1995 'to study overseas Chinese globally'. Interestingly, this impressive publication expressly avoids the word 'diaspora' in its title (even though it is used liberally in the text), and is called *The Encyclopedia of the Chinese Overseas* instead (Pan 1998). This suggests that there is something problematic about the politics of naming and use of the label 'Chinese diaspora' – an issue I will return to shortly.

Of course, the transnationalization of the imagination afforded by the notion of diaspora can be experienced as rather liberating indeed. By imagining oneself as part of a globally significant, transnational Chinese diasporic community, a minority Chinese subject can rise, at least in the imagination, above the national environment in which (s)he lives but from which (s)he may always have felt symbolically excluded. I would contend that much of the current popularity of 'Chinese diaspora' among ethnic Chinese around the world is fuelled precisely by this emotive desire not just to belong, but to belong to a respectable imagined community, one that instils pride in one's identity precisely because it is so much larger and more encompassing, in geographical terms at least, than any territorially bounded nation. Global diaspora, in this context, signifies deliverance and release from territorialized national identity, triumph over the shackles of the nation–state.

In the economic realm, the rising power of what Ong and Nonini (1997) call 'modern Chinese transnationalism', whose subjects are jetsetting business men criss-crossing the Asia-Pacific to enhance their commercial empires, has received much attention. This transnational Chinese capitalist class, mythically held together by supposedly unique Chinese cultural characteristics such as *guanxi*, grew substantially since the opening up of mainland China in the mid-1980s (e.g. Chan 2000). It is a well-known fact that the Chinese economy owes much of its astonishingly rapid growth in recent years to the multi-million dollar investments of overseas Chinese capitalists from across the Asia-Pacific region, in no small part encouraged and enticed to do so by the communist authorities in Beijing who are determined to establish a 'capitalism with Chinese characteristics' with the help of China's diasporic sons, all in the name of 'cultural solidarity, filial piety and everlasting loyalty to the motherland' (Ong 1999: 45). The creation of new overseas Chinese business networks operating on a global scale has accelerated in the 1990s as traditional overseas Chinese voluntary associations, in the past organized mainly under principles of native place, kinship and dialect and dedicated to traditional obligations such as ancestor worship, were transformed into modern, globally operating organizations specifically committed to expanding economic opportunities and strengthening diasporic cultural ties across national boundaries (Liu 1998). The World Chinese Entrepreneurs Convention, established in 1991, is only one of the most prestigious new organizations embodying the new, self-confident and capitalist elite face of the Chinese diaspora in the era of globalization.[2]

But the strengthening of global Chinese identification goes far beyond the level of economic cooperation and trade connections: it is a transnational *cultural* movement involving many ethnic Chinese whose concerns are mainly of a personal-political nature, dealing with basic issues of identity and belonging. An example of this is one of the most well-known popular Chinese diaspora institutions in recent years, the website Huaren (www.huaren.org). As I have discussed in Chapter 3, this organization, which presents itself explicitly as a grassroots movement independent from the official overseas Chinese organizations, gained some international notoriety when it galvanized an unprecedented level of diasporic Chinese militancy in response to what came to be known worldwide as the anti-Chinese riots in Indonesia in May 1998. More generally, the site's main stated objective is 'to promote kinship and understanding among all Overseas Chinese' – a task hugely facilitated by the quintessential technology of contemporary transnationalism: the Internet. The site's Homepage depicts the Chinese diasporic experience specifically in terms of loss of identity, and the need and opportunity to restore it through the electronic assertion of a proto-familial, ethnic/racial community:

> Chinese diaspora had existed for many centuries and spread far and wide. Early mistreatments had caused many descendants to feel confused, indifferent, or ambivalent toward their heritage. With modern communication technology, this is the right time to bring us together and to promote the sense of kinship.
>
> (www.huaren.org Homepage)

They contine:

> Chinese are estimated to be living in over 136 different countries, making it perhaps the most widespread ethnic group in the world. Such diversity is indeed awe-inspiring. Yet, it is the same diversity which creates gulfs among peoples. We often encounter Chinese-Americans or Chinese-Canadians who know or care little of their counterparts elsewhere. Such ignorance and indifference should be corrected.
>
> (www.huaren.org About Us)

Put briefly, then, Huaren's activist desire is to unite the Chinese Diaspora (it is not insignificant that the word diaspora is generally capitalized in Huaren's editorial statements). They wish to counter the fragmenting effects of centuries-long spatial scattering through a reaffirmation of historical continuity and perpetuity of a proto-familial blood connection which crosses geographical borders and dividing lines imposed by nation–states. Unlike the business networks, which can be said to have instrumental reasons to capitalize on co-ethnic identification (i.e. economic opportunity), for Huaren, the affirmation of Chinese identity is an end in itself: in this sense, it practises pure identity politics on a global scale. Naturalized notions of fictive kinship and racial belonging are the basis of Huaren's contribution to the active *production* of the transnational community of diasporic Chinese. In his book *Global Diasporas* Robin Cohen (1997: ix) notes that 'a member's adherence to a diasporic community is demonstrated by an acceptance of an inescapable link with their past migration history and a sense of co-ethnicity with others of a similar background'. It is precisely this acceptance of one's primordial Chineseness that Huaren wishes to strengthen or instil in anyone who has some Chinese ancestry. From this point of view, any Chinese-American or Chinese-Canadian would do well, to all intents and purposes, to be Chinese first, and American or Canadian only second, and so help bolster the internal cohesion and solidarity of the global Chinese diasporic community.

It is clear what is involved in this particular instance of diaspora politics. First of all, it is based on the premise that historical origin is – or stronger, *should be* – ultimately more important than the geographical present in determining one's contemporary identity and sense of belonging. It is also premised on the notion that the signifier 'Chinese' alone, whatever its meaning, is sufficient to differentiate between people who do and those who do not belong to this massively large diasporic community, and to somehow seal and define the commonality of all those who do belong. Further, the motivation for diasporic solidarity is implicitly and explicitly justified by a stance of moral high ground: it is past and present 'mistreatments' (read: anti-Chinese racism) which urges 'us' to stick together. Thus, apart from a commitment to document 'Indonesian atrocities against Huaren' the Huaren website significantly dedicates much of its cyberspace to the Nanjing Massacre of 1937 (Sun 2000). Finally, it is assumed that the move toward transnational alignment with co-ethnics elsewhere provides an emancipatory lever which enables diasporic Chinese 'to circumvent disciplining by nation–states' (Nonini and Ong 1997: 3) and, in the end, to racial harmony between 'Chinese' and 'non-Chinese'. This stated idealism, however, is contradicted by the actual hostility expressed towards various non-Chinese others (as I have discussed in Chapter 3) and the hardening of the boundary between Chinese and non-Chinese produced by it.

It should be pointed out that the production of the Chinese diaspora, as exemplified by Huaren, is first and foremost a matter of collective self-representation. The interactive and participatory nature of Internet communication is a very efficient vehicle through which a global sense of community and collective identity is created: this very process helps bring the Chinese diaspora into being. As Tölölyan puts it, 'the diasporic collective subject [is] a figure that mobilizes dispersion into diaspora and is fleshed out in the course of that mobilization' (1996: 29). One can object, of course, that only relatively few diasporic Chinese would ever take part in the cyber-communication of Huaren and other similar organizations. However, according to Tölölyan the (re)production of any diaspora worthy of that name depends on a small number of political leaders and, most importantly, intellectuals and artists who produce the cultural works and discourses that fuel the diasporic consciousness and identity. And, the fact that the committed, activist and militant diasporists rarely form more than a small percentage of old ethnic or new immigrant dispersions now emerging as diasporas does not prevent them from claiming the now-valorized 'diaspora' label for the social formation in whose name they strive to speak to dominant groups.

(Tölölyan 1996: 19)

In short, the re-description of a dispersed people *as* a diaspora is not an innocent act of name-change but a transformative political move – a move which Tölölyan himself cautions against celebrating too uncritically. What, then, are its pitfalls? Wang Gungwu, the great doyen of overseas Chinese historical scholarship, has recently expressed his disquiet about the use of the term diaspora, especially in relation to overseas Chinese. His reservations are not theoretical but primarily political and ultimately existential.

The more I think about it, the unhappier I am that the term has come to be applied to the Chinese. I have used the term with great reluctance and regret, and I still believe that it carries the wrong connotation and that, unless it is used carefully to avoid projecting the image of a single Chinese diaspora, will eventually bring tragedy to the Chinese overseas.

(Wang 1999: 15)

A transnational nationalism

Wang's sense of foreboding, which he expressed with the recent difficulties faced by Chinese-Indonesians in mind, is informed by a profound knowledge of overseas Chinese history and an awareness of the problems raised by earlier manifestations of Chinese diaspora politics, even if that term was not used as such. Specifically, Wang's concern is induced by the controversial historical role played by the ambiguous term *huaqiao* (Chinese sojourner) in the production of the Chinese diaspora. The term emerged in China in the 1890s and came into general use to describe all overseas Chinese after the Revolution of 1911 (Wang 1992). It remained prevalent until well into the 1950s, when its use ran into trouble as newly independent postcolonial nation–states began to assert control over the Chinese minority populations within their borders. *Huaqiao* carried strong political and emotive connotations, implying the unity of overseas Chinese communities as one people and their unbroken ties with the Chinese homeland. This is how Wang sums up the problematic political career of the term:

From China's point of view, *huaqiao* was a powerful name for a single body of overseas Chinese. It was openly used to bring about ethnic if not nationalist or racist binding of all Chinese at home and abroad. In the countries which have large Chinese minorities, the term had become a major source of the suspicion that the Chinese minorities could never feel loyalty towards their host nations.

(Wang 1999: 2)

In other words, the term *huaqiao*, with its reference to temporariness of residence outside China and its wholesale application to all Chinese abroad, evoked a scenario of 'militant commitment to remaining Chinese or restoring one's "Chineseness"' (Wang 1992: 7). This ideological China-centredness and obsession with Chineseness helped fuel anti-Chinese suspicion and discrimination in foreign lands, whether in South-East Asia or in European immigrant societies such as Australia and the United States. The question lingering in Wang Gungwu's mind is: 'Will the word diaspora be used to revive the idea of a single body of Chinese, reminiscent of the old term, the *huaqiao*?' (1999: 2).

The power of these words – *huaqiao* then, diaspora today (not to mention *huaren*) – is not solely associated with their capacity to consolidate the collective imagination. They also spur people into action: they buttress and legitimize organizing practices aimed at mobilizing dispersed communities around a singular point of cultural and political identification: real and imagined 'China', the centre of authentic 'Chineseness'. Thus, the hegemony of *huaqiao* discourse in the first half of the twentieth century was closely connected to the activist practices of mainland Chinese nationalists, who sought to resinicize overseas Chinese communities in South-East Asia who, in their eyes, had 'lost' their Chineseness. Through ideological apparatuses such as Chinese language education and the unifying narratives of race and fictive kinship, the self-identification and identification by others of these communities *as* Chinese were reinforced and affirmed. The controversial history of overseas Chinese nationalism – a diasporic nationalism designed to support and strengthen the nation–state of China – does not have to be recounted here; suffice it to say that its overall ideological effect was a general reification of the very idea of Chinese identity as something fixed and indisputable. As Prasenjit Duara has argued, before the intervention of the Chinese nationalist activists, the majority of Chinese outside China lived with a flexible and ambiguous sense of Chineseness which had relatively open and soft, permeable boundaries. The activists, in Duara's words, 'sought to transform these multiple, mobile identifications into a Chineseness that eliminated or reduced internal boundaries, on the one hand, and hardened the boundaries between Chinese and non-Chinese, on the other' (1997: 41).

It is this ideological effect, associated with the term *huaqiao*, which Wang Gungwu finds intellectually and politically debilitating, and which he sees as in danger of being repeated in the current valorization of the Chinese *diaspora*. Indeed, there is little doubt that the global discourse of diaspora, *pace* Huaren, is a powerful instrument in stimulating the (desire for) transnational integration and essentialist homogenization of overseas Chinese communities and individuals around the world as ultimately Chinese, and by implication, as ultimately distinct from non-Chinese. In this sense, the language of diaspora is fundamentally nationalist: it feeds into a *transnational nationalism* based on the presumption of internal ethnic sameness and external ethnic distinctiveness. Unlike the nationalism of the nation state, which premises itself on a national community which is territorially bound, diasporic nationalism produces an imagined community which is deterritorialized, but which is symbolically bounded nevertheless. Its borders are clearly defined, at least in the imagination, and its actual and potential membership is finite: only certain people, notionally 'Chinese' people, can belong to the 'Chinese diaspora'.

It is this particularist vision inherent in the diasporic imagination that Benedict Anderson has scathingly criticized as lacking in 'universal grounding'. In his view, it 'represents a certain contemporary vision of cosmopolitanism based on a quasi-planetary dispersion of bounded identities', attractive to some, Anderson suggests, because it makes them feel 'entitled to belong to ancient bounded communities that nonetheless stretch impressively across the planet in the age of "globalization"' (Anderson 1998: 131). According to Anderson, this vision distorts the way global migrations and historical change form real social subjectivities because it assigns particular people *a priori* to particular diasporic groupings: 'Wherever the "Chinese" happen to end up – Jamaica, Hungary, or South Africa – they remain countable Chinese, and it matters little if they also happen to be citizens of those nation-states' (ibid.). One does not have to share Anderson's dismissive rejection of identitarian notions of ethnicity *per se* to agree that the discourse of diaspora is authorized in principle by a fundamental notion of closure: it postulates the existence of closed and limited, mutually exclusive universes of ethnic sameness.

Seen this way, then, diasporas cannot simply be counterposed to nation–states: interestingly, a cultural nationalism – in the sense of the proposition of an imagined cultural community with clear boundaries, whether territorial or ethnic – underpins the construction of both. But if this is so, then we can ask the question whether diasporas – no longer to be seen as unambiguous sites of liberation in opposition to the presumably oppressive site of the nation–state – can exercise their own forms of disciplinary power on their members. If one of the key modes of power nation–states have over the people in their respective territories is that of inclusion and exclusion, don't diasporas apply similar mechanisms in patrolling *their* boundaries? This, indeed, is how Duara (1997: 40) describes the work of the early twentieth-century nationalist activists who, 'with a totalizing vision of community seek to eliminate these permeable boundaries [of local overseas Chinese communities] or transform them into the hardened boundaries of a closed community'. In this light, practices of resinicization aimed at re-imbuing those who apparently had 'lost' their Chineseness with their 'true' cultural identity, can be interpreted as practices of *forced inclusion*: they are attempts to prevent those who had dispersed themselves from the homeland from 'going astray' and to sharpen the boundaries of the Chinese diaspora. Ironically, these very migrants cannot help but blur these boundaries through their everyday interactions with and adaptations to their non-Chinese environments.

In today's diasporic activism, similar tendencies can be detected. Remember, for example, the Huaren lament that many Chinese-Americans or Chinese-Canadians 'know or care little of their counterparts elsewhere' and the added militant directive that 'such ignorance and indifference should be corrected'. To be sure, the very suggestion that Chinese-Americans should consider any other 'Chinese' group elsewhere in the world as their 'counterparts' cannot be taken at face value as a natural and logical demand. It is one instance of the imposition of fictive kinship which is part and parcel of the production of the Chinese diaspora as an imagined trasnational community. The claimed need for correction of trans-national ignorance and indifference only stresses the desire for integrating, if not unifying the diaspora.

One could object, of course, that unlike nation–states, diasporas do not in general have the institutional resources to impose their disciplinary power on their members: they are, after all, stateless.[3] Furthermore, one could point to the fact that many people with Chinese ancestry today voluntarily identify with their Chinese 'roots' – a development in sync with the emergence of identity politics and the rise of multiculturalism, mostly in Western nation–states, especially the United States. Indeed, novels by Amy Tan and many other Chinese-American writers have popularized the stories of young and old second-, third- or even fourth generation Americans with Chinese ancestry who derive profound meaning and joy out of the rediscovery of their Chinese heritage, often underscored by return visits to China the motherland.[4] But these developments only confirm the empirical observation that the social and discursive production of the Chinese diaspora is in full swing, a process driven by a passionate identification with and reification of 'Chineseness' as a globally relevant marker for identity and difference, and for which 'China', which, as I have discussed in Chapter 2, can be culturally defined as much as geographically located, forms the centre. The power of the diaspora here is ideo-logical and emotional rather than institutional: it works through the imagination (Appadurai 1996a).

We can now return to Wang Gungwu's unhappiness about the upsurge in the application of the word *diaspora* to the overseas Chinese. Wang's concern focuses on the danger that the expression 'Chinese diaspora', just like the word *huaqiao* in earlier times, would create the false image of a single global Chinese community which would be ultimately loyal to China, to the detriment of the autonomy and specificity of local Chinese communities in different parts of the world. As Wang remarks: 'I have long advocated that the Chinese overseas be studied in the context of their respective national environments, and taken out of a dominant China reference point' (1999: 1). To counter the homogenizing tendencies of 'diaspora', Wang wishes to emphasize the large variety of overseas Chinese experiences, the real historical effects of the process of dispersal. For Wang, this emphasis on difference and diversity within the diaspora opens up the perspective of a diasporic pluralism, one that recognizes that there are 'many kinds of Chinese', even 'many different Chinese diasporas' (ibid.: 17), variously settled in and oriented towards their new countries of residence.

Indeed, Wang is acutely aware of the pressure brought about by this emphasis on proliferating diversity, predicting that:

> the single word, Chinese, will be less and less able to convey a reality that continues to become more pluralistic. We need more words, each with the necessary adjectives to qualify and identify who exactly we are describing. We need them all to capture the richness and variety of the hundreds of Chinese communities that can now be found.
>
> (Wang 1999: 16)

Unlike Anderson (1998), however, Wang does not go so far as problematizing the use of the term 'Chinese' as such. And yet precisely in light of the pluralization of diaspora advocated by Wang it is instructive to reiterate Anderson's disturbing query: why would 'Chinese' who happened to end up in the most far-flung corners of the world – Jamaica, Hungary, or South Africa – still count as Chinese, even if they are now citizens of those nation–states? What makes them still Chinese and when, if ever, can or do they stop being Chinese? This question drives us right into the question of the border: the boundary between 'Chinese' and 'non-Chinese' which, as we have seen above, is liable to manipulation and redefinition, moulded from soft to hard.

Undoing '(the) Chinese'

What I am trying to get at is this: not only the word diaspora needs to be problematized, but also the word 'Chinese'. While Wang's concern focuses on the need to diffuse the China-centredness of Chinese overseas (even though 'China' remains inevitably central to the imagining of the diaspora, the imaginary homeland that ultimately binds the diaspora together symbolically), Anderson's question points to the need for a serious examination of the outer border of the diaspora, that shifty, peripheral area where 'Chinese' transmutes into 'non-Chinese'. Of course, this very image of core and periphery captures the central hierarchy that is key to the transnational nationalist imagination which carries dominant renderings of the Chinese diaspora.[5] Take, for example, this visual resprentation of the Chinese diaspora in the *Encyclopedia of the Chinese overseas*, which displays all the paradoxes of the diasporic imagination I have discussed here (see Figure 4.1).

The centrality of China and Chinese within China is dramatically represented in Figure 4.1, with Taiwan and Hong Kong slightly decentred. The *Encyclopedia* deals mainly with those in circle C. The definition of this group is quite comprehensive:

> [it] encompasses those unequivocally identified as 'overseas Chinese' (or 'Chinese overseas'). Examples of these are the so-called 'hyphenated' Chinese: Sino-Thais, Chinese Americans, and so on; people who are of Chinese descent but whose non-Chinese citizenship and political

85

allegiance collapse ancestral loyalties. If this book may be said to have a constituency, these foreign Chinese are it.

(Pan 1998: 15)

Note this peculiar term 'foreign Chinese'! The most interesting segment, however, is circle D, the 'assimilated'. These are described as 'those of Chinese ancestry who have, through intermarriage or other means of assimilation, melted into another people and ceased to call themselves Chinese'. To which is added: 'Whether they will call themselves Chinese at some future date must be left an open question, however, because it has been known to happen' (ibid.: 15). Here then the ambiguous and uncertain boundary between 'Chinese' and 'non-Chinese' is most clearly spelt out and acknowledged. Circle D is the nebulous and fuzzy border zone where the Chinese/non-Chinese boundary is decidedly up for grabs, indeterminate and unsettled.

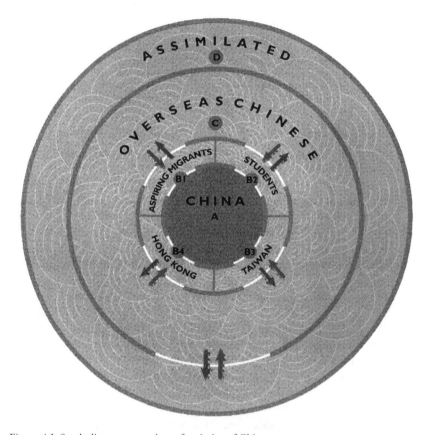

Figure 4.1 Symbolic representation of varieties of Chinese

Source: Pan (1998). Reproduced with permission from the Chinese Heritage Centre, Singapore.

Those interested in the Chinese diaspora would typically consider this border zone either as of peripheral significance – too far removed from the 'pure' Chinese core in the inner circle – or as a danger zone, where Chinese people are at risk of losing their Chinese characteristics. However, I would argue that it is precisely by focusing on this soft and porous border zone, which is only peripheral if one accepts the hierarchical model of concentric circles as the only valid representation of reality, that we can move beyond the nationalist imagination – territorial or deterritorialized ethnic – shared by both nation–states and diasporas. Indeed, in this era of global-ization, where the mixing and interconnecting of people from different ethnic and cultural backgrounds are becoming increasingly commonplace, even in the still relatively closed and homogeneous nation–state of China, one could suspect that the border zone, where identities are unfixed and destabilized, will only become increasingly crowded, and gain in size and significance. This border zone, the actual and symbolic contact zone of intercultural encounter and negotiation (Pratt 1992), is where processes of hybridization transpire on a regular and ordinary basis.

It is my argument throughout this book that if we are interested in analysing cultural globalization today it is these processes of hybridization that need to be the centre of our attention (Garcia Canclini 1995; 2000; Hannerz 1996). One of the merits of the concept of hybridization is that it undermines the binary and static way of thinking about difference which is dominant in theories of cultural pluralism, which are premised on the *distinctness* of cultures and ethnicities. However, as Garcia Canclini remarks, '*Diversity* and *heterogeneity* are terms that serve to establish catalogues of differences, but they do not account for intersections and mixings between cultures' (2000: 41, emphasis in original). The importance of highlighting processes of hybridization is that it provides us with a conceptual 'point of departure from which to break from fundamentalist tendencies and from the fatalism of the doctrines of civilizing wars' (ibid.: 48). Crucially, the cut-and-mix circulation of cultural meanings activated by hybridization illuminates the relatively arbitrary and contingent character of all culture, its dynamic flexibility and profound open-endedness.

Taking processes of hybridity seriously as productive of 'a field of energy and sociocultural innovation' (ibid.: 49) has of course become commonplace in contemporary cultural studies. What has been less emphasized, however, is that pervasive hybridity also has radical ramifications for how we think of different 'peoples'. Indeed, as hybridization consists of exchanges, crossings, and mutual entanglements, it necessarily implies a softening of the boundaries between 'peoples': the encounters *between* them are as constitutive of who they are as the proceedings *within*. These encounters are not always harmonious or conciliatory; often they are extremely violent, as the history of colonialism has amply shown. Nevertheless, they have to be gone through 'when a collection of men and women feels challenged by another culture and has to choose between hybridisation and confrontation' (ibid.: 50). Even in the most oppressive situations, then, people thrown into intercultural encounters, whether by force or by will, would seek to negotiate their differences if they are to avoid war. The result, after many centuries of contact history, is a throroughly hybridized world where boundaries have become utterly porous, even though they are artificially maintained. As Garcia Canclini asserts:

> It is not possible to say where the British end and where the colonies begin, where the Spanish end and the Latin Americans begin, where Latin Americans begin and where the indigenous do. None of these groups still remain within their original limits.
>
> (ibid.: 49)

In parallel, we can say that centuries of global Chinese migrations have inevitably led to a blurring of the original limits of 'the Chinese': it is no longer possible to say with any certainty where the Chinese end and the non-Chinese begin. Indeed, the very attempt to draw such a line would amount to a form of discursive reductionism, if not symbolic violence, which disparages the long history of profound imbrication of Chinese peoples in the world as they have dispersed themselves all over the globe. Obviously '(non-)Chinese', here, is to be defined in more than strictly biological terms, not just as 'race' with all its complicated connotations (see Chapter 2), but in cultural terms, in terms of the meanings and practices that we have over the centuries come to think of as what sets 'Chinese' culture apart from others. Wherever notionally Chinese communities and individuals routinely enter into relations with others, live and work together with 'non-Chinese', processes of hybridization are set in motion which inevitably transform everyone involved. It is in these border zones that the fuzziness of the identity line, the fundamental uncertainty about where the Chinese end and the non-Chinese begin(s), can be best recognized and empirically examined.

Hybridity and Chineseness in the global city

In methodological terms, this means an interesting shift of our focus back to the space of the territorial nation–state, or more precisely, to the physical space of territorial co-presence. In this era of globalization, nation–states are no longer the enclosed beacons of ethnic and cultural homogeneity. Indeed, the very proliferation of diasporas in the past century or so has thoroughly undermined the nineteenth-century apartheid fantasies of 'a place for each "race"' so favoured by nationalists (Cohen 1997: 196). Instead, many nation–states today, especially those which are destination points for the mass migrations of the past century or so, are undergoing a process of what Kobena Mercer (2000: 234) calls 'multicultural normalization' – a massive process of social transformation which makes it increasingly more appropriate for nation–states to be described as multicultural states, consisting of many different, overlapping and intertwined groups and identities with multiple loyalties and attachments, exchanges and interactions both within and across the border.

The metropolitan space of the contemporary global city is more representative of this state of affairs than the nation–state as a whole (where non-metropolitan areas, such as rural Australia, are typically still more characterized by real and imagined homogeneity, and militantly protective of it). A crucial difference between nation–states and cities is that the latter, spaces characterized by the constant circulation of various types of locals and non-locals, cannot police their territorial boundaries: there is no border patrol at the perimeter of cities. At the same time, many metropolitan cities today are becoming so deeply internationally oriented, sustained by the rampant border-crossing activities of their dynamic and hetero-geneous populations (in trade, finance, media, tourism, and so on), that they can be described as 'translocalities', spaces with a sense of place and identity which is 'substantially divorced from their national contexts' (Appadurai 1996b: 44). In this sense, the global city may indeed be appropriately described as a transnational formation *par excellence*, in the sense that at any one time its 'membership', both permanent and temporary, typically consists of individuals and groups of myriad ethnic and racial backgrounds with ongoing connections all over the world. But in contrast with global diasporas (named by Tölölyan as the exemplary communities of the transnational moment), the imagined community of the global city is principally unbounded and open, in the sense that no one is *a priori* excluded from its space on the basis of predetermined kinship criteria such as race and ethnicity.[6] Indeed, as transnational formations global cities and diasporas may stand as contrasting metaphors, as Figure 4.2 shows.

Diaspora	Global city
Ethnic unity, spatial scattering	Ethnic diversity, spatial convergence
Transnational nationalism	Local hybridity
Virtual deterritorialized space	Actual social/territorial space
Sameness-in-dispersal	Together-in-difference

Figure 4.2 Diaspora and global city as transnational formations

While diasporas are constituted by ethnic unity in the face of spatial scattering, global cities are shaped by ethnic diversity through spatial convergence. While what matters for a diaspora is a connection with a symbolic 'elsewhere', a long-distance, virtual relationship with a global community of belonging, what grounds the global city is its firm orientation towards the 'here', the local, *this* place. While the transnationality of the diasporic community is one of 'sameness in dispersal' across global space, the transnationality of the global city is characterized by intense simultaneity and co-existence, by territorial 'togetherness in difference'. The global city, in this sense, is one large and condensed contact zone in which borders and ethnic boundaries are blurred and where processes of hybridization are rife inevitably because groups of different backgrounds, ethnic and otherwise, cannot help but enter into relations with each other, no matter how great the desire for separateness and the attempt to maintain cultural purity.

So what happens to Chineseness and Chinese diasporic communities in the global cities of today? This, of course, is an empirical question that needs to be examined on a case-by-case basis, taking into account not just demographic features and population movements but also the socio-cultural contexts and ideological currents which influence the formation of local identities and communities. Singapore and Sydney, to name but two global cities in the Asia-Pacific region, provide two very different examples. Let me finish this chapter with a brief exploration of Chinese/non-Chinese hybridization in the two cities.

Singapore is an odd case because it is both a nation–state and a global city. Here, the 'Chinese' are the majority ethnic group in an explicitly multiracial and multicultural city–state context – a unique situation in the Chinese diaspora. However, the Chineseness of the Singaporean Chinese has been a persistent object of significant concern to the PAP government, which has been insistent on the necessity to stop what they see as the gradual erosion of Chinese cultural characteristics among its Chinese population. Hence, the famous Speak Mandarin Campaign and other government policies to inculcate those of Chinese 'race' with Chinese 'culture' (Clammer 1985; Chua 1995; Ang and Stratton 1996). In other words, in Singapore there is an officially orchestrated desire to soften, if not counter the effects of hybridization as people of Chinese descent mix with others on a daily basis in a modern urban environment which has grown out of a British colonial legacy. As a result, a constant concern, if not obsession, with Chineseness is an enduring part of the Singaporean state's cultural mindset, even if the distinction between what is and what is not Chinese is often impossible or nonsensical to make in the hybrid conditions of everyday social practice. Such a climate, as Geoffrey Benjamin remarked in an early analysis of Singaporean multiracialism, 'puts Chinese people under pressure to become more Chinese . . . in their behaviour' (1976: 118). Chineseness, then, becomes a prescription, a project, an artificially imposed cultural identity rather than a lived, uncontrived one. But this desire to manage the Chineseness of Chinese Singaporeans, which is a project of the Singaporean nation–state, runs up against the actual processes of hybridization which proliferate in Singapore the global city.

In 1999, a storm of indignation and apprehension erupted in the global city–state when the results of a sociological survey were revealed in the press indicating that more than one in five young Chinese Singaporeans would rather be of another race – primarily white or Japanese – than Chinese. The survey was conducted by Dr Chang Han Yin of the National University of Singapore, who in an interview with *The Straits Times* expressed alarm over the lack of ethnic pride and confidence in Chinese culture that he read into his data (15 December 1999). Not the results of the survey as such (whose interpretation is contestable) but the fact that they caused so much consternation and anxiety is of most significance here. It could well be that precisely the heavy-handed insistence on the importance of being Chinese in the nation–state of Singapore generates a desire among a large number of young people, whose lives are presumably most immersed in the processes of everyday hybridization in the global city, to explore other identities beyond the bounds of their own 'race'. Indeed, as one commentator suggests, against the litany of recommendations on 'what can be done to strengthen the young's pride in their own race', the survey may show that 'race is not such a big issue' for young Singaporeans. The fact that many of them, given the chance, would identify with Caucasians or Japanese not only reflects a sound recognition of the global cultural power of Japan and the West, but also, according to Han Fook Kwang (1999), 'shows a certain openness to the world, and willingness to accept new ideas, no matter from which ethnic grouping'. In other words, in the globalizing world of today hybridization is increasingly a fact of life, altering if not diminishing the significance of Chineseness in any 'pure' sense as a marker of cultural identity. Thus, despite the persistence of the Speak Mandarin Campaign, which was launched in the late 1970s and has been relaunched every year since, the number of families using Mandarin at home has been dropping steadily as English is becoming increasingly the language most frequently spoken (from around 20 per cent in 1988 to more than 43 per cent in 2000) (*The Straits Times*, 12 September 2000).

Sydney is a very different environment for the formation of (non-)Chinese identities in the contact zone of the global city. Sydney is located within the nation–state of Australia, but its status as a transnational global city is affirmed by the fact that it receives by far the largest proportion of all migrants from all over the world coming into the country every year. Many of these are of Chinese descent in some particular fashion. Surveys of 'the Chinese in Australia', whose numbers have increased substantially in the past few decades, now point routinely to the diversity of the Chinese population, having migrated to Australia from different previous countries of residence (Ho and Coughlan 1997; Inglis 1998). Thus, Chinese from the PRC, Taiwan, Hong Kong, Malaysia, Indonesia, Vietnam, or East Timor, as well as those born in Australia, now share the metropolitan space of Sydney (together with many other ethnic groupings originating from all over the world). The global city, then, is a meeting place of large sections of the dispersed diaspora, where 'Chinese' of very different and largely unconnected histories have the opportunity to intersect and interact not in virtual cyberspace (as is the Huaren website), but in actual social space. It should not come as a surprise that these disparate groups have hardly recognized themselves as belonging to a singular Chinese community, even if the predominant mode of categorizing would insist on it. As Christine Inglis observes:

> Attempts to bring the plethora of [Chinese] groupings together within a unifying structure or umbrella at either the national or local level have so far been unsuccessful. The diversity of interests and backgrounds, as well as personal competition, has made it difficult to develop an organizational structure acceptable to all, and to identify individuals able to represent, or speak on behalf of, the Chinese community as a whole.
>
> (1998: 282)

In this regard, one might ask whether it makes sense to speak of a unitary 'Chinese community as a whole' in the first place!

Indeed, the very meaning of Chineseness, and who can or should be included in this category, can be the object of intense contestation among and between these groups. Here, then, we have a clear case where what counts as Chinese (or not) is torturously uncertain. Inglis remarks that one of the most isolated groups is the East-Timorese Chinese, who after more than two decades in Australia are 'only gradually developing contacts with other Chinese' (1998: 285). The tricky formulation here is 'other Chinese', which too hastily serves to stress the presumed *commonalities* of East Timorese of Chinese ancestry with, say, Hong Kong Chinese or Vietnamese Chinese. But most East-Timorese Chinese speak Hakka (if they still do), not a very widely used language in the other Chinese groups. Moreover, under the influence of the Portuguese who were the colonial rulers of East Timor until 1975, most East-Timorese Chinese are Catholic and do not observe many traditional Chinese customs. I have been told that the East-Timorese Chinese community in Sydney a few years ago decided to celebrate Chinese New Year in February together with some other Chinese groups in the city. This is a festivity which the East-Timorese Chinese had long dropped from their annual calendar, so their taking it up can be described as a small but meaningful instance of resinicization. After one year, however, they abandoned the event again because they didn't feel comfortable partying together with the other Chinese. Instead, they decided to celebrate something akin to 'Chinese New Year' (signified by typical paraphernalia such as dragon dances) among themselves, but on the 'regular' Christian New Year's day, the first of January.[7] One might wonder whether 'Chinese' is still useful to describe this very hybrid cultural practice? Is the category Chinese meaningful to label the East-Timorese Chinese at all, and if so why? The same questions can be asked, *inter alia*, about the Indonesian-Chinese, most of whom speak Indonesian not Chinese, and do not feel much affinity with other Chinese groups at all. To put it bluntly, why are they so readily counted in the Chinese diaspora, as the Huaren website and others have so insistently done, not the Indonesian diaspora?

In the hybridized and hybridizing environment of the global city, then, it is the continued validity of the label 'Chinese' itself that comes under scrutiny. In Singapore, it is pushed officially as a desirable and preferred Identity (with a capital I), which has led paradoxically to its problematization by significant numbers of young Singaporeans. In Sydney, the coming together of many different groups who have carried the label 'Chinese' to describe themselves has exposed its contested nature and its failure to operate as a term of diasporic integration. In this sense, 'Chineseness' is put under erasure, 'not in the sense of being written out of existence but in the sense of being unpacked' (Chow 1998b: 24), denaturalized and stripped of its self-evident cogency as a category of social and cultural classification. The hybridizing context of the global city brings out the intrinsic contradiction locked into the concept of diaspora, which, logically, depends on the maintenance of an apparently natural, essential identity to secure its imagined status as a coherent community. The global city is the space of diaspora's undoing.

Part II

BEYOND THE WEST
Negotiating Multiculturalism

5

MULTICULTURALISM IN CRISIS

The new politics of race and national identity in Australia

With Jon Stratton

Multiculturalism is a centrepiece of official government policy in Australia. It is a top–bottom political strategy implemented by the state to accommodate the inclusion of ethnic minorities within the national culture and to 'manage cultural diversity'. This policy has been in place since the early 1970s – a few years later than Canada, where the term 'multiculturalism' was first introduced into state discourse – and it has been widely touted as a repudiation of an exclusionary, homogenizing, even racist past, in favour of an inclusionary, pluralist and equitable recognition of the diverse ethnic groups living within the boundaries of the nation. In this sense, multiculturalism in Australia can be seen, to an important extent, as a form of symbolic politics aimed at redefining national identity. By the early 1990s, the description of Australia as a 'multicultural nation' had become commonplace in public discourse, and then Prime Minister Paul Keating could characterize the country fondly as 'a multicultural nation in Asia'. This official discourse of multiculturalism revels in the 'enrichment', both economic and cultural, provided by the presence of a plurality of cultures within the nation, and appeals to the citizenry by asking them to join in the chorus of 'celebrating our cultural diversity' (Hage 1994). Multiculturalism, in this sense, is ideologically inscribed in the very core of the 'new Australia', a key element of national cultural policy which could draw active support from Liberal and Labor governments alike from the early 1970s onwards.[1]

In the late 1990s, however, a backlash against multiculturalism gathered pace, coming mainly from conservative circles. During the 1996 elections, Keating's Labor Government suffered a crushing defeat. Keating's exuberant extolling of the virtues of multiculturalism – together with his enthusiasm for Australia's integration with Asia and his high-minded commitment to reconciliation with Aboriginal people – was widely cited as one major explanation for the defeat. These same elections brought to the fore reactionary populist forces which explicitly

95

denounced multiculturalism. A fish-and-chip shop owner-turned-politician, Pauline Hanson, gained a seat in Parliament as an Independent, on an election campaign which attacked the core of Keating's political agenda on the grounds that it did not represent the interests of ordinary, white Australians like herself. She slammed the special treatment of Aboriginal people (whom she considered were getting privileges not accessible to people like herself) and condemned Asian immigration because, as she put it, 'they don't assimilate and form ghettos'. On top of this, she wanted the policy of multiculturalism 'abolished' (Hanson 1997a).[2]

Hanson struck a chord, especially among white Australians living outside the big metropolitan centres, where she quickly gained a considerable following.[3] Not surprisingly, political criticism against her was loud and clear, reflecting a general tendency in Western liberal-democratic societies to position right-wing populist voices such as Hanson's outside the domain of political respectability (although what she is saying would have been perfectly respectable even in the 1950s). Analysts and activists have repeatedly compared Hanson with right-wing radicals such as David Duke in the United States and Jean-Marie le Pen in France in order to discredit her. However, while such international comparisons may be useful (enlightening the transnational dimensions of 'white panic' in the post-Cold War world),[4] it is important also to understand the specificity of the so-called Hanson phenomenon in the historical context of contemporary Australia, and the particular effectivity of her rhetorical strategy in that context. An important aspect of that strategy has been her self-representation as an *ordinary Australian*, and on her tireless claim that she speaks on behalf on 'the Australian people'. In her own words, she speaks 'not as a polished politician but as a woman who has had her fair share of life's knocks' (Hanson 1997a). Again and again she criticizes government policies which, in her view, promote 'a type of reverse racism applied to mainstream Australians' by supporting 'various taxpayer funded "industries" that flourish in our society servicing Aboriginals, multiculturalists and a host of other minority groups' (ibid.). Aware of the controversial nature of her views, she vigorously denies that she is a 'racist', claiming instead that she is only anxious to see Australia preserved as a strong and united country. The name of her political party, One Nation, is an indication of her bottom-line concern: 'To survive in peace and harmony, united and strong, we must have one people, one nation, one flag' (ibid.). This emphasis on 'oneness' reflects Hanson's nostalgic desire for national *homogeneity* (be it social, cultural or racial) – a desire which is clearly antagonistic to the pluralist celebration of diversity in multiculturalism.

Pauline Hanson has been a sensational phenomenon in *fin-de-siècle* Australian politics but, while her views do certainly reflect a significant strand in contemporary popular consciousness, her political power will arguably remain limited to that of an extreme, radical fringe. More important and more disturbing than the rise of Pauline Hanson is the stance taken by Keating's successor as Prime Minister, John Howard. Howard won the 1996 elections for the conservative Liberal Party on a campaign bearing the slogan 'For All of Us', a motto with a clear subtext that Keating's policies were *not* for 'all of us' but privileged special, minority interests.

The slogan itself bears an uneasy resemblance to Hanson's idea of 'one nation', and Howard's ideological inclination revealed itself when he failed to come up with a quick denunciation of Hanson's views, arguing that she had a right to speak her mind. This convenient, evasive recourse to the dogma of freedom of speech raised the suspicion that Howard privately sympathized with her views – a suspicion which he significantly has never explicitly tried to counter.[5] Howard has made it very clear that he is not a great fan of multiculturalism. Significantly, as soon as he gained governmental power he abolished the Office of Multicultural Affairs, severely slashed the migrant intake, and tightened up English proficiency requirements for new migrants. He also restricted access for new immigrants to social welfare and other benefits. His dislike of the very word 'multiculturalism' is so great that he would have preferred to scrap it from the national vocabulary. For example, in preparing a joint parliamentary resolution against racism in October 1996, which was instigated by the increasingly loud calls for an official, high-level denunciation of Pauline Hanson, he insisted on deleting the word 'multiculturalism' from the text.

Howard's reluctance to defend multiculturalism unambiguously, which, as we have said, has had bipartisan political support for more than two decades, has created an atmosphere of controversy around what came to be commonly referred to as 'the M-word'. In a government-commissioned discussion paper entitled *Multicultural Australia: The Way Forward*, the National Multicultural Advisory Council (1997) formulated the key question thus: 'Is multiculturalism an appropriate term to describe a policy for managing cultural diversity or has it outlived its usefulness?' Given what is known about the Prime Minister's own feelings on the issue, his likely answer to the question would be quite predictable. This is despite Howard's reassurance that 'the absolute, unqualified embrace of a culturally diverse, harmonious and tolerant Australian community is not in question' (Howard 1997). In other words, while Howard, unlike Hanson, does not express an explicit desire for a return to monocultural homogeneity – as the leader of a democratic country in the late twentieth century he simply would not be able to do that – but acknowledges the sociological reality of diversity, he refuses to use the term 'multiculturalism' to refer to that diversity.[6] The discussion paper itself elaborates on some of the difficulties of the use of the word: it reports that some people (it doesn't mention who) are 'uncomfortable' with the term, or feel 'threatened' by it, and that there is a general 'confusion' about its meaning.

Journalistic responses have been overwhelmingly critical of Howard: major newspapers have generally declared in favour of 'keeping the M-word'. As one commentator says: 'The simple fact is, when you have 150 different cultures, 80 religions and 90 languages living on one island, you need a welcoming phrase, a word that promotes inclusion, tolerance and parity. Multiculturalism is such a word' (Carruthers 1997). In all the consternation around the word, however, there has been little critical reflection on what it is about 'multiculturalism' that has created the confusion and uneasiness about it; on how and why negative perceptions of multiculturalism could have grown in the past decade or so to the point that it could have become the target of such massive attack, not only from the radical right (of which Hanson has been the most prominent face) but also from such a powerful, middle-of-the-road politician such as John Howard. In this chapter we will attempt to provide a partial answer to these questions, emphasizing multiculturalism's complicated role in the construction of Australian national identity.[7]

Multiculturalism as ideological discourse

Multiculturalism in Australia has operated as an *ideological discourse* designed to provide Australians with a favourable, flattering, even triumphant representation of the national self in two respects. First, in historical terms, it tells the Australian people that with the adoption of multiculturalism the nation has discarded an important part of its shameful, racist past. Second, in symbolic terms, it presents the people of Australia with a public fiction that they live in a harmonious, tolerant, and peaceful country where everyone is included and gets along. Again and again public figures, including John Howard himself, have announced with pride that Australia is one of the most successful multicultural societies in the world. Here is an example from a speech he delivered in 1997:

> Australia has been a remarkable success story. We are sometimes, as a community, not assertive enough about how successful we have been. We sometimes think, well, maybe we can't really be so confident about how successful we have been. When you look at what has occurred elsewhere, when you look at what Australia has faced, when you look at the 140 to 150 different ethnic groups and nationalities which now make up this remarkable country of ours, we have been an astonishing success story. And we should never cease to say that to ourselves and, frankly, we should never cease to say it to the world.
>
> (Howard 1997)

In so far as such rhetoric is addressed to the Australian population as a whole, it operates as an ideological project which interpellates all Australians to be proud of this 'astonishing success' and to rejoice in their own imaginary 'unity-in-diversity'. However, it is in the nature of ideological interpellations that they may fail to resonate with the concerns, aspirations and desires of the interpellated, in which case the latter will resist identifying with the ideology's representations. This, we argue, is what happened with the discourse of multiculturalism in Australia around 1996. While there had been enthusiastic support for the creation of a 'multicultural Australia' among the governing and intellectual elites, *popular* support for it has always been less than whole-hearted. Indeed, what the crisis around multiculturalism signified, at least in part, is the fact that sections of ordinary people – mostly referred to by the highly problematic term 'Anglo-Celtic' Australians, or sometimes simply as 'old Australia' – could not recognize themselves in multiculturalism's rosy narrative of the 'new Australia'.

The term 'Anglo-Celtic' was originally used in the 1880s/1890s by Irish Catholic Australians as an amendation to the term 'Anglo-Saxon', in order to incorporate themselves within the Anglo-Saxon-dominated power structure. While the term did not gain much currency then, its use has re-emerged and surged since the advent of multiculturalism to describe the so-called 'core culture' of Australia that is claimed to have existed before the post-war mass European and Levantine immigration. As Ken Inglis (1991: 21) notes, 'If non-English-speaking migrants and their children are to be called "ethnic", [then Anglo-Celtic is] the name . . . given to the old host population.' However, it should be pointed out that the category 'Anglo-Celtic' is a homogenizing, assimilationist one, implicitly natural-izing the historical domination of the English Protestant elites over Irish Catholics in the national culture. Furthermore, the term implicitly denies the existence of diversity within 'old Australia' itself (e.g. migrant groups from Wales, Scotland, Northern Europe and, especially, Germany) and disallows the possibility for descendants of these pre-War European migrants to claim their ethnic heritages. Thus, the term 'Anglo-Celtic' itself perpetuates culturally the discursive break between an assimilationist and a multicultural Australia.

As a result, there is a gap between the neat official representation of 'multicultural Australia', on the one hand, and the contradictory everyday experiences and historical memories of these people, on the other – experiences and memories which remain unaccounted for, or are even denied and disclaimed, by the official discourse. It is not surprising therefore that many ordinary, 'Anglo-Celtic' Australians are seeking refuge in alternative narratives to account for their experiences and memories, some of them with deeply nostalgic and reactionary overtones such as Pauline Hanson's and, in a more subtle and therefore more damaging way, John Howard's. As Peter Cochrane (1996) observes: 'Hanson is the voice of old Anglo-Celtic Australia, resentful of its displacement from the centre of Australian cultural life by the new ethnic Australians and nostalgic for a time when it imagined its identity was both secure and central.' Howard, as we will discuss below, hints at a similar resentment in his championing of what he insistently calls 'mainstream Australia' (Brett 1997; Johnson 1997).

The ideological project of multiculturalism has entailed a fundamental re-description of the nation away from racial and cultural homogeneity in the direction of ethnic and cultural diversity. Such a redescription, of course, can only be successful if it manages to win over 'the hearts and minds of the majority of ordinary people' and enter 'as a material and ideological force into [their] daily lives' (Hall 1988: 6). Only then can an ideological project become hegemonic (in the Gramscian sense of the term); that is, win popular consent and, in the words of Stuart Hall (1988: 7), secure 'a social authority sufficiently deep to conform society into a new historic project'. We are not suggesting here that the project of multiculturalism has entirely failed in Australia. On the contrary, support for it has remained widespread and almost universal, especially among the educated, urban middle classes and the business community, for whom cultural diversity is deemed an economic asset. But we must remember that hegemony is never complete and is always in a process of renegotiation. The Hanson/Howard ascendancy is a clear indication that more than two decades of official government policy has not led to the generation of a deep and pervasive nation-wide commitment to multiculturalism. Why? It is not our intention to provide a comprehensive analysis of this situation, which would obviously need to take the interplay of complex economic, political, institutional, demographic and other factors into account (see Stratton 1998). Here, we would like to single out one problem with the discourse of multiculturalism as it has been constructed in Australia. The problem is that this discourse is incapable of providing a convincing and effective narrative of Australian national identity because it does not acknowledge and engage with a crucial ideological concern in the national formation's past and present, namely, that of 'race'.

In brief, we want to argue that the Australian discourse of multiculturalism does not recognize, confront or challenge the problematic of 'race' but rather represses it. In so doing a very significant province of Australian historical experience, which, as we will show, is replete with a concern, if not obsession with 'race', has been simply set aside, as if it were never of any importance. At the same time, this repression of 'race' in multiculturalist discourse cannot prevent the persistence of 'race' as a key marker of absolute and unacceptable cultural difference in everyday understandings, a persistence which, we will argue, resonates with common unreflexive notions of an 'Australian way of life' and, a term used insistently by John Howard, 'mainstream Australia'. Such notions not only marginalize so-called 'ethnic' cultures, but also, damagingly, creates a situation in which white or 'Anglo-Celtic' Australians are encouraged to construct themselves as *outside* 'multicultural Australia'. One aspect of this is the unthinking and automatic association of multiculturalism with (non-English-speaking) migrants, as if it has nothing to do with the 'core culture'. What is made impossible to imagine and narrate as a result are the very real changes in the way ordinary white, 'Anglo-Celtic' Australians are positioned in the new, 'multicultural Australia', as well as the daily conflicts and contradictions involved. In other words, the discourse of multiculturalism has failed to provide 'old' Australians with ways of re-imagining themselves as an integral part of the 'new' Australia. On the contrary, what has been constructed is a struggle between the 'old' and the 'new' Australia, a divisive tug of war which John Howard has insisted on resolving in the interest of 'all of us'.

To understand how 'race' plays a central part in this discursive struggle, which, it has to be emphasized, is part and parcel of a larger social, economic and cultural struggle over the changing place of the Australian nation–state in the global order (see Ang and Stratton 1996), we will give a brief historical account of the construction of a distinctively Australian national identity from the moment that the colonial settler society became a quasi-independent nation–state.

Creating White Australia: 'race' as absent centre

When the Commonwealth of Australia was established in 1901, it immediately adopted an Immigration Restriction Bill, which became the basis for the infamous White Australia Policy. This bill prohibited the immigration into Australia by 'non-Europeans' or 'the coloured races'. The fact that this bill was the very first major legislative issue dealt with by the parliament of the newly-created nation–state suggests the perceived importance of 'racial purity' as the symbolic cement for the imagined community of the fledgling nation (Markus 1979). This bluntly exclusionary policy on the basis of 'race' should not simply be interpreted, with the wisdom and political correctness of hindsight, as the mere expression of white supremacist prejudice. After all, the policy was implemented at a critical moment in the development of a new nation. In this respect the White Australia policy can be seen, in an important sense, as a *nationalist* policy, reflecting the new nation–state's desire to construct a modern national identity based on (a British-based) racial and cultural homogeneity (see further Stratton and Ang 1998). In light of this modernist desire – not unusual in a time of intense European nationalism and hegemonic imperialism (Hobsbawm 1990) – the exclusion of non-white racial/cultural Others was logical and inevitable. In other words, philosophically speaking, the White Australia policy implied the official and explicit *racialization* of Australian national identity, based on a discourse of homogeneity that collapses culture into race.

It is important to remark here that at the beginning of the twentieth century Australia deemed itself extremely well placed to achieve a racially pure, and purely white, utopia. The rhetoric of white racial purity was constantly rehearsed in speeches and editorials surrounding the birth of the new nation, and was a crucial element of the national popular consciousness. As Richard White observes:

> In a society which dreaded the mixing of races as debilitating in the struggle for survival, in a society which was becoming more and more obsessive in its desire to protect . . . racial 'purity' . . . the outlook of 1901 was promising. It could be proclaimed that the new nation was 98 per cent British, more British than any other dominion, some said more British than Britain itself.
>
> (1981: 112)

According to the 1901 census, the largest non-British migrant groups were the Germans (1 per cent) and the Chinese (0.8 per cent). In this context, in contrast to, for example, the United States where 'race' was historically always-already an internal national issue because of the uneradicable legacy of slavery, in Australia the salience of 'race' was elided in daily life: it was the 'absent centre' which made it possible to imagine the national community as virtually completely white, where the very issue of 'race' could be relegated to the realm of the outside world, far removed from the national domestic sphere. In a very straightforward way, 'race' marked the conceptual limits of the national imagined community, sanctioning

101

the state to exclude or, in the case of the Aborigines, who were considered a 'doomed race', to extinguish those considered racially undesirable, that is, those who are not 'white' (McGregor 1997). In Markus's words:

> Australians rejoiced that they were able to deal with racial problems through a policy of exclusion: they looked forward to the realisation of a 'white Australia', expecting that the inferior Aboriginal people would die out and that the small, largely male, non-European populations still left in the country would not be able to reproduce themselves.
>
> (1988: 18)

Of course, we know all too well now that the indigenous people of the land did not die out, as widely predicted at an earlier age, despite concerted efforts to speed up this process through the compulsory assimilation of Aboriginal children into the dominant, white culture by taking them away from their Aboriginal families (the so-called Stolen Generation).[8] The increasingly powerful self-assertion of Aboriginal Australia in Australian national discourse since they were awarded citizenship in 1967 shattered the illusion that white Australia would be spared the return of the repressed. Indeed, if the issue of 'race' looms large in contemporary Australia, it is first and foremost in connection with the unresolved political status and social condition of Aborigines and Torres Strait Islanders within the nation. In this respect it is significant that Aboriginal people are not generally included in debates about multiculturalism, not least because Aborigines themselves have generally refused to be treated as 'another ethnic minority'. In this sense, the framing of indigenous politics in terms of the discourse of 'race' – more precisely, in relation to what is commonly called black/white reconciliation – signifies the strategic importance of 'race' as a point of self-identification for Aboriginal people, an identification which, ironically, was initially imposed on them by the European colonizers. Today, however, their status as a 'race' enables them to make their distinct political claims as the original inhabitants of the land, and not to be lumped into the non-distinct liberal pluralist imaginary of multiculturalism.

Our focus in this chapter, however, is not on how White Australia attempted, unsuccessfully, to extinguish the trace of 'race' *within* the geographical boundaries of the nation–state, but on the consequences of the attempt to prevent non-white 'races' from coming into the country during the White Australia policy. For non-white here, read, first and foremost, 'Asian'. It is important here to stress that support for a 'white Australia' was activated in large part through popular campaigns against 'coloured' workers, mostly Chinese, in the late nineteenth century (Curthoys and Markus 1978). However, the anti-Chinese movement was a broad alliance across all classes, reflecting the deeply ingrained nature of racism through-out the population, and the central role of the idea of the 'yellow peril' in the cementing of national unity. These ideological links between racism, populism and nationalism were sanctioned by the state, for whom racialist nationalism became a central ideological project and policy instrument. With the official adoption of the White Australia policy the number of Chinese and other 'coloured' people in the country dwindled significantly in the course of the first half of the twentieth century. This trend was not reversed until the final dismantling of the racially discriminatory immigration restrictions, which took place around the same time as the introduction of multiculturalism, in the early 1970s.

While similar policies were, of course, in place in other European settler societies such as Canada, there is a specificity about the political and ideological desire to be a 'white nation' in early twentieth-century Australia. Australia's antipodean geographical location as a 'far-flung outpost of Europe', its spatial detachment and the seeming naturalness of its borders as an island-continent promoted the idea early on that in Australia 'it was possible to control contact with the rest of the world in a manner not possible for most other nations' (Evans *et al.* 1997: 205). At the same time, as David Walker (1997: 133) puts it, 'the need to live in relatively close proximity to awakening Asia lent a certain drama and intensity to the Australian situation, it conferred a special status on Australia as a continent set aside for the development of the white race'. Indeed, the desire to keep Asians out was an important rationale for the massive population build-up after World War Two (about which more below). As demographer Charles Price wrote about the early post-war period: 'the country felt that the best answer to the international cry that it should open its unused land and resources to Asia's crowded millions was to populate the continent and develop its resources with as many white persons as possible' (quoted in Brawley 1996: 237).

Gradually dismantled in practice from the mid-1960s, the official abolition of the White Australia policy was formalized only in 1972, when the Labor Government of Gough Whitlam finally scrapped all references to 'race' from immigration law. This was, of course, the same government which introduced multiculturalism as a diversity-oriented population management policy. That these two radical policy shifts – the scrapping of racially discriminatory immigration policy and the official sanctioning of cultural diversity through a policy of multiculturalism – took place around the same time, the early 1970s, has made it easy for them to be conflated in the national cultural imaginary. From this time on, it is constantly reiterated, Australia no longer discriminates 'on racial grounds' when it comes to selecting potential immigrants. John Howard too, for example, has always insisted that 'non-discrimination is a non-negotiable element of Australia's immigration programme' (1997). This shift was indeed a qualitative change, which made it possible for large numbers of people generally classified as 'non-white' – particularly from Asian countries – to migrate to Australia, and which has resulted in the multiracial outlook of Australian society as we know it today.[9]

What we want to highlight here is that the very deletion of the reference to 'race' in immigration law in the early 1970s represented a *radical epistemological break* in the official national discourse on who could now be included in 'the Australian people'. While 'race' was all-important in earlier times, now 'race' was officially, suddenly, declared completely unimportant, at least in principle.[10] The symbolic importance of this break for the redefinition of the nation's imagined community should not be underestimated. It has enabled the production of a new national narrative which tells the reassuring story that Australia has now relinquished its racist past, and embraced a non-racist and non-racial national identity. Raymond Evans *et al.* (1997: 188), for example, remark: 'Today, the concept of "White Australia" is an anachronism in multicultural Australia. It is an embarrassment, and difficult for 1990s Australians to understand'. However, embarrassment is hardly a productive affect if one is to come to terms with what could be described as a major change of heart in the life of the nation. It signifies a tendency to disavow, rather than confront and come to terms with the racist past of the nation, and with the central importance of racial differentiation in the very historical constitution of Australia as a nation–state. Instead, this past is reduced symbolically to a childhood sin, as it were, which doesn't have anything to do with the mature Australia. It is worth noting here that the embarrassment is likely to be felt most acutely by the liberal intelligentsia, for whom anti-racism has become an article of faith. It is here that the ideological project of multiculturalism – as an alternative and a replacement for the narrative of 'white Australia' – comes into play, in a manner however which, in our analysis, turns out to be less than effectual.

From white nation to multicultural nation: repressing 'race'

The assumption that the notion of a 'white Australia' has become an anachronism in 'multicultural Australia' has been made possible by the common conflation of multiculturalism with non-racialism. That is, the very statement that Australia is now a 'multicultural nation' is often implicitly put forward as evidence that the notion of a 'white Australia' is no longer current in the national imaginary, as if the adoption of multiculturalism were by definition an act of anti-racism.

This view is extremely problematic. First of all, it is important to stress that multiculturalism is a policy that recognizes and confirms cultural diversity, not non-racialism. The distinction is crucial. In fact, a brief look at how and why the policy of multiculturalism was introduced in Australia will clarify that multi-culturalism was originally never intended to be equated with multiracialism. In the post-World War Two period, as we have noted, Australia embarked on a programme to build up its population rapidly. Recovering from World War Two and in the face of an increasingly strong Asian 'near north', Australia, in the words of its first Minister for Immigration, Arthur Calwell, felt it needed to 'populate or perish'. One consequence of the desire to increase immigration was a liberalization of the White Australia immigration policy. As there was not enough supply of immigrants from Britain, immigrants were recruited first in Northen Europe (Scandinavia, the Netherlands, Germany), and later Southern and Eastern Europe (Italy, Greece, Poland, Croatia, Macedonia, and so on). Importantly, this liberalization did not overturn the racially-based two-tiered structure which distinguished Europeans from non-Europeans, white from non-white, included and excluded. It did, however, introduce an element of diversity *within* the category 'white'. That is, with the admission of non-British European migrants, *racial* homogeneity ('whiteness') could no longer be equated with *cultural* homogeneity (i.e. the British-based, Anglo-Celtic Australian culture). However, the pursuit of a homogeneous national community remained government priority well into the 1960s. It was to ensure cultural homogenization that the new immigrants were forced, officially, to adopt the existing 'Australian way of life' and assimilate into the dominant culture, the notional core culture of 'Anglo-Celtic' Australia. In other words, the policy of assimilationism was aimed at the maintenance of a culturally homogeneous white Australia (Castles *et al.* 1990: 45).

The later introduction of the policy of multiculturalism has widely been seen as a response to the failure of the policy of assimilationism. Indeed, the fact was that non-British European migrants – Italians, Greeks, and so on – were simply not divesting themselves of the cultural practices which they brought with them from their national 'homelands' (for example, drinking coffee and wine rather than tea and beer, and speaking their incomprehensible 'national' languages) and cloning themselves into the Anglo-Celtic dominant culture as the assimilation policy required. The shift toward a policy of multiculturalism in the 1970s implied a recognition of this failure and an embrace of the notion of 'cultural diversity', which the policy itself is aimed to 'manage'. But it was a cultural diversity within a single 'white race': it was 'white' multiculturalism, not multiracialism. In other words, logically speaking there is no reason why multiculturalism should be race-blind. The fact that it was tacitly assumed to be the case – i.e. that multiculturalism was synonymous to an overcoming of racism – is a key element in the repression of the discourse of 'race' from official and dominant rhetoric.

One important indication for the way 'race' has been repressed is the fore-grounding of the term 'ethnic communities' in the discourse of multiculturalism in Australia. The rhetorical shift from 'race' to 'ethnicity' signifies Australia's local contribution to the post-World War Two movement away from the biological essentialism of classical racial discourse and the espousal of a more culturally-oriented approach to human diversity (de Lepervanche 1980). Thus, when in the decade after the fall of Saigon in 1975, some 80,000 Vietnamese were allowed into Australia, their integration into Australian culture, supported by multicultural policies, was never discussed openly in terms of their 'racial' difference. Officially, the Vietnamese were simply added to the growing list of 'ethnic groups' making up the increasingly heterogeneous multicultural mix in the nation. In the Australian discourse of multiculturalism new migrant groups are designated an ethnic identity (defined generally in terms of national origin), not a racial one. Thus, the Australian census classifies people according to 'birthplace' and 'language spoken at home' and as such, distinguishes between people from 'Vietnam', 'China', 'Malaysia', 'Lebanon', 'India', 'Fiji', 'Japan', 'Korea', or 'the Philippines, as well as 'Britain', 'New Zealand', 'Italy', or 'Germany', and so on. The racial term 'Asian' (or 'white' for that matter) does not officially appear at all: the bureaucratic imagination does not, in Australia, make use of 'race' as a means of categorizing people. This is in sharp contrast, for example, with the United States, where the discourse of 'race' is excessively salient. In the USA, individuals are routinely asked, in application forms, questionnaires, etc., to slot themselves into one of the five ethno-racial categories of white (or Euro-American), African American, Asian American, Hispanic or Native American (Hollinger 1995). As a result, Americans are always officially reminded of 'race' as a primary marker of differentiation among themselves.

Not so in the Australian context, at least in the case of non-indigenous Australians. Here, the erasure of racial categorization from official discourse has constructed an equivalence between disparate groups such as the Vietnamese and the Dutch, the Chinese and the Italians. Since the introduction of multiculturalism, all these groups have the same categorical status as 'ethnic communities'. In the past they would have been racially differentiated – as either white/European or not – and considered qualitatively, absolutely distinct from each other *because* of their purported racial differences, but today these racial differences are, at least in the official language, made irrelevant. As a result, there was no vocabulary any longer to describe the real changes in the social and cultural landscape, as new migrant groups whose entry into Australia was made possible by the formal ending of the White Australia policy, and who would previously have been described as 'non-white', 'non-European', 'coloured' or by any other racial term, began to fill the streets. The officially colour-blind discourse of multiculturalism could not appropriately address the bewildering cultural heterogeneity produced by the settlement of these new groups within the social life of the nation, especially in the large cities. We must remember, as we have noted earlier, that the way in which multicultural policy – i.e. the recognition of 'cultural diversity' – in Australia implied some degree of commonality, some affinity or family resemblance between the cultures concerned, signalled by the term 'European'. No similar implication was there for the cultures of later 'non-white' migrant groups, most prominently those from 'Asia'.

It is as if the extension of the cultural diversity sanctioned by official multiculturalism to groups other than those classified as white/European, was accompanied by a tacit denial, or an embarrassed silence, that these groups were previously not allowed to enter the country precisely *because of* their 'racial' difference. In other words, a kind of disavowal is at stake here. But it is not this disavowal as such that is problematic. What is problematic is its effects on the national imaginary, on how it robs the nation of an effective and acceptable way of narrating the national self anew in the context of these changes. That is, by simply silencing this history of exclusionism the official discourse also represses the more general and more significant fact that 'race' has been of crucial constitutive importance for the very creation of the Australian national identity. There was virtually no attempt to reconcile the fact that the admission of many people from Asian countries represented a qualitative turnaround of magnificent proportions, an historical shift which completely overturned Australia's crucial and long-standing self-definition as a 'white nation' (Hage 1998). From one moment to the next, as it were, ordinary people were forced, without much positive explanation, to ditch the way they have for generations conceived of themselves as a nation. As Peter Lawrence (1983) remarks, the admittance of thousands of Vietnamese 'boat people' from the mid-1970s onwards 'forced many [Australians] to accept that the days of Australia as a purely white European outpost were finally over'.

What we are arguing here is this. Giving up an idea which for generations has been a key element of the meaning of Australian nationhood – the idea of Australia as a 'white nation' – requires the development of a new national narrative which can account for the change, and gives the people a new, livable sense of national identity. The discourse of multiculturalism does attempt to provide Australians with such a narrative through the constant confirmation and reiteration of the success, cultural richness and tolerance of 'multicultural Australia'. But it has failed to offer white Australians, especially, the discursive means to articulate their experience of the tensions and contradictions associated with the loss of their racial monopoly. One reason for this failure, we have argued, lies precisely in the repression of the discourse of 'race'. Given that 'race' has been so formative to the Australian national imaginary, it cannot be erased from that imaginary simply by making it disappear from the textual surface of respectable discourse. In other words, for all of the state's efforts to re-imagine the nation in the image of a non-racial paradise of 'cultural diversity', the trace of 'race' continues to lead a subterranean life which remains effective in people's everyday understandings of what's happening in their country.

'Race': return of the repressed

As we have noted, today 'race' has returned from the repressed with a vengeance in Australian political discourse, especially in relation to the issue of indigenous rights. A second key index for the continued effectivity of racial discourse is the connotative loading accrued by the term 'Asian', particularly, in the context of multiculturalism, 'Asian' immigration. As we have remarked, 'Asian' immigration has been one of Pauline Hanson's main political targets. As she puts it: 'I and most Australians want our immigration policy radically reviewed and that of multiculturalism abolished. I believe we are in danger of being swamped by Asians' (Hanson 1996). Clearly, 'Asians' and 'Australians' are mutually exclusive categories for Hanson, as they have been for a long and formative period in Australian history.

When Hanson speaks about 'Asians', she clearly transgresses the preferred, 'colour-blind' framework of the discourse of multiculturalism. To put it differently, in using the term 'Asian' she invokes a *racial* discourse which was supposed to have been banished from the Australian cultural imaginary with the introduction of an officially non-racial immigration policy. While Chinese, Vietnamese, Malaysian, Singaporean and other migrants from the geographical region called 'Asia' are now considered an integral part of Australia's multicultural ethnic mix, these groups are collectively *racialized* by Hanson in order to single them out and amass them as the Other that threatens the national Self. This signals the continued operation of racial thinking in the minds of many Australians in articulating their responses to changes within the national social formation. 'Race', here, in Stuart Hall's (1998: 290) words, operates as a discursive logic which 'gives legibility to a social system in which it operates', by producing, marking and fixing 'the infinite differences and diversities of human beings through a rigid binary coding'. The binarism constructed here is that of 'white' versus 'Asian', and by invoking it Hanson reintroduces precisely the marker of exclusion that was in place during the White Australia policy. Hanson appeals to a very old discourse of racial differentia-tion to patrol the limits of the inclusiveness of the Australian imagined community in a time when the politics of inclusion has become part of the *doxa* of 'multicultural Australia'. As she revealingly puts it: 'Of course, I will be called racist but, if I can invite whom I want into my home, then I should have the right to have a say in who comes into my country' (Hanson 1997a). Here the Australian 'home' is implicitly coded 'white', in full continuity with the old fantasy of a 'White Australia' where 'race' operated to mark the external boundary of the nation, not distinctions within it.

We have to point out here that Pauline Hanson did not come out of the blue in Australia. She has an illustrious predecessor in Geoffrey Blainey, a distinguished Professor of History, who in 1984, hardly ten years after the formal ending of the White Australia policy and the arrival of the first Vietnamese 'boat people', sparked a heated controversy by launching a virulent attack on 'Asian immigration'. Arguing that immigration policies were now biased in favour of 'Asians' and against migrants from Britain and Europe, Blainey stated that 'too many Asians were undesirable because they might endanger Australia's social, economic and political structures' (Ricklefs 1985: 37). Significantly, Blainey did not call for a complete stop to Asian immigration, but for a significant reduction of it. It is also worth noting that John Howard, too, took a stance against Asian immigration during the 1980s. In the wake of the 'Blainey debate' he said in a radio interview in 1988: 'I do believe that if [Asian migration] is in the eyes of the community, it's so great, it would be in our immediate term interest and supportive of social cohesion if it were slowed down a little, so that the capacity of the community to absorb was greater' (quoted in Kelly 1992: 423). This statement, which explicitly conjures up 'race' as a marker for what he saw as the limits of community tolerance, caused such a furore among the political establishment, both left and right, that Howard has since refrained from making any such explicitly race-related comments. As the present Prime Minister, he now uses much more cautious, coded and ambiguous language to articulate his point of view.

A dozen years after Blainey, Hanson repeated history almost farcically by mimicking him and Howard's earlier incarnation, and by insisting that she is not against Asian migrants as such, although she does want their numbers significantly reduced to 'restore the balance'. A close reading of her speeches makes it clear that her main objection is against 'Asians' who 'have their own culture and religion, form ghettos and do not assimilate', and not those who 'have wholeheartedly embraced the Australian way of life'. This qualification is put forward by Hanson herself as evidence that she is not a racist (as she is not against 'Asians' *per se*). Indeed, strictly speaking she is not a racist in the old, biological determinist sense, but a culturalist, in the sense that her anxiety is targeted at what she sees as alien *cultures*. In this sense Hanson can probably best be described as a multiracial assimilationist. As she put it, 'Australians are sick of imported problems be they crime, disease or aspects of cultural difference that will never be able to accept the Australian life' (Hanson 1997b). In drawing the line of acceptable cultural difference by using the term 'Asian', however, she exemplifies what James Donald and Ali Rattansi (1992: 2), in discussing 1980s' Britain, have called 'a new racism, based not on ideas of innate biological superiority but on the supposed incompatibility of cultural traditions'. As Professor Blainey put it bluntly in 1984: 'Asians were people from a variety of cultures who don't belong to our present mainstream culture' (quoted in Ricklefs 1985: 40). The continuity from Blainey to Hanson indicates that in contemporary multicultural Australia, where 'cultural diversity' is supposedly accepted and even cherished, 'race' – as operationalized in the term 'Asian' – is still effective as a marker of the limits of tolerable diversity, of what, from the point of view of the new racists, goes beyond the acceptable boundaries of Australian national culture and identity. In other words, it is through the rhetoric of 'race' that the political right has consistently challenged multiculturalism. The term 'Asian' stands here for unassimilable, unabsorbable difference, too different to be integrated into the 'Australian way of life'. But because the discourse of state multiculturalism does not have a way of talking about 'race' it cannot deal with the elements of diversity which, for Hanson, Blainey and the Howard in his earlier incarnation, are 'too much' and therefore a threat to the 'Australian community'.

Here, then, we reach the point where the discourse of multiculturalism cannot offer an effective counter-attack. The pluralist discourse of 'cultural diversity', which emphasizes the harmonious co-existence of a variety of ethnic groups, is simply not capable of counteracting the divisive and conflict-ridden imaginary produced by discourses of racial tension as exemplified by Hanson's. Indeed, the discourse of multiculturalism may be so ineffectual precisely because it glosses over experiences of disharmony and conflict, leaving it to racial discourses as enunciated by Hanson to capture and give meaning to those experiences. Surveying the character of Australian racism and ethnocentrism in the 1980s, a few years after the 'Blainey debate', Andrew Markus remarks:

> Compared with the 1950s there is a much greater tolerance for ethnic diversity, particularly amongst the more affluent, but this tolerance does not entail majority support for multiculturalism. The Anglo-Australian sense of the superiority of their culture, previously manifested in the policy of assimilation, is disowned by governments but remains a significant factor in the community.
>
> (1988: 21–2)

By the late 1990s, the popularity of Pauline Hanson among some sections of Anglo-Australians (or Anglo-Celtic Australians) testifies to the lack of change since the

1980s, although the Anglo-Celtic Australian sense of 'superiority' may be tinged more with anxiety and defensiveness than with confidence and arrogance. In fact, Markus suggests as much when he notes that the failure of government after government to gain popular support for the reformed immigration and multi-cultural policies has to do with a failure 'to allay unreasonable fears of the dangers of multiculturalism, and to create a climate of confidence that the legitimate interests of Anglo-Australians were being protected' (ibid.: 22).

But what, so we can ask, are those 'legitimate interests'? Surely a purported desire to return to a 'white Australia' among some Anglo-Celtic Australians can no longer be recognized as 'legitimate' by any government, not even John Howard's? We are returned here to Howard's ambivalence about multiculturalism. Having explicitly argued against 'too many Asians' in the 1980s, a position he had to disavow in order to save his political career, by the mid-1990s he said that under his government, 'the views of all particular interests will be assessed against the national interest and the sentiments of mainstream Australia' (Howard 1995a). It is reasonable to argue that the sentiments Howard refers to here are those of ordinary 'Anglo-Celtic' Australians. By describing this group as 'mainstream Australia' he implicitly marginalizes people of non-Anglo-Celtic backgrounds, and opposes the latter's particular interests to the 'national interest', which presumably represents the legitimate interests of the Anglo-Australian 'mainstream'. In another speech (Howard 1995b), he attacks what he calls 'minority fundamentalism', which, he says, 'is based on the assumption that if you extol mainstream practices or values then you must automatically be intolerant of the values or circumstances of minorities – despite overwhelming evidence to the contrary'. Thus Howard (1995a) sings the praises of mainstream tolerance: tolerance is a virtue of the mainstream. 'Tolerance', he says, 'has been one of our distinguishing features for a very long time.'

However, as Ghassan Hage (1994: 23) has observed: 'the popular language of acceptance, often encountered in the form of "they're just as Australian as we are" or "they're Australian too", reinforces the placing of the Anglo-Celtic Australians in the position of power within the discourse of tolerance.' Thus it is the Anglo-Celtic Australians – or, in Howard's ex-nominating terminology, 'the mainstream' – which has the power to put limits to its tolerance, presumably at that point where minority interests are so 'out of the mainstream' that they are no longer 'in the national interest'. In this discursive move Howard, without making any explicit racial references, manages to reorient the policy of multiculturalism closer to the assimilationist concerns of the old White Australia policy. Thus the government now emphasizes the need for 'ensuring that cultural diversity is a unifying force' (National Multicultural Advisory Council 1997), a statement which clearly signals a tendency to see 'diversity' and 'unity' in terms of a binary opposition and not, as in the multiculturalist slogan of 'unity-in-diversity', as mutually reinforcing.

What should now be apparent is that this assimilationist move is also, in practice, if implicitly, a racializing one. In Australia 'Anglo-Celtic' or 'mainstream' culture is historically British in origin and, most importantly for our argument, 'white'. By repressing the discourse of 'race' rather than acknowledging its power in the Australian cultural imaginary, and dealing with its ideological implications, multiculturalism has allowed, contrary to its intentions, the possibility for the conservative renovation of racializing discourses as an aspect of a renewed emphasis on assimilation and on a 'mainstream culture' whose whiteness is unspoken but undeniable.

6

ASIANS IN AUSTRALIA

A contradiction in terms?

The late 1990s have seen the publication of not one, but two edited collections with the generic title of *Asians in Australia* (Inglis *et al*. 1996; Coughlan and McNamara 1997). Both books single out a particular group of people – amassed as 'Asians' – whose presence in Australia seems to merit special consideration. Otherwise, why dedicate whole volumes to it?

The issue of 'Asians in Australia' is historically complex, and continues to be an ideologically loaded and politically and culturally sensitive one. The sub-titles of the two collections above – respectively emphasizing the 'dynamics' and the 'patterns' of migration and settlement – are remarkably similar and they give a fair indication of the dominant intellectual framework in which public discourse on 'Asians in Australia' is cast. Thus, both books focus on themes which have pre-occupied Australian governments and public commentators alike in the past few decades: succinctly, the macro-sociological concern with the overall process of *integration* of 'Asian' immigrants into Australian society.

'Asians', in this context, are defined first and foremost as those born in an Asian country, concordant with the way the Australian Census categorizes the 'ethnic' diversity of the population, i.e. by country of birth. Using this definition, an estimated 4.9 per cent of the total population could be categorized as having been born in an 'Asian' country by 1991, more than eight times as many as in 1966. By 1996, the estimated proportion of the Australian population born in Asia is reported to have increased to 6.2 per cent (see Mackie 1997: 13). What these figures clearly reveal is a strong and steady rise in the number of Asians in Australia in the past thirty years, and it is this very rise – so bluntly stated through these objectivist statistics – that has intensified the politicization of 'Asians in Australia' as a theme in public discourse and debate.

But these statistics are rubbery figures given the flexibility and ambiguity of the meaning of the term 'Asia' and, as a consequence, who counts as 'Asian'. As a geographical entity, 'Asia' is an artificial construct with uncertain boundaries, especially on its western front where its border with 'Europe' has never been firmly established by European geographers from whose meta-geographical imagination the very idea of 'continents' had sprung (Lewis and Wigen 1997). Significantly, then, as Jon Stratton (1998: 59–61) has observed, people from what is commonly called 'West Asia' (including Turkey, Cyprus, Lebanon and the Middle East) are sometimes included in the broad category of 'Asians' in Australian public discourse, sometimes not. Today, in the popular imagination at least, 'Asians' are generally associated only with those coming from East, South-East and, to a lesser extent, South Asia, reflecting what Lewis and Wigen (1997: 55) call an 'eastward displacement of the Orient' in the global geography of the latter half of the twentieth century.

Lewis and Wigen go on to remark that 'Oriental peoples' have come to be defined 'by most lay observers as those with a single eye fold'. This visual emphasis on corporeal difference betrays the inescapable *racialization* of 'Asians' in the dominant cultural imaginary: the lumping together and homogenization of a group of people on the basis of a phenotypical discourse of 'race'. In Australia, as elsewhere, common-sense notions of 'Asianness' are inevitably, impulsively associated with some notion of visible racial difference, even though contemporary official discourse (such as that used in the Census) generally avoids the use of explicitly racial categories. As we have seen in the previous chapter, in the early 1970s, when the infamous 'White Australia' policy was finally fully abolished, a so-called 'non-discriminatory' immigration policy was introduced and a policy of multiculturalism established. In the process, the discourse of 'race' was erased in Australian discussion about population and immigration in favour of a discourse of ethnicity, in which people were categorized in arguably less contested and contestable terms such as 'birthplace' or 'language spoken at home'. The racial term 'Asian' disappeared from official classificatory systems such as the Census, even though the term remains salient in the public mind, which cannot easily be censored.

It is not surprising, therefore, that the silence about 'race' in official discourse has not prevented the repeated eruption of racialist and racializing voices into the public sphere. Thus, 'Asians' are regularly and often unthinkingly, taken-for-grantedly, talked about *en masse* as if they were a single, homogeneous group. In most cases this proto-racial rendering is harmless enough, signalling no intended racist othering. In some historic instances, however, racialist reference to 'Asians' is made explicitly to problematize and question the legitimacy and desirability of their status as residents of Australia. The most recent example is that of Pauline Hanson and her One Nation Party, the white populist political movement which swept the country in the years 1996–98. While Hanson has always strenuously denied being a racist, she has not stopped claiming that Australia is being 'swamped by Asians' and that the influx of immigrants should be halted – a code message that there are already 'too many Asians' in the country. Hanson's brief but sudden surge to popularity rocked the nation, rudely awakening many Australians to the virulent persistence of xenophobic forces in their midst they had thought were long extinct. Yet the 'Hanson phenomenon' illuminates the fact that the issue of 'Asians in Australia' is profoundly entangled in the continuing significance of 'race' in the Australian cultural imagination. This is an uncomfortable message for a nation that has attempted very hard, in the past few decades, to efface its legacy as an explicitly and self-consciously racist nation–state.

Let's put this in a broader historical frame. The issue of 'Asians in Australia' must be seen as an intense site of symbolic contestation in contemporary Australia, which points to larger issues pertaining to the changing role, status and viability of the nation–state as we enter the twenty-first century. Of course, each nation–state has to deal with the myriad sociological complexities which have inevitably arisen with the entry of thousands of new migrants with unfamiliar cultural practices, experiences and values. Some of these issues are discussed in the two edited collections I have referred to above in relation to Asian immigration into Australia. My focus here, however, will not be on the actual social reality of Asians in Australia today, but on what 'Asians in Australia' stands for, symbolically, for the present and future of the Australian nation as an 'imagined community' in transition, struggling to adapt to the changing environment and requirements of a globalizing world. Lisa Lowe (1996) and David Palimbo-Liu (1999) have made similar assessments about the positioning of peoples of Asian background in the United States.

What the so-called Hanson phenomenon has highlighted is the profound unease experienced by a significant part of the population with the far-reaching social and cultural changes of the past few decades. These changes were effected not just by the liberalization of immigration policies since the 1970s, which enabled many migrants from Asian backgrounds to settle in the country, but are associated more generally with the changing status of nation–states in an increasingly globalized world. Globalization – the increasing interconnectedness and interdependence of the world as a result of intensifying transnational flows of goods, capital, infor-mation, ideas and people – has decreased the capacity of national governments to control and maintain effective territorial sovereignty. It is a process which has had a deep impact in Australia where governments since the early 1980s have been determined, through rigorous neo-liberal economic policies, to open the country up to the forces of the global capitalist economy (Wiseman 1998).

The significance of Pauline Hanson, who was swept into Parliament in March 1996 but lost her seat in the 1998 election, lies not so much in her influence on the formal political process. What made her politics acutely pertinent, as well as infuriatingly transgressive, was her articulation of everyday, ordinary Australian fears and anxieties, which official politics has been unable, even unwilling to address and represent.[1] These fears and anxieties reveal a deep concern about the real and perceived loss of control over the nation as globalization marches on. As Hanson herself has warned, 'Unless Australia rallied, all our fears will be realised, and we will lose our country forever, and be strangers in our own land' (quoted in Wilkinson 1998). Hanson's One Nation Party has been making announcements against big business, the United Nations, cosmopolitan elites and other symbols of globalism, but by far the most controversy has been raised by the way Hanson has directed her fear and resentment against those she believes will rob her of her country: Aboriginal people and Asians, and their supporters in the intellectual and political elites. Not surprisingly, critics have routinely accused her of 'racism'. But the moral(istic) critique of racism doesn't take account of the deeper, more pervasive sense of identity panic that underlies her call for the nation to be 'one'.

114

Just before the October 1998 elections I spoke with a middle-aged woman, wife of a senior manager, at a university function. The deeply common-sensical nature of Hanson's world view was brought home to me when this woman said, with some timidity, 'But we do have to be one nation, don't we?' From her perspective, this longing for 'oneness' seemed perfectly natural, and who could blame her, in a country where the ideology of homogeneity and assimilation has been so actively pursued as a national project until only thirty years ago? If Hanson and her supporters feel anxious, then, I would argue, it is not so much about 'race' as such, but with the uncertainty about the future that 'race' represents: both Aborigines and Asians put the moral and economic future of the nation in doubt, and, consequently, the white (Anglo-Australian) sense of entitlement and 'home' (Curthoys 1999).

The projection of a multiracial future for the nation is articulated with the growing sense of insecurity among many ordinary Australians as the process of globalization continues apace. The fact that this is a *global* development, not just affecting Australia alone, is generally lost in popular discourse, resulting in a sense of local/national victimization unchecked by a clear understanding of the larger dimensions of change and transformation that are subsumed under the umbrella term 'globalization'. One important aspect of globalization is that it has exposed and intensified 'the deep tensions between global migrations and the sovereign borders of the 190 members of the United Nations' (Wang 1997: 16). As the Indian American anthropologist Arjun Appadurai has observed: 'The isomorphism of people, territory, and legitimate sovereignty that constitutes the normative character of the modern nation-state is under threat from the forms of circulation of people characteristic of the contemporary world' (1996a: 43).

The symbolic significance of 'Asians in Australia' should be read in light of the disjuncture of people, territory and sovereignty that globalization has effected on the nation–state of Australia. In this sense, Australia is going through a process of partial unravelling – a painful process, to be sure – similar to many other nation–states with a large influx of migrants. But the way in which this process is experienced and worked through in Australia is particular to its history, especially its history as a white settler nation in the far corner of 'Asia', a product of European, or more specifically, British imperialism.

Asians out/Asians in

The rise of Pauline Hanson's One Nation Party has demonstrated that the old sentiments of 'White Australia' – the notion that Australia should be a pure European nation, particularly of people of 'British stock' – still linger in the contemporary Australian unconscious. It is important to remember that the idea of a White Australia was foundational to the establishment of the new nation–state of Australia in 1901. As Janeen Webb and Andrew Enstice (1998: 140) remark, 'The twin concepts of Australian Federation and a White Australia of pure British stock became inextricably linked in the popular imagination.' Indeed, racial and cultural homogeneity was seen as a necessary precondition for the new imagined community of the Australian nation, and the desire for homogeneity inevitably implied the exclusion of racial/cultural others.[2]

Due to Australia's geographical location, these 'others' were generally imagined as coming from the 'near north', that is, from Asia. Indeed, one of the most salient motives for the unification of the five separate colonies into a federated Australia was the common desire of the colonies to develop more effective policies to keep out Chinese immigrants (Markus 1979; Rolls 1996). The Chinese, who came to Australia from 1848 onwards, were increasingly resented because they proved to be highly efficient, hard-working and economically competitive. This was experienced as a threat to the livelihood of the European settlers, who were themselves recent arrivals in the antipodes and were still struggling to make a living in a new, unfamiliar and barely developed environment. Webb and Enstice put it this way:

> Where Aborigines had been dismissed quite early as incapable of being absorbed into a European economic model, the Chinese were vilified for the very efficiency with which they fitted in. Cultural and racial differences were merely convenient ways of identifying and attacking what – from the point of view of the individual European immigrant trying to establish a sound economic base – was soon perceived as the economic enemy.
>
> (1998: 131)

If anti-Chinese sentiment in nineteenth-century Australia was born of economic anxiety, the solution to 'the Chinese problem' *then* was an aggressive politics of exclusion – an exclusion which was legitimated through the language of 'race'. Australia was emphatically appropriated 'for the White Man', as the masthead of *The Bulletin*, the national current affairs magazine, had it until it was finally removed as late as 1960 (Lawson 1983). Ever since the goldfield days more than a century ago, white Australians were afraid of being 'swamped by Asians', as Pauline Hanson puts it in the 1990s. This fear could be repressed, or at least held at bay, as long as self-protective policies could be maintained which would secure keeping Australia white. 'The ideology of race', observes historian Luke Trainor (1994: 89), 'met the needs of many elements of Australian society' during this period.

Since the introduction of the Immigration Restriction Act in 1901, which formed the basis for what came to be known as the White Australia policy, the number of Chinese and other 'coloured' people (or, to use another term of exclusion, 'non-Europeans') in the country dwindled significantly – a trend not reversed until the final dismantling of the White Australia policy in the early 1970s, when a so-called 'non-discriminatory' immigration policy was finally introduced.[3]

Interestingly, as about one hundred years ago, economic considerations are pervasive in justifications for today's determined elision of 'race' as a marker of distinction in immigration regulations. However, in contrast with one hundred years ago, today the official rhetoric states that it is important to *include* Asians rather than exclude them because of the rise of Asian capitalism and the progressive integration of Australia's economy into the Asia-Pacific region. In this respect, the radical symbolic shift from 'White Australia' to Australia as a 'multicultural nation in Asia' (to use former Prime Minister Paul Keating's famous phrase) was a matter of *realpolitik*: in a postcolonial, globalized capitalist world cosmopolitanism – the cultural habitus of 'free trade' – is not just more chic and sophisticated, but simply more likely to enhance Australia's economic well-being than xenophobia, arguably the cultural appendix of 'protectionism'.

But these pragmatic considerations, influenced strongly by changing global conditions and geopolitical relations, had a profound impact not only on how Australia saw its own place in the world (it finally had begun to recognize and accept its geographical location), but also on whom it considered welcome within its borders (that is, it finally relinquished its racially discriminatory immigration policies). The fact that this was a dramatic sea change in the history of the young nation cannot be overstated. This turnaround, which took place over the course of the century, has been succinctly discussed by Freeman and Jupp (1992). I quote them at length:

> Precisely because it was small and relatively insignificant on the world stage, Australia was able to maintain a racialist control policy until relatively recently. Defended militarily by Britain and then the United States, Australia's geographical isolation was its real defence until World War II. It could ignore its location in the Asian Pacific region because its economic, political, and cultural ties were with Europe and North America. White Australia was an embarrassment, but it caused few serious consequences. [However] . . . [w]ith Britain's entry into the European community and the emergence of Asian capitalism, Australia has had to rethink its position. One reason that is often advanced as a justification not only for a non-discriminatory immigration policy, but also for a multi-culturalism at home, is that it is an essential component of good trading relations with rising Asian economic giants (Garnaut 1989). How far these changes of attitude have gone to relax Australian policy is hard to say; in their public utterances officials imply they *have little choice* given the sensibilities of their Asian neighbours.
>
> (Freeman and Jupp 1992: 18–19)

The overhaul of immigration law in the early 1970s represented a radical break in the official national discourse, not just on who could now formally be included in 'the Australian people', but also on the nation's preferred self-image. As I have already remarked in Chapter 5, the symbolic importance of this break for the redefinition of the nation's imagined community cannot be underestimated. It was accompanied by the production of a new national narrative which tells the reassuring story that Australia has now relinquished its racist past and embraced a non-racist and non-racial national identity. As a result, the central importance of

117

racial discrimination in Australia's very historical constitution as a nation–state is now often simply discarded as belonging to the past, no longer relevant to the present. This is the reasoning, for example, behind Prime Minister John Howard's refusal to express a formal apology on behalf of the (white) Australian people to the so-called Stolen Generation of Aboriginal people: again and again, Howard has insisted that 'we' cannot be held responsible for the 'mistakes' made by past generations.

But the rise of the One Nation Party makes it all too painfully clear that the legacy of the past cannot simply be done away with. Indeed, one could reasonably speculate that the sense of guilt, shame or disgust about the country's 'racist' past is a structure of feeling confined mostly to the educated urban middle and upper-middle classes, whose moral and cultural orientation has converged with the 'regime of value' that has become dominant in the post-1960s' international Western world (Frow 1995). This progressivist, liberal regime of value favours equality for all, tolerance and cosmopolitanism, it celebrates the enrichment derived from cultural diversity, and, in general, it raises the sentiments of a universalist humanism to the ideal standard of moral virtue. Within this regime of value, the White Australia policy was irredeemably morally wrong – at least in principle. However, one cannot assume that this liberal structure of feeling is shared across the whole spectrum of the population. Indeed, the backlash against 'political correctness' – uttered by both Pauline Hanson and John Howard – speaks to the contrary.

Hanson has insisted, rather querulously, that 'the people of Australia were never consulted' about Asian immigration and multiculturalism. As she said in one of her speeches, 'Australians are tolerant but their patience is being sorely tested by their politicians who have never allowed a full and open debate on immigration and multiculturalism' (Hanson 1997a: 20). This expression of populist resentment speaks to the great divide that has grown between 'the cosmopolitan elites' and 'ordinary people' on this issue, especially those of Anglo-Celtic background. When Hanson argued against the 'special treatment' of Aboriginal people and against immigration (especially of Asians) and multiculturalism, and at least implicitly in favour of a return to the 1950s, when the White Australia policy was still firmly in place and when Australians were still encouraged to feel proud and lucky about their country's status as a far-flung outpost of Europe, we can read her appeal *culturally* as a refusal to submit to the dominant regime of value which discredits the past and offers an alternative, progressivist national narrative from which she and her supporters feel alienated. In Peter Cochrane's (1996: 9) words: 'Hanson represents the grief that goes with the loss of cultural centrality and the loss of identity that happens when a cosmopolished (Anglo) elite lines up with the new ethnic forces on the block.' In short, Hanson's politics is a politics of resistance, but an irrevocably reactionary one.

It is not surprising, given Hanson's fear-driven rejection of Australia's multiracial future, that One Nation's first policy document was on immigration policy. The populist paranoia and distrust are evident in this passage:

The government's unspoken justification for immigration and the result of the policy will lead to the Asianisation of Australia. Our politicians plan an Asian future for Australia. As the then Immigration Minister, Senator Bolkus said, on 6/12/1994: 'We cannot cut and should not cut immigration because it would jeopardise our integration with Asia.' Do we need to change the ethnic/racial make up of Australia for trade? Trade comes and goes, but our identity as a nation should not be traded for money, international approval or to fulfil a bizarre social experiment.
(Pauline Hanson's One Nation 1998: 11)

What is interesting to note here is Hanson's resistance to the discourse of economic opportunism in favour of an idealistic, if reactionary, discourse of national identity. Harking back to the notion of a separate, sovereign, 'White Australia' as the nation's common destiny, it was defined explicitly against the threat of a possible 'Asian invasion'. This inward-looking notion of Australian national identity is nothing new; indeed, it was a hegemonic rendition of the national self, in the Gramscian sense of being almost universally accepted as common sense and as naturally right and good, until well into the 1960s. Its establishment was backed by an over-whelming consensus which brought together white Australians of all classes; it was a key aspect of what journalist Paul Kelly (1992) called 'the Australian Settlement'.

The move away from the idea of 'White Australia' during the 1960s was less based on a broad national popular will. An important role was played by political pressure from activist intellectual groups such as the Immigration Reform Group, who called for a gradual relaxation of the racially discriminatory policies of the government. In the end, the abolition of the White Australia policy was almost exclusively a matter of strategic governmental decision-making, not underpinned by national popular conviction but by 'wide-ranging elite consensus' (Viviani 1996: 8). In the new postcolonial world of East and South-East Asia the 'White Australia' ideal was increasingly seen as untenable, 'especially at a time when Australia was trying to find friends and allies there' (Mackie 1997: 19).

The admission of many migrants from Asian countries after 1966 (when the first, crucial immigration reforms were quietly introduced) represented a qualitative turnaround of magnificent proportions, an historical shift which completely overturned Australia's crucial and long-standing self-definition as a 'white nation'. From one moment to the next, as it were, Australians were expected, without much positive explanation, to ditch their entrenched self-conception as a sparsely populated 'white nation' in a threateningly yellow and brown region, which governments and political leaders of all persuasions had so passionately promoted for decades. The matter came to a head with the Indochinese refugee crisis in the second half of the 1970s. Australia simply had 'no alternative', observes Jamie Mackie (1997: 27) in an overview article on the politics of Asian immigration, but to take in its fair share of Indochinese refugees, as it needed to work closely with the ASEAN countries and as the international world attempted to achieve a solution to the refugee problem. In short, the opening up of Australia to non-European – especially Asian – new settlers and its dramatic implications for the nation's racial and ethnic make-up were in an important sense a not-quite-intended consequence of international pressure; it was a sign of the impact of globalization, of the increasing interdependence and entanglement of nations and states in the integrated world system and 'family of nations' that were slowly emerging after World War Two.

These developments took place without the existence of active popular consensus. There was, at most, a grudging acceptance, a submission to powerlessless in the face of overwhelming, external influences. Indeed, one of the most prominent elements in the history of immigration in Australia has been the persistent unease on the part of policy-makers and others about adverse 'public opinion', and the perceived need not to 'alarm' the general public by letting 'too many' refugees and other (Asian) immigrants in. In other words, the Australian people were constructed as generally incapable of coping if the changes were introduced too rapidly – a 'fact' corroborated by opinion polls which regularly asked people whether 'too many' Asians were allowed into the country (see Mackie 1997: 13–18). Politicians are ever mindful of a possible electoral backlash and therefore have generally avoided exhibiting active political leadership on the issue. As a result, as Nancy Viviani (1996: 11) has observed, 'politicans and bureaucrats became hostage to their own reinforcement of an adverse and divisive contest of public opinion'. As no credible narratives were presented to people to come to terms with these developments, those feeling uncomfortable were left to themselves in trying to understand why their beloved, old 'white Australia' should be abandoned and why, for the matter, their political leaders had abandoned *them*. By the 1990s, government officials and the cosmopolitan elite more generally simply sang the praises of 'cultural diversity' and 'tolerance', and ignored popular disquiet which, as we have seen, was regularly evidenced in opinion polls and popular controversies.

Benedict Anderson (1991: 6) once made the useful remark that national communities are 'to be distinguished, not by their falsity/genuineness, but by the style in which they are imagined'. To this we can add that some nations may, in the course of their history, be compelled to *change* the style in which they imagine themselves as a national community. Think, say, of modern Germany, where after the humiliating experience of Hitler's Nazism and the subsequent erection of the Berlin Wall, not to mention the latter's 'fall' many decades later, Germans had to constantly readjust to new meanings of being German. Think, to give a very different example, Taiwan, where the older idea of being part of a larger 'Chinese' nation has been replaced slowly by a much more vigorous and assertive sense of being a separate, Taiwanese nation. Or South Africa, where the demise of apartheid has ushered in a fundamental transformation of South African nationhood from a white supremacist to a 'multiracial' imagined community. In Australia, a similar transformation was designed in a less dramatic fashion, but it is fair to say that the end of the White Australia policy signified a monumental, state-led change in the style the Australian nation was to be imagined.

But changing the style in which a nation is imagined so fundamentally without the consent of the people, those whom the state claims to represent, is a tricky business. Consent, here, is a profoundly cultural-political issue and should not be defined in narrow empiricist terms, i.e. as reflected in referendums or public opinion polls. Buci-Glucksmann (1982), in summarizing Gramsci's theory of hegemony, distinguishes between passive and indirect consent and active and direct consent. While the latter involves participation and continuous engagement of the masses, the former implies a bureaucratic repressive relation between leaders and led, corporate integration of the led, and a reduction of democracy solely to its legal aspect. One does not have to adhere to Gramsci's Marxian romanticism to recognize that popular consent to the new, multicultural and multiracial Australia – as it has emerged since the 1970s – was much more passive than active, more indirect than direct. Active and direct consent, after all, cannot be taken as given, but has to be produced, created, fought for through careful ideological work, through cultural education and persuasion. While governments have certainly undertaken some of this work, for example, through multicultural education in schools, the encouragement of multicultural festivals and the organization of so-called 'harmony days', the social effectivity of much of this work remains doubtful especially as they tend to overlook the everyday experiences of the white majority.

The populist suspicion of 'ordinary Australians' against 'the elites' as expressed by Pauline Hanson and her followers is a manifestation of the failure of strategic leadership to engage in the production of consent, in the cultural struggle for a re-imagining of the nation away from 'White Australia' and in the direction of a multicultural/multiracial Australia. To put it differently, the ideological work necessary to actively *disarticulate* racism and nationalism (where the two were previously so firmly connected and popularly supported) and to win consent from the population at large for this disarticulation has remained undone.[4] I would suggest that this is one crucial reason why the presence of Asians in Australia remains, for better or worse, an object of anxiety – or at least of anxious concern – and why 'Asians in Australia', as a theme, can still become so easily, and so repeatedly, a focus of white populist anger and resentment.

In One Nation's immigration policy statement, this is how the anger is expressed. The strategic use of statistics is of particular interest here:

> 70 percent of our immigration program is from Asian countries. Consequently Australia will be 27 percent Asian within 25 years and, as migrants congregate in our major cities, the effect of Asianisation will be more concentrated there. This will lead to the bizarre situation of largely Asian cities on our coast which will be culturally and racially different from the traditional Australian nature of the rest of the country. In a democracy, how dare our government force such changes on the Australian people without their consent and against their often polled opinion.
>
> (Pauline Hanson's One Nation 1998: 11)

121

Hanson can be so self-righteous here because she feels she can rightfully speak from a position of entitlement, itself an enduring product of white settler colonial history. Ideologically, the White Australia policy was not just a declaration of racial exclusivism, it was also a claim of symbolic ownership. The very act of establishing procedures to ensure the maintenance of a 'white Australia' – through explicitly discriminatory immigration criteria designed to keep non-Europeans out – was a form of power to control who was or was not entitled to live on this island-continent. Implicit in this statement of power, then, was a sense of territorial entitlement, a self-declared authority to appropriate and own the land, a claim to what Ghassan Hage calls a 'governmental belonging' to the nation: 'the belief in one's possession of the right to contribute (even if only by having a *legitimate* opinion with regard to the internal and external politics of the nation) to its management such that it remains "one's home"' (Hage 1998: 46). Hanson herself put it more straightforwardly: 'Of course, I will be called racist but, if I can invite whom I want into my home, then I should have the right to have a say in who comes into my country' (Hanson 1997a: 7). The important point here, however, is not so much Hanson herself, whose One Nation Party has lost clout in the official political world remarkably quickly, precisely because it has always operated in the liminal space of (il)legitimacy. What is at issue here is the more deep-seated and long-term structure of feeling which determines who has symbolic ownership of 'Australia' – a structure of feeling spectacularly embodied by Hanson but arguably a much more pervasive, if implicit motivator of the national consciousness.

Of course, the moral quandary of white appropriation of the land is most drama-tized in relation to Aborigines and Torres Strait Islanders, the indigenous people of the country, whose increasing assertiveness in claiming their rights as the original inhabitants of the country has destabilized white Australians' sense of entitlement. In this regard, the sense of uncertainty – so prominently featured during the native title debate which raged around the same time as Hanson's rise to prominence[5] – must be related not just to the uncertainty with regard to the materiality of land claims, but more symbolically, the uncertainty of one's own legitimacy as occupiers of the land. Historian Ann Curthoys (1999: 2) has argued that 'beneath the angry rejection of the "black armband" view of history, lurks a fear of being cast out, made homeless again, after two centuries of securing a new home far away from home'. This clarifies Hanson's repeatedly made, emphatic statement that 'I am indigenous, and "indigenous" means "native of the land". I am Australian as much as any Aboriginal' (*Sydney Morning Herald* 1998). It is the white claim on Australia as home which needs to be upheld and defended in the face of Aboriginal and Torres Strait Islander resistance.

As to 'Asians', however, the relationship is different. As the exclusion and expulsion of Asians were central to the very formation of the modern Australian nation, their increasingly visible presence today, especially in the large cities, is still deeply associated with the foreign, the strange, with alien otherness, and with invasion. While Aboriginal people are now more or less universally, if sometimes reluctantly, recognized as belonging to Australia, Asians would never seem to be capable of acquiring the same status. As Lisa Lowe (1996: 6) has remarked about the analogous situation in the United States, 'the Asian American, even as a citizen, continues to be located outside the cultural and racial boundaries of the nation'. She goes on to observe that despite the relaxation of immigration laws, which has placed Asian people within the US nation–state in the workplace and in its markets, Asians remain stubbornly defined as 'foreign' and 'outside' the national polity in linguistic, cultural and racial terms (Lowe 1996: 8). Such a contradiction is also clearly at work in the Australian national imagination.

In a recent speech, Hanson restated her opposition to what she sees as the 'Asianization' of Australia by saying: 'If we were to have too many of one race coming in that weren't assimilating and becoming Australians, it would take over our culture, our own way of life and our own identity, and that's what I'm protecting' (quoted in *Sydney Morning Herald* 1998). Here, Hanson exemplifies the continuing force of the hegemonic assumption that 'Australian' culture/identity and 'Asian' culture/identity are mutually exclusive, antagonistic categories: the two cancel each other out, they are a contradiction in terms. One cannot, from this point of view, be Asian and Australian at the same time. While Hanson has always been careful to leave some space open for racially Asian people provided that they assimilate into Australian culture, she is adamant about the incompatibility of Asian and Australian *cultures*. In this sense, Hanson is a cultural racist, or 'culturalist' (Stratton 1998: 64). An 'Asianization' of Australia would therefore inevitably mean its de-Australianization. In a clear reference to her fear of being 'Asianized', Hanson once sketched a future in which Australian farmers can no longer stay in business. She asked, ominously, 'Will the Government then import even basic crops, perhaps rice, to get us more used to it?' (quoted in Wilkinson 1998: 43).

Beyond the politics of numbers

'Too many of one race.' We are returned here to the politics of statistics, the very vehicle of establishing what is 'too many'. Critics of Hanson, including Immigration Minister Philip Ruddock, have been quick to point out that her figures are incorrect. Thus, in response to the Hanson phenomenon Ruddock's Department of Immigration published several fact sheets and a brochure 'Dispelling the myths about immigration' (http://www.immi.gov.au). In this brochure the minister responds to questions such as, 'Why do we take in people who don't speak English?', 'Why do we see so many foreign faces in Australia?', and 'Is Australia being swamped by Asians?' To the last question, Ruddock's response is a reassuring: 'no. Only about 5 per cent of Australia's population were born in Asia.' He goes on to say that 'if immigration levels and selection processes remain about the same, the proportion of Asian-born people is projected to be about 7.5 per cent in 2041'. Never mind the 'exact' figures; what matters here is the suggestion that we are not being 'Asianized', that the number of Asians coming into this country is much *lower* than Hanson claims. Thus there is, so we are implicitly told, no need to be afraid of being 'swamped by Asians'.

The provision of 'objective' information such as this is of course well intentioned. However, the danger of this kind of statistical skirmishing is that it may actually *confirm* the assumption that 'too many' Asians would be a problem in Australia. But how much is too many, and who has the authority to determine how much is too many? Indeed, the constant repetition of the question whether there are 'too many' Asians or not, as in opinion polling practices, for example, only legitimizes the framing of the issue in this way. As a consequence, the issue of 'Asians in Australia' is reduced to a politics of numbers in which the voice of Asians themselves is completely absent. In this discourse of reassurance, Asians are reduced to the status of *objects to be counted*, they are excluded from active participation in a conversation which implicitly takes it for granted that the overall whiteness at the core of Australian identity should not be jeopardized, not now nor in the future. Asians can come in, but in moderation, because they are never to be allowed to dilute the nation's predominantly white racial/cultural identity: Ruddock tacitly agrees with Hanson on this, just as they are effectively in agreement about their authority, as white Australians, to speak for the country as a whole.

To illuminate the restrictiveness of the discursive field in which the problematic of 'Asians in Australia' is being debated across the cultural political spectrum, we can contrast this discursive consensus with the radically oppositional voice of someone like Eric Rolls, historian of the Chinese in Australia. While Rolls remains within the discursive frame of economic advantage, he provocatively argues for *more* Asians in Australia, because only such an increase of the Asian population would secure the country's future:

> We need to increase immigration by Chinese and other Asians. They do not drain our resources, they generate their own businesses to Australia's profit. Australia will have little chance in the next century unless we are at least 30 percent Chinese and Asian. Then we will be able to accept where we are and prosper accordingly. Our new people will generate our future.
> (Rolls 1996: 599)

The question here is not whether Rolls is right or wrong. The question is, how many Australians today would feel threatened about such an imagined Eurasian future for the nation? The fact that voices such as Rolls's are virtually unheard of in the public discourse, suggests that the issue of '(too many) Asians in Australia' remains cast as an uncomfortable problem in the national imagination, condensing fears and anxieties too difficult to contemplate.

As we enter the twenty-first century, however, the nation–state's power to determine its racial make-up will become ever more anachronistic. As Alistair Davidson (1997: 6) remarks, 'the world becomes increasingly a place of multi-ethnic states, with up to 30% of the population coming from other societies'. In this light, the important task here is to deconstruct the very desire for 'one nation' – a modernist ideology which can no longer be sustained in a postmodern, globalized world. In this context, national unity cannot be based on a sense of common history and collective memory, or a sense of racial kinship, a sense of 'Australian family'. What is at stake, then, is a reconfiguration of Australian nationalism, from its earlier, racially exclusionary form – the nation as 'one' – to a new, inclusive, and open-ended form – the nation as a porous container of multiple, criss-crossing, intersecting flows of different peoples and cultures (Turner 1997). This is not by any means an easy task: it involves a whole new style of imagining the nation, for which there are no proven established models. Meaghan Morris has put the hard questions this way:

> The old nationalism was a *protectionist* as well as a racist settlement that thrived on Australia's cultural and physical isolation. What sort of unity can be projected for a free-trading nation at the mercy of world economic forces that no government can control? For a society unable effectively to legitimize its norms with reference to a common culture, yet with large numbers of citizens yearning to do so?
>
> (1998b: 209)

To be sure, Australia is not the only country faced with this predicament – a predicament intimately bound up with the accelerating process of globalization, which has unsettled the real and imaginary stability and immanence of all nation–states. The increasingly frequent reference to 'multiculturalism' and 'cultural diversity' is symptomatic of the quest for a new national culture suitable for globalizing times. In this, the task is to develop viable ways of 'living together' in which differences cannot be erased, only negotiated, and where notions of belonging no longer depend on an allegiance to a given 'common culture' (under-girded by racial sameness) but on the *process* of partial sharing of the country, a process that will necessarily imply give and take, mutual influencing, and ongoing cultural hybridization. As long as acceptance of such processual and open-ended nation-building is not forthcoming, 'Asians in Australia' will remain a contradiction in terms.

7

RACIAL/SPATIAL ANXIETY

'Asia' in the psycho-geography of Australian whiteness

Pauline Hanson is known for representing herself as 'only a fish and chip shop lady' speaking for 'the Australian people'. But for her not all people living in Australia belong to 'the Australian people'. In her infamous maiden speech, which she delivered in the Federal Parliament in August 1996, she singled out two groups as targets for her resentment and hostility: Aboriginal people and 'Asians'. On Aborigines, she said among others:

> I am fed up with being told, 'This is our land'. Well, where the hell do I go? I was born here, and so were my parents and children. I will work beside anyone and they will be my equal but I draw the line when told I must pay and continue paying for something that happened over 200 years ago. Like most Australians, I worked for my land; no-one gave it to me.
>
> (Hanson 1997a: 4)

About 'Asians', she had this to say:

> I believe we are in danger of being swamped by Asians. Between 1984 and 1995, 40% of all migrants coming into this country were of Asian origin. They have their own culture and religion, form ghettos and do not assimilate. Of course, I will be called racist but, if I can invite whom I want into my home, then I should have the right to have a say in who comes into my country.
>
> (ibid.: 7)

The juxtaposition of these two comments illuminates a crucial strand in the worldview of Hansonism: a claim of ownership of the Australian land, and a strident sense of entitlement adhering to that ownership. In presenting herself as the rightful proprietor of this country, Hanson does two things. First, she disavows the implications of Aboriginal dispossession which formed a founding moment of the creation of modern Australia with the arrival of the British in 1788. Second, as the 'hostess', she claims the right to act as a gatekeeper for any newcomers,

126

especially when they are 'Asian'. What is important in this latter case is not so much that Hanson is anti-Asian *per se*, but the fact that she feels entitled in wanting to keep Asians out, especially if they 'do not assimilate', that is, if they do not behave according to the rules and habits of the house, to 'the Australian way of life' that Hanson herself claims to represent. Hanson, in other words, has appropriated 'the native's point of view'. The true natives of Australia, for Hanson, are not the Aboriginal people, but people like herself, ordinary, white Australians. Implicit in the ideology of Hansonism is a suppression of the history of colonization which was foundational to modern Australia, the indigenization of the white presence in this land, and the postulation of its demographic and cultural dominance as *natural* – and therefore, naturally legitimate.

The emergence of Pauline Hanson on the political stage has been an uncomfortable reminder of a shameful aspect of the nation's political and cultural past, a past many Australians would rather forget about. But it should have become clear from the previous two chapters that Pauline Hanson is not a 'phenomenon' that can be conveniently relegated to the distant Other realm of Australia's past. On the contrary, she is very much a symptom of a problematic aspect of the national present – one that is not simply going to go away. As Ann Curthoys and Carol Johnson have rightly remarked,

> Hansonite politics, in one form or another, whether or not it revolves around Pauline Hanson herself, or around One Nation specifically, is a form of politics of the future not the past. . . . It is a politics that is here to stay at least as a significant minority factor in Australian political life.
>
> (1998: 97)

It is therefore important to understand the more long-term and enduring underpinnings of the views and sentiments expressed by Hanson and her followers.

The recent surge of Hansonism in Australia represented a disturbing but undeniable return of the repressed. What were repressed are deep-seated and deeply ingrained anxieties – often articulated as racial anxieties – which have underlain the peculiar structure of feeling of 'white Australia'. Obviously, as so clearly articulated by Hanson herself, these anxieties have far from vanished, despite the official ending of the White Australia policy in the early 1970s. What is the nature of these anxieties? I want to suggest that simple accusations of lingering 'racism' do not suffice here. Hanson's hostility against Aborigines and Asians is not merely and simply a matter of racial hatred. As her statements quoted above clearly indicate, the anxieties she has given expression to do not merely and simply revolve around 'race', but also, significantly, have to do with land, with territory or more precisely, with *claims* on land and territory. In other words, what is at stake here is a problematic articulation of race and space. The recognition of Native Title after the Mabo and Wik decisions, which has given such a jolt to the Aboriginal and Torres Strait Islander land rights movement, makes this glaringly clear. Perhaps less evident is the fact that anti-Asian sentiment in Australia also has a spatial, as well as a racial, dimension. This is what I would like to illuminate in this chapter.

As a nation, Australia has a relatively short and peculiar history. As we all know, the modern nation–state of Australia grew out of a violent history of settler colonialism, which was literally a process of land-grabbing on a huge scale. Once the British Europeans had colonized the country, they claimed it as their own. Moreover, they proceeded to claim *exclusiveness* of posession: Australia was to be for them only, that is, for 'the white man' (as the famous slogan of *The Bulletin*, Australia's premier news magazine, stated). The very idea of a 'white Australia' was an assertion of racial and spatial symbiosis, or at least the desirability thereof. The fantasy was that the entire territorial space of Australia was to be for one race only, the white race. The presence of all those who were not white was considered undesirable, on the grounds that a superior race – the white race – should not mix with inferior races. The seriousness of the matter was debated extensively in Parliament in 1901, where most politicians were in agreement that, in the words of one member , it is 'our duty to preserve this island continent for all eternity for the white race' (King O'Malley, quoted in R. Hall 1998: 138). Measures were therefore put in place to ensure, as much as possible, their removal from the continent (for an overview, see Hay 1996). Conveniently, the original inhabitants of the land, the Aborigines, who according to the racial theories that prevailed in the late nineteenth century were placed on the lowest rank on the racial hierarchy, were assumed to be a doomed race that would soon die out, assisted by actively genocidal policies and practices of the British colonizers (McGregor 1997). On the other hand, the 'coloured races', in particular the Chinese, Japanese and other Asians, had to be kept from entering and settling into the country (and many of those already in the country were thrown out). A central mechanism in the pursuit of this objective was the Immigration Restriction Bill, implemented in 1901 as soon as the new, federated nation–state of Australia was established. This measure came to be known as the White Australia policy.

Of course, white racism was nothing extraordinary at the turn of the twentieth century. It was, after all, a hallmark of the European sense of racial superiority at a time when European imperialist hegemony was at its height. However, white racism in the Australian context has peculiarities which have to do with the spatial dimensions of this settler colonial project. Geographically, modern Australia was on the other side of the (European) world from which it was born. The contradictions of being 'a far-flung outpost of Europe' were deeply ingrained on the white colonial Australian mind: the 'mother country' was so far away and yet so emotionally overpowering. This produced a particularly antipodean sense of place, a spatial consciousness of self and of the world moulded by the experience of occupying this vast, distant land, which was perceived as nearly empty. The fact that the gravity of settlement was largely in the southeast corner, where Captain Cook first landed, only added to the sense of isolation and separateness.

After 1788, the great Southern land was progressively claimed by the expanding British Empire until it annexed the entire Australian landmass in 1829. This huge territorial claim was an act of supreme imperial might: unlike, for example, Canada, which to this day has to negotiate the legacy of two competing European colonial powers within its national framework, the whole territory previously known as *terra Australis incognita* had come under the control of a singular world power. (Indeed, had history run another course, what is now Western Australia could easily have become either a Dutch or a French state.) As it happened, the totalizing nature of the British annexation and control paved the way, several decades on with Federation in 1901, for the creation of 'one Australia', encompassing the whole territory of the island-continent and imagined in terms of a transplanted British homogeneity. In other words, what was produced here was the collapsing into one of physical geography and human geography, which had a powerful imaginative effect on the white settlers. It provided the fledgling settler society with a singular sense of spatial identity, the integrity of which coincided with that of the whole island-continent.

It should be noted that the idea of Australia as an 'island-continent' is by no means an innocent one. This idea absolutizes the disconnection of the territory from the rest of the world and downplays the fluidity of the border zone between the northwest coast and the southeastern islands of what is now Indonesia (including Timor), for example, as testified by the centuries-old links between Aborigines and Malays in that region. In their book *The Myth of Continents*, Martin Lewis and Kären Wigen remark that for a long time there was no agreement among (Western) geographers on how to represent the space of Australia: in eighteenth- and nineteenth-century world atlases, Australia 'was sometimes colored as a portion of Asia, sometimes as a separate landmass, and sometimes as a mere island' (Lewis and Wigen 1997: 30). The fact that the idea of Australia as a separate and distinct 'island-continent' is now completely naturalized, is the historical outcome of a world-political process which has produced and legitimized the boundaries of the nation–state of Australia as we know it today. More importantly, it has elicited a national geopolitical vision shaping some peculiarities of Australia's view of itself and its relationship to the world (Dijkink 1996).

The absence of internal cultural/political fracture within the territory as a result of its entire appropriation by the British, and the imaginary closure provided by the sense of continental wholeness and insularity, must have intensified – together with the distance from Europe – a feeling among the inhabitants of the new white nation that they were dangerously exposed to external threats. Documenting the period around Federation in 1901, Raymond Evans *et al.* remark: 'Australia was an isolated continent, far from Europe, in the midst of Asia and the Pacific Islands. Settlers in Australia constantly felt vulnerable, fearing that some other world power would come and ruin their Austral-British tranquility' (1997: 180). Throughout the nineteenth century that 'other world power' was by turns identified as France, Germany or Russia, but Japan's victory over Russia in their war of 1904–5, as one author observes, 'appeared to link the presumed threat from a *foreign great power* – till then a European monopoly – with the *non-European demographic*' (Fitzpatrick 1997: 98, italics in original).

What we have here is a crucial determinant of what I want to call, to borrow a term from Morley and Robins (1995: 8), the 'psycho-geography' of white Australia:

the fear of invasion. This fear was intensely heightened when the invader was imagined as 'Asian': so geographically proximate, so threateningly multitudinous, and not least, so alienly non-white. It is important to dissect the cultural logic of this fear, as it still informs contemporary sentiments and attitudes towards 'Asia'. In a paper on settler colonialism and national security ideologies in Australian history, Fitzpatrick (1997) speaks about the 'threat ethos' which has traditionally informed Australia's security obsession. This experience of threat is profoundly bound up, according to Fitzpatrick, with Australia's development as a European settler society on the southeastern fringe of Asia. This situation produced a mindset which sought to guarantee Australia's security 'through the support of culturally similar but geographically distant powerful friends', first Britain, later the United States (ibid.: 116). Implicit in this scenario is the construction of Australia's geographical neighbours – 'Asia' – as an utterly distrusted Other. In other words, at the heart of modern Australia's sense of itself lies a fundamental tension between its white, European identity and its Asian, non-European location. As historian Andrew Markus has remarked:

> The non-Europeans of the 'near north' were seen as posing a threat to the social and political life of the community, to its higher aspirations. The perception of this threat was heightened by a consciousness of race, a consciousness that innate and immutable physical characteristics of certain human groups were associated with non-physical attributes which precluded their assimilation into the Australian nation.
>
> (1979: 256)

What becomes clear here is that *racial* anxiety is articulated with a distinctively Australian, equally formative *spatial* anxiety. David Walker (1997: 133) puts it this way: 'the need to live in relatively close proximity to awakening Asia lent a certain drama and intensity to the Australian situation, it conferred a special status on Australia as a continent set aside for the development of the white race'.

Thus, white Australia's anxiety about 'Asia' was not accidental to its history, nor merely based on racialist prejudices which have now become outdated (and therefore easily discardable). On the contrary, in a fundamental, one could say, ontological sense, anxiety about 'Asia' structurally informed the antagonistic relationship of its history and its geography. In Walker's (1997: 141) words, 'what was meant by "Australia" and what was meant by "Asia" were not unrelated questions'. The establishment of the settler colony, dependent as it was on the appropriation of the vast territory of the island-continent and on the legitimization of its claim to exclusive possession, was conceived as the creation of a white European enclave in an alien, non-European part of the world. In other words, 'Australia' was defined, foundationally, *against* 'Asia', what Meaghan Morris (1998a: 245) describes as 'a deliriously totalized "Asia"'.

Almost a century later, the official rhetoric has made a complete turnaround, at least on the surface. Australia now proclaims itself a *part* of the Asia-Pacific region.

Furthermore, the abolition of the White Australia policy, which began in the 1960s and was finally formalized by the Whitlam government in 1973, has made it possible for many people from Asian countries to migrate into Australia and thus to become co-inhabitants of Australian territorial space. While these changes are significant, however, I would argue that to an important extent the shift has not been a qualitative, paradigmatic one but merely one of valence: Australia no longer turns it back against 'Asia' (because it can no longer afford to), but is now for 'Asia' (because it thinks it has to be). Much of the engagement with 'Asia' today remains caught within a paradigm of mutual exteriority: 'Australia' and 'Asia' continue to be imagined as absolutely separate, mutually exclusive entities, even if their relationship may be conceived differently, though still one entered into with less than full conviction.

The establishment of White Australia was, as I have indicated above, a statement about Australia's place in the world: it stated that Australia felt entitled to quarantine itself from its immediate surroundings in the interest of a much desired internal homogeneity and white racial purity. Strict control over who could or could not come into the country was therefore deemed necessary to protect the kind of civilization that the new settler society imagined itself to develop and maintain. Its territorial insularity and the seeming naturalness of its borders promoted the idea that in Australia 'it was possible to control contact with the rest of the world in a manner not possible for most other nations' (Evans *et al.* 1997: 205). Thus, a self-righteous, self-protective parochialism, a determined commitment to provincialism and anti-cosmopolitanism, has played a founding role in the formation of white Australian culture. It should be stressed that this was a *positive* commitment: it was born of the idea that the new society had a paradisiac, 'lucky country' potential if it remained set apart from the world. But the other side of this fierce, self-chosen isolationism is a deep discomfort about the outside world, an outside world which is the source of danger, threat, insecurity, and which had to be kept at bay as much as possible. In this sense, Australia is and has remained an 'anxious nation' (Walker 1999).

Pauline Hanson's rhetoric clearly draws upon this contradictory, anxious strand of white Australian settler identity. Hanson's is a paranoid discourse that is predisposed to be deeply suspicious of everything that is marked as foreign, imported, international. Indeed, some of Hanson's political demands were that Australia repudiate all its international obligations (such as those related to United Nations treaties) and cease all foreign aid. The idea of multiculturalism, a policy which Hanson wanted to see abolished, is denounced in *Pauline Hanson – The Truth*, the book published under her name, as a 'foreign import' (from Canada and later the United States), as are ideas of a liberal multiracial society, free trade and economic rationalism (Hanson 1997a: 73ff.). In short, what Hansonism stands for is an extreme protectionism in defence of an embattled, fortress identity, not only economic but also cultural and racial, a tenacious desire to hold on to the dream of an insular, closed, wholesome 'white Australia'.

That this dream turned out to be an illusion, however, had become clear many decades ago, especially after World War Two, when Australia found itself caught within a changing configuration of international relations. If the international acceptability of (the desire for a) White Australia depended on the hegemony of the Colonial World Order within which it was conceived (see Lowe 1997), the post-war process of decolonization and the emergence of a postcolonial world unsettled the political, not to say the moral legitimacy of Australia's policy of racial exclusivism, which was, in Sean Brawley's (1996: 242) words, 'a bright red rag to Asian sensibilities'. The dismantling of the British Empire 'no longer offered Australia a security umbrella' (Goldsworthy 1997: 155), while the newly decolonized nation–states in Australia's near north posed an unprecedented challenge to the very tenets of faith on which White Australia was built. Australian authorities were intensely aware that the White Australia policy was liable to international challenge in a post-Holocaust world grown more sensitive to the injustices of racial discrimination and intolerance. But the emotional attachment and ideological commitment to a White Australia were so great that they long remained a dominant factor in post-war population policies.

Thus, the decision for a massive increase in immigration intake with people from Europe – which, incidentally, implied a dilution of the definition of 'whiteness' beyond the preferred notion of 'Britishness' – was driven explicitly by a desire to keep Australia white, and to keep Asia out. There was a strong belief that without a massive population build-up Australia was in danger of facing annihilation: 'populate or perish'. As demographer Charles Price wrote about the early post-war period: 'the country felt that the best answer to the international cry that it should open its unused land and resources to Asia's crowded millions was to populate the continent and develop its resources with as many white persons as possible' (quoted in Brawley 1996: 237). Seen from this perspective, the post-war immigration policy, which provided the seeds for the future policy of multiculturalism some three decades later, was negatively motivated, inspired by fear, not by the positive envisioning of a new, more inclusive future.

The gradual decline of the White Australian dream was given a massive impetus in the late 1960s, when the Aborigines were finally recognized as full citizens in 1967. But it was in the mid-1970s when the social impact of the end of the White Australia policy was only truly felt, with the admission of thousands of Indochinese refugees in the wake of the war in Vietnam. It should be noted that Australia's decision to take in these refugees, too, was made in the context of high level international pressure (Viviani 1996). The so-called 'boat people' 'jarred Australians living in their peaceful and stable society to a greater awareness of how near they were to a turbulent South-East Asia' (Lawrence 1983: 26). Their arrival marked the effective beginning of Australia's willy-nilly transformation into a multiracial (and not just multicultural) society. This development was an unintended consequence of world events beyond the nation's own control; it was not something actively willed by the Australian community itself.

There was, then, over the years a slow but inevitable erosion of Australia's sovereign capacity to retain a sense of racial/spatial singularity and separateness, as the world changed quickly and irrevocably. The (idea of) White Australia was established in a time when European imperialism was at the height of its world hegemony, and when Australians could count on 'a predominant European influence interposed between themselves and "Asia"' (Lowe 1997: 1). But clinging to the idea of a White Australia became more and more untenable as the colonial world was dismantled and Asian assertiveness became stronger. As Lowe (ibid.) remarks, 'What Robert Menzies . . . described in 1935 as a strong sense of "imperial destiny", came under pressure – not in any gradual or easily discernible way, but with shocks and jolts which undermined assumptions about Australia's role and identity in international affairs.' Little could Menzies have known that by the 1990s, Australian elites would imagine national survival and prosperity not in terms of protection *from* 'Asia', but in terms of becoming integrated *with* 'Asia'!

The rising global importance of East and South-East Asia in the last decades of the twentieth century has been of particular significance to Australia, especially in economic terms. In this context governments have greatly welcomed the role of Asian migrants within Australia, who are seen as human assets providing the contacts, linguistic skills and cultural knowledge to promote Australia's (primarily economic) 'integration with Asia'. There has been an overwhelming consensus among economists, politicians and business leaders that Australia's future 'lies in Asia', something not diminished by the economic crisis which swept across the region in the latter half of the 1990s. In other words, for Australia the globalization of the world economy has primarily meant an 'Asianization': as global capitalism operates increasingly through the creation of regional alignments, Australia found itself excluded from 'Europe' (or the European Union), on the one hand, and from 'America' (or NAFTA), on the other, Australia had no choice but to attempt to define itself as 'a part of Asia' (as has been evidenced in Australia's leading role in the establishment of APEC, the Asia Pacific Economic Forum).

This geo-economic imperative has necessitated a fundamental transformation in the way Australians perceive the place of their own country in the world. Australia's traditionally dominant self-image as a white European enclave, which implied a denial and disavowal of its actual physical location at the edge of a world region much more proximate in geographical terms, but alien, unfamiliar and generally considered inferior in cultural terms, has gradually become an anachronism. It is for this reason that the rising power of 'Asia' poses such a challenge for Australia, not just in economic terms but, more importantly, in *cultural* and *psychic* terms. After all, 'Asia' used to stand for that which was to be emphatically excluded from the Australian imagined community, and whose otherness – that of its people, cultures, its societies – was to be kept at bay at all cost, not allowed to contaminate the white national self. To represent 'Asia' now as the inescapable destiny for Australia, requires an enormous adjustment in the national sense of self. This is a not ironic turn of events which most Australians have hardly come to terms with.

Indeed, it is the spectre of 'Asianization' – an ill-defined but widely used term in Australian public debate whenever the future of the nation is discussed – which is central to the politics of fear expressed in the discourse of Hansonism. As Hanson herself succinctly put it: 'I don't want to be Asianised.' The fear, then, is about a coming future which Hanson and her many followers desperately want to keep at bay: a future in which the island-continent can no longer be preserved as white territory. With an alarmist tone she invokes a scenario in which a barely containable fear of an 'Asian invasion', a fear of being obliterated by 'Asia', is all too palpable. 'Time is running out,' she said in her maiden speech:

> We have only 10 to 15 years left to turn things around. Because of our resources and our position in the world, we will not have a say because neighbouring countries such as Japan, with 125 million people; China, with 1.2 billion people; India, with 846 million people; Indonesia, with 178 million people; and Malaysia, with 20 million people are well aware of our resources and potential. Wake up, Australia, before it is too late.
>
> (Hanson 1997a: 10)

Racial/spatial anxiety is expressed here through the invocation of the teeming Asian millions who threaten to engulf the antipodean land that was supposed to be reserved for whites. In Pauline Hanson's One Nation policy document on immigration, which was issued in 1998, the apocalyptic image was sketched of an island-continent where white Australians were marginalized into the dead centre of the island-continent. The fact that Asian migrants congregate in the major cities, so it conjectured, 'will lead to the bizarre situation of largely Asian cities on our coast which will be culturally and racially different from the traditional Australian nature of the rest of the country.' (Pauline Hanson's One Nation 1998: 11). In other words, the fear is not just that Australia will no longer be 'one nation'; more terrifyingly, white Australia will slowly but surely be swallowed up by the Asian hordes! This scenario operates, as Morris has noted, in 'a register of paranoid anticipation' whose psychological effect is all the more powerful because it evokes 'a chain of displacement': 'something we did to others becomes something that happened to us and could happen all over again'. Enunciating the dark conscience of the white Australian settler subject, Morris notes wryly that 'on the beach, we replay our genocidal past as our apocalyptic future' (Morris 1998a: 247). It is for this reason that the simultaneous assault on white certainties by the new assertiveness of indigenous Australia, on the one hand, and by the spectre of Asianization, on the other, creates such an intense anxiety, the anxiety expressed in Hanson's desperate 'Where do I go?' It is the anxiety of someone who feels trapped, with no way out.

By expressing this anxiety – with its clear racial/spatial overtones – so explicitly, Hanson has unearthed a suppressed but pervasive element in the psycho-geography of Australian whiteness. Indeed, it is a powerful force in Australia's political unconscious, a force transcending differences in political positions which might superficially, at the level of conscious opinion, appear poles apart. To illustrate this, let us briefly look at Stephen FitzGerald's book *Is Australia an Asian Country?*, published in 1997, precisely at the moment when the Hanson controversy was at its height. FitzGerald is a former ambassador to China and known as one of the staunchest proponents of a profound and committed Asianization of Australia. His political position can therefore not be further removed from that voiced by Pauline Hanson: he berates Australians for 'laziness in coming to terms with the fact of Asia' (FitzGerald 1997: 57) and welcomes the stream of Asian immigrants into the country, which he sees as essential to 'bringing Asia into our social and cultural landscape' (ibid.: 67). In his view, 'the Asian challenge for Australia is not economic or commercial. It is intellectual, and the issues are political and cultural' (ibid.: 4). And he adds a sense of urgent necessity to this: 'the question of how we make our future with Asia, or whether we *have* a future, depends on how well we can apply our minds' (ibid.: 5, my italics). He warns that if Australia doesn't massively increase its ability to function in the new dynamic East Asian world it will be left outside – as the back cover of *Is Australia an Asian Country?* puts it, 'an unregarded nation in a region dominated by a powerful and confident Asian confederation'.

In such warnings we can begin to trace an unmistakable undercurrent of fear and anxiety in FitzGerald's ostensibly Asia-embracing discourse. The sub-title of his book makes this painfully clear. It asks ominously, 'Can Australia survive in an East Asian future?' And here we come to the crux of the matter. The message that Australia should become a 'part of Asia', of which FitzGerald's own book is a prime example, has been sold to the people with the prospect of a threat to Australia's very survival as a country. In this era of rapid globalization, the emergence of regional trade blocs and the troubled rise of Asian, especially East Asian economic prominence, so the message goes, Australia *must* embrace its geographical neighbours. To put it dramatically: 'Asianize or perish'. Alarmist pronouncements have abounded, especially before the financial crisis hit the region in 1997. Author Ross Terrill, for example, admonished that 'Australia would be doomed if it turned the clock back against Asian influence' (1996: 17). And Stephen FitzGerald himself packaged his message with the insistent reiteration that Australia had to step up its engagement with Asia if it is not to be left behind. He invoked the dramatic image of a lonely island-continent cut adrift, deserted by its parent-protectors:

> the great global shift in the balance of power is in their favour. The world has changed forever. It no longer belongs to the European or the North American. And we are alone, exposed. Nowhere to go but Asia.
>
> (1997: 14)

The undertow of anxiety is all too palpable in this geopolitical vision of Australia in the twenty-first century: Australia's future is tied to Asia, whether it likes it or not. The Asian financial crisis has not changed this sense of inescapability; if anything, it has only increased it. Thus, in the wake of the crisis, journalists asked questions such as, 'have we made a big mistake pursuing an economic strategy hinging on Asian prosperity?' (Wood 1997: 28). Whatever the answer to this question, commentators agreed that Australia could not evade its interdependence and interconnection with Asia: geography is destiny. Not surprisingly therefore, when the economic indicators turned bullish hardly two years later, those same commentators could barely suppress their journalistic enthusiasm – an enthusiasm tinged with a sense of relief and, to be sure, a sense of anxious urgency. In the words of one *Sydney Morning Herald* observer: 'Something big is happening in Asia in the wake of its financial crisis – and its creating a great investment opportunity for Australian business if it is smart enough, and quick enough, to take advantage of it' (Burrell 1999: 22). FitzGerald, on his part, would probably protest that Australians would only be able to be smart and quick enough if their engagement with Asia was more than merely opportunistically economic.

A very disturbing double bind begins to emerge here. Stephen FitzGerald and Pauline Hanson may be diametrically opposed in terms of philosophy, values and politics, but they are both passionately driven by a sense of emergency about Australia's future. With equal insistence they both claim that 'time is running out'. But while the informed, elite view (as exemplified by FitzGerald and many others) pronounces that Australia will be doomed if it doesn't 'Asianize', the popular/populist Hansonite view is that Australia will be doomed if it does. As antagonistic as they are, both positions remain strong currents in contemporary Australian imagination, an indication of the fact that the key contradiction in Australian national identity – history *versus* geography – is still an agonizing force in the national culture. How to overcome it, or at least come to terms with it? A minimum requirement, I would argue, would be the overcoming of the register of fear and anxiety itself. As Meaghan Morris has observed,

> If panics over immigration from Asia seem (as they do in 1996) to be recurrent in Australian public life, how surprised can we really be – when so much official rhetoric of 'Asianization' addressed to us in recent years has been marked by the very same panic, prompted now by economic rather than racial anxiety about the future?
>
> (1998a: 255)

Australians routinely overestimate the number of 'boat people', always marked in the imagination as 'Asian', even though many in recent years come from equally alien Middle Eastern countries such as Iraq and Afghanistan, signalling 'their persistent fear and suspicion of Asian invaders' (Phelan 1997).[1] Against this kind of psycho-geographic anxiety, expressed and amplified by the neoracism of Hanson, former Prime Minister, Malcolm Fraser, said of his own country, with a tone of resignation bordering on self-hatred, that 'the idea of a European enclave at the edge of Asia is unrealistic and offensive' (quoted in Editorial *Sydney Morning Herald*, 6 May 1997). But it is clear that a nation cannot live with such a verdict of illegitimacy on itself. Obviously, what is needed are positive visions of a new future in which Australia resolves its unease with its geographical location. A different kind of reconciliation is called for here. If reconciliation with Aboriginal people requires white Australia to come to terms with its past, the challenge of Asia, both inside and surrounding the territory claimed by and for whites only somewhat more than two hundred years ago, requires white Australia to come to terms with its future. In this future, the alignment of race and space – part and parcel of the project of white settler colonialism – will have to be disarticulated. The Australian land can no longer be the exclusive possession of one 'race', but will be a space of sharing and coexistence. FitzGerald actually comes up with an image for such a future of togetherness, a future he romantically describes as 'honey-coloured':

> If race is to be one thing which identified what is Asia, then with immigration and intermarriage, and the prospect this brings of a honey-coloured society (honey ranging as it does all the way from white to black), the heritage of the Australian Australian will be an enriching blend of European and Asian, a cosmopolitan truly fitted to be a member of an Asian regional community.
>
> (1997: 71)

We can end, however, with a positive note. For all the panic, fear and anxiety expressed in public rhetoric left and right, large pockets of Australian society are already acquiring, through daily interaction and ordinary interconnections, the multi-colours of honey.

8

THE CURSE OF THE SMILE

Ambivalence and the 'Asian' woman in Australian multiculturalism

Throughout most of the 1990s, Australia has prided itself on being one of the most successful and progressive multicultural nations in the world. For example, in 1995, the year which the United Nations dubbed the International Year for Tolerance, the Australian government hosted a lavish Global Cultural Diversity conference in Sydney, in which distinguished international guests were invited to take part in 'celebrating our cultural diversity' – one of the central mottoes of the conference, and of the highly pro-multiculturalist Keating government of that time. Of course, this upbeat, self-congratulatory rhetoric received a severe beating when One-Nationist Pauline Hanson exploded onto the political stage one year later. Hanson's popularity, as we have seen in the previous chapters, resulted in a period of doubt about Australia's commitment to multiculturalism, not least because the new Prime Minister, John Howard, has been known quite explicitly for his scepticism about the M-word and his generally more conservative vision for the nation, drawing as he does on images of a more uncomplicated, homogenous past, when diversity was not yet an issue nor something to pride oneself upon (Allon 1997). Nevertheless, by October 2000, when Sydney hosted the Olympic Games and all the eyes of the world were upon Australia, the theme of the happy and successful multicultural nation – as colourfully represented during the spectacular extravaganza of the opening ceremony – was once again trumpeted as Australia's main selling point. And a few months later, during the festivities of the 100th anniversary of Australia's birth as a nation on 1 January 2001, Prime Minister Howard himself in his ceremonial speech highlighted the importance of diversity in the story of the making of the Australian nation diversity – without, however, mentioning the word 'multiculturalism' – when he boasted about 'the remarkable way in which this country has absorbed people from 140 nations around the world, in a social experiment without parallel in modern history which has produced a degree of social cohesion which is the envy of the rest of the world'. It is fair to say that this kind of rhetoric, in which diversity is represented as a crucial building block of national unity and prosperity, is part of the grand narrative of late twentieth-century Australian nationalism, and in all likelihood will remain so long into the twenty-first, as nation–states will increasingly see themselves internally diversified by intensifying global flows of people.

Thus, the 'celebration' of cultural diversity has become one of the ideological catch cries of societies which recognize themselves as 'multicultural' today. The very assertion that 'cultural diversity' whatever this means is a cause for celebration, rather than something to be rejected or feared, is worth a pause. The discourse of celebration, evoked again and again at official commemorations of the nation (see e.g. Spillman 1997), has the effect of repressing the expression of some of the darker, more conflictual, less harmonious reverberations of living together in a culturally diverse society (of which Pauline Hanson herself is a dramatic manifestation). So often do we hear official spokespersons make the claim that Australia as a nation has discarded its shameful racist past and embraced the values of cultural pluralism and tolerance that we are compelled to wonder what is at stake in the repetitive and insistent, ritualistic enunciation of such a rosy and 'politically correct' image.

The forces of desire propelling this utopian social imaginary have power effects of their own. Australia's *desire* to be (seen as) a tolerant, multicultural nation in which cultural diversity is celebrated tends to vindicate a redemptive national narrative designed to come to terms with its explicitly racist history of Aboriginal annihilation and of the White Australia policy, which barred non-white peoples, particularly 'Asians', from entering the country. That is, an influential narrative of progressive transformation circulates in Australia today in which the nation is claimed to be on the road from a racist, exclusionary past to a multicultural, inclusionary present, with an emphatic pride of place for the nation's indigenous people (Stratton and Ang 1998). I am not concerned here with the sociological validity of this narrative. Rather, I am interested in how the truth value accorded to this narrative has the unfortunate effect of suppressing a plain dealing and unsentimental consideration of the continuing constitutive role of processes of racialized and ethnicized othering in contemporary Australia. I want to suggest in this chapter that these processes of othering have been transformed in the multicultural era: racially and ethnically marked people are no longer othered today through simple mechanisms of rejection and exclusion, but through an ambivalent and apparently contradictory process of *inclusion by virtue of othering*.

Featured in a mid-1990s' government poster encouraging immigrant residents of the country to take up Australian citizenship, which arguably would seal their permanent and definitive inclusion within the imagined community of nation, is the image of a visibly Asian woman, that is, a female with East Asian features. The poster says: 'Come and join our family.' Such is the nation–state's determination to be perceived as pursuing an inclusive policy towards its subjects irrespective of race, ethnicity or gender, that an Asian woman can now stand for the Australian population as a whole, a full member of the Australian 'family'. But we may ask, why an Asian, and why a woman rather than a man? And does her selection as a symbolic representative of the Australian citizenry really mean that she is no longer marginalized in Australia's national space and no longer occupies the position of 'other'?

Indeed, in light of the fact that only thirty years ago Asians were still considered *persona non grata* in this country, there is a certain irony to the fact that, in a peculiar way, Asians have, by the mid-1990s, become Australia's pet people. I know this from personal experience. My earliest memory of Australia dated from the mid-1960s, when my parents wanted to get out of Indonesia, my country of birth, because of the volatile political situation there. We ended up migrating to the Netherlands, but there were other possibilities: in a tight labour market quite a few countries in the world would have been willing to give my father, an engineer, a job – Brazil, America, Singapore. Why not Australia? I asked my father. As a child growing up in Indonesia, I was very aware of Australia's proximity as the Great White Land to our direct south. It was on Australian radio that I could listen to exciting music such as the Beatles and Elvis Presley – virtually banned from Indonesian radiowaves because they were considered 'western decadence'. I wouldn't have minded moving to Australia then. But that was simply not an option because, so my father told me, 'They only let white people in.' It is therefore not a little ironic that thirty years on I am not only living and working in this country, but also, from time to time, receiving extremely 'welcoming' comments. As one very friendly taxi driver recently said to me, 'We need people like you here.'

'People like me' were, so I gathered, 'Asians' (although, as I will clarify below, not all Asians, but only particular kinds of Asians). The driving force behind this change of attitude towards Asia and Asians has been primarily economic, related to Australia's belated realization that in an increasingly globalized world and as transnational regional economies become more and more important, it should exploit its geographical closeness to its populous, and increasingly prosperous, northern neighbours. What I want to explore here, however, are the more complex and contradictory *cultural* aspects of this renewed acceptance of Australia's inevitable regional context, enshrined as it is in the image of the Asian woman on the government poster for Australian citizenship. In this sense, multiculturalism as propagated by the state can be seen, at least in part, as an instrument of Australia's desired 'integration with Asia'. This does not mean that people of diverse Asian origins living in Australia are no longer constructed as other to the Australian self but, as I will argue, that the status of that otherness has changed.

I want to trace the specific forms and mechanisms of this change because it has, I believe, major consequences for the way we think about the distinctiveness of 'race relations' in a society which avowedly adheres to multiculturalism. What I want to argue is that the historical tensions within these 'race relations' are not solved by the rhetoric of multiculturalism, but, instead, made more complex and complicated. This does not mean that I am against multiculturalism. But I do want to suggest that the notion of a 'multicultural Australia' creates problems of its own, which we need to address if we are to pursue a critical 'politics of difference' – arguably one of the most urgent issues in contemporary critical theory (see e.g. Anthias and Yuval-Davis 1992; Pettman 1992; Gunew and Yeatman 1993). In much late twentieth-century critical theorizing, including feminist theory, the ideal of 'living with difference' has been put forward as a way beyond homogenizing definitions of identity politics. As Sneja Gunew (1993: 17) put it, 'the issue of cultural differ-ence has become an inevitable qualifier of any questions to do with gender or class'.

This book is written in the spirit of that ideal, but it also articulates a profound ambivalence towards it – an ambivalence which, I hope to show in this chapter, is both necessary and inevitable.

To be sure, many critics have emphasized the fact that Australia remains a deeply racist society despite its apparent commitment to multiculturalism (and, for that matter, to reconciliation between indigenous and non-indigenous Australians). Indeed, it seems fair to say that an acceptance of the values of pluralism and tolerance does not guarantee a disappearance of racism (Hage 1994; Stratton 1998). It is in recognition of this perceived incomplete abolition of the racist taint that the Labor government has initiated the adoption of racial vilification laws, for example. One problem with such avowedly 'anti-racist' measures (and the discourses that go along with them) is that they tend to be formulated from the implicit assumption that it is possible to make racism disappear. In this way, racism is tacitly conceived as deviant from the non-racist norm, an extremist aberration, something that, like a cancer, can be removed from the social body. What is constructed as a consequence is the image of a society which, in the end, will be free of racial prejudice and discrimination. But I want to argue that the idealized fantasy of such a purified, squeaky clean utopia only blinds us to the always less-than-perfect messiness of daily life in social space, where 'cultural diversity' can have many different, complex and contradictory meanings and effects.

The myth of pluralist tolerance (or tolerant pluralism) itself plays an important role in upholding such a fantasy. While Australians are now interpellated as being tolerant and as seeing tolerance as a virtue, the discourse of multiculturalism has by and large relegated intolerance to the realm of the forbidden, the 'politically incorrect'. Stronger still, precisely because intolerance (except in exceptional cases) has been legislated against as violating the preferred, multicultural order, the expression of actual and real tensions resulting from living in a culturally diverse society – and the feelings of resentment and animosity they can induce – cannot be done without risking being branded as evidence of 'racism', and explained away in the process. In other words, as the case of Pauline Hanson has abundantly proven, the imaginary construction of 'multicultural Australia' depends on a demonization of the racist other. It is based on the assumption that when all intolerance has finally been purged, the non-racist, tolerant utopia will be realized.

The problem with this representation lies in the simple binary oppositioning and separating out of (good) tolerance and (bad) intolerance, and in the illusion that we can have one without the other. It should be noted, however, that tolerance itself is irrevocably dependent on intolerance, insofar as it can only establish itself through a fundamental intolerance towards intolerance. As Slavoj Žižek has remarked:

> The traditional liberal opposition between 'open' pluralist societies and 'closed' nationalist-corporatist societies founded on the exclusion of the Other has thus to be brought to its point of self-reference: the liberal gaze itself functions according to the same logic, insofar as it is founded upon

the exclusion of the Other to whom one attributes the fundamentalist
nationalism, etc.

(1993: 223)

This suggests that the cutting-edge problematic of 'race relations' in the context
of liberal-pluralist societies – such as 'multicultural Australia' – should be cast
analytically and politically in terms of the *limits* of the discourse of tolerance. As
both Zygmunt Bauman (1991) and Ghassan Hage (1994) have persuasively
argued, the structural hierarchy between majority (singular) and minorities (plural)
is not nullified by the very elevation of tolerance as a value: indeed, in the ideology
of tolerance the dominant majority is structurally placed in a position of power
inasmuch as it is granted the active power to tolerate, while minorities can only
be at the receiving end of tolerance, or, if they are for some reason (e.g. having the
'wrong' religion) considered beyond the realm of the tolerable, deemed unworthy
of being tolerated. This power-laden division between the tolerating and the
tolerated lies at the heart of Australian multiculturalism, a division which is all
the more pernicious as it generally remains unacknowledged and unrecognized. In
other words, while raw and direct expressions of racism are no longer condoned,
the attempt to eliminate such expressions by preaching tolerance paradoxically
perpetuates the self–other divide which is the epistemological basis of the very
possibility for racism in the first place.

For example, as Hage (1994) points out, while the presence of the minority
subject is valued in the discourse of multiculturalism for the 'cultural enrichment'
s/he supposedly provides, precisely this function keeps her/him positioned in the
space of objectified otherness.

> For the Anglo-Celtic Australian who accepts it, the discourse of enrich-
> ment still positions him or her in the centre of the Australian cultural map.
> . . . More importantly, this discourse assigns migrant cultures a different
> *mode of existence* to Anglo-Celtic culture. While Anglo-Celtic culture
> merely and unquestionably *exists*, migrant cultures *exist* for the latter.
>
> (ibid.: 31–2; emphasis in original)

From this point of view, the new visibility of the Asian woman in representations
of Australian nationhood should be interpreted in more complex terms than in
those of a happy familial inclusion, because that inclusion comes at a cost.

Hage uses the provocative phrase 'tolerant racism' to refer to this relational
asymmetry. But I hesitate to use the word 'racism' here because of its strongly
moralistic negative connotations and, as such, its tendency to invite simplistic
political Manicheanism. Indeed, as the example of cultural enrichment indicates,
we should recognize the *difficulty* of determining where racism begins and ends,
and of establishing a clear dividing line between tolerance and intolerance in a
self-declared multicultural nation such as Australia. As Hage himself suggests,
the acceptance and enjoyment of 'other cultures' signalled in the idea of cultural

142

enrichment still contrasts favourably – as they at least create a space for divergent cultural expression – with the ethnocentric rejection of all signs of cultural difference predominant in older, more homogenizing and assimilationist discourse of culture and society. In other words, if tolerance as a value is fundamentally limited, its pursuit is still better than intolerance. At the same time, precisely because tolerance is never unconditional, it is never sufficient as a guarantee for acceptance or equality.

The contradictory nature of tolerance suggests that if we are to become more aware of the intricacies of what it means to be living in a 'multicultural' world and the different ways in which we are all positioned within it, we need to analyse what happens in those instances of interracial, inter-ethnic and intercultural tensions which cannot be sufficiently understood in terms of the secure binary oppositions of racism/anti racism and tolerance/intolerance, and to a certain extent, even that of dominant/subordinate. To put it differently, what I want to foreground here is the complex and profound *ambivalence* that is inscribed in the liberal-pluralist notion of a multicultural society.

This ambivalence operates at two interconnected levels. At a structural level, it is a force which destabilizes the boundary lines between the two sides of the binaries, which must be fought and suppressed if the assumptions of the multicultural worldview are to be upheld. The self-congratulatory insistence on 'celebrating our cultural diversity' in Australian multiculturalism is one clear instance of the suppression and repression of the structural ambivalence inscribed in the very idea of a multicultural nation. After all, what this idea generally disavows is the fact that there are always differences which cannot be easily subsumed within the neat and tidy enclosure of a harmonious 'unity-in-diversity'. As Homi Bhabha (1990b: 208) has remarked, the discourse of multiculturalism entails simultaneously 'a *creation* of cultural diversity and a *containment* of cultural difference'. And it is because the containment of cultural difference can never be completely successful that ambivalence can never be totally suppressed from the multicultural universe. This is the structural ambivalence created by the ongoing tension between difference as benign diversity and difference as conflict, disruption, dissension. This tension has manifested itself in a host of difficult cultural-political issues created by multiple cultural incommensurabilities (such as those to do with the management of gender and sexual relations), and it is widely recognized that there can be no easy solution to this tension.

But ambivalence also operates on a second, more subjective level. Precisely because the discourse of multiculturalism implies a suppression of the structural ambivalence inscribed in it in favour of an imposed 'celebration' of cultural diversity and of 'tolerance' as a prescribed virtue, it produces ambivalent subject positions for majority and minority subjects alike, while it also heightens the ambivalence of the *relations between* majority and minority subjects. As a result, ambivalence pervades the micropolitics of everyday life in a multicultural society. While the dominant ideology of multiculturalism both reinforces and obscures this ambivalence, it is important to examine these ambivalent moments because they have significant consequences for the prospect of our capability to be 'living with difference'. That is, the problem is not so much that people cannot 'deal with difference' (Pettman 1992), but that they often do not know *how* to deal with it, which is to say that they deal with it *ambivalently.*

The contradictory nature of tolerance itself, as I have described above, produces countless moments of ambivalence in everyday settings. This is the case, for example, when a majority subject is suspended in the unassuming (and mostly unconscious) moments of indecision over whether to tolerate or not to tolerate a minority subject. Carmen Luke (1994), a white woman married to a man of Chinese descent, describes the experience of being on the receiving end of such ambivalence in this way:

> In the company of my partner, I have been named by others in racist terms. Racist positioning has occurred through various comments but what is more difficult to describe and make explicit are the subtle social mannerisms of exclusion from conversations, the avoidances, the 'looks', people turning around on the streets to 'look again', people staring in restaurants, and so forth.
>
> (1994: 54)

As a white woman, Luke is identified as 'other' by association with her non-white partner. As an Asian woman, I have been the object of similar penetrating treatment and, like Luke, what I find most infuriating about these moments is precisely their elusive, undecidable nature, the fact that one cannot prove any 'hard' racism here while still feeling objectified, subjected to scrutiny, othered. This indicates that when it comes to 'race relations', the problem most often confronting minority subjects is not direct racial assault or straightforward discrimination (although this still happens a great deal as well, particularly to those with little social power such as most Aboriginal people and disadvantaged 'ethnics'), but something much less tangible than that. Luke (1994) cites a study of people's responses to white women in interracial relations which found that in by far the largest number of social encounters (with workmates, neighbours, shopkeepers, children's teachers, and so on), people were unsure how to react and gave ambiguous signals, their reactions falling 'midway between complete acceptance and complete rejection'. As Luke says, what these women found most difficult to deal with is 'the way they were made to feel marginal through begrudging acceptance' (ibid.: 59). Here, the ambivalent benefit of 'being tolerated' is resoundingly obvious.

Ambivalence also marks the apparently innocent question 'Where are you from?' which racially and ethnically marked people living in Australia are confronted with over and over again. Many of us have become extremely (over-)sensitive about this question because (we know that) it is often asked in the context of a denaturalization of our status as coinhabitants of this country, and in the automatic assumption that because we don't fit into the stereotypical image of the typical Australian, we somehow don't (quite) 'belong' here. As a result we anticipate, often correctly, that the (white) person asking us the question would expect the

144

answer to be some distant, alien or exotic land. (Several people of Chinese descent who have lived in this country all their lives and speak in a clear Australian accent have told me that even they get questioned in this way.) Is such a presumption racism? And by extension, is the question itself necessarily tainted by a racist attitude? The irritation and frustration we feel at having to explain again and again 'where we are from' incline us to answer 'yes' to these questions. 'White' friends I have spoken to about this issue generally deny any racist motivation implied in this question, and defend it as a sheer expression of interest; but, then, what triggered the interest in the first place, if not a certain curiosity about otherness – a curiosity which is implicated in our very construction and positioning as other? On the other hand, should the question not be asked at all? Wouldn't a lack of genuine interest in our 'difference' be just as frustrating and insulting? In short, what we have in this very simple instance of social exchange is an acute moment of awkwardness, which points to a semiotic realm beyond the simple binaries of acceptance and rejection, tolerance and intolerance, racism and anti-racism – a realm of profound ambivalence shared by both sides of the party, but keeping them worlds apart, a true moment of 'communication breakdown'.

In Australia, the celebratory preoccupations of official multiculturalism and the ongoing national obsession with Asia overdetermine the way in which this ambivalence is articulated in relation to Asians. In my experience, a significant number of white Australians have internalized the 'Asia-mindedness' so promoted by the government and have moved beyond 'mere tolerance' in their attitudes towards Asians in the direction of a more enthusiastic excitement of sorts. Indeed, due to Australia's geographical proximity to Asia I have encountered many (white) Australians who have actually become quite familiar with some of the countries to the north: they've been 'there' on holidays or on their way to Europe, or they do business with Malaysians, Chinese, or Japanese, and so on. Thus, as someone who looks visibly Asian, I am quite often asked 'Where are you from?', but with a curious inflection of liking or fondness for 'Asia' rather than suspicion and mistrust:

> 'Where are you from?'
> 'I was born in Indonesia.'
> 'Oh, I really like it there; it's such a spiritual country!'

This snippet of conversation reminds me of Ruth Frankenberg's observation in *White Women, Race Matters* (1993) that while American white women mainly see nonwhite 'cultures' as lesser, deviant or pathological, they sometimes see these 'cultures' as somehow better than their own, for example, as more 'interesting', more 'natural', or indeed more 'spiritual'. But these 'positive' evaluations, as Frankenberg (1993: 199) rightly notes, are still based on dualistic conceptions of self and other.

At a party, I was introduced to a man who, upon giving me his hand, immediately started to blurt out some words in Cantonese, then Japanese, then Malay. Did he want to show off or something? It surprised and frustrated him that I understood nothing of what he said and that I refused to speak to him other than in English. Unfortunately, the conversation was doomed to be extremely brief because I couldn't think of anything to say to unlock me from the pigeonhole of Asianness in which he insisted on placing me, continuing to say how much he loved Asia. What takes place in such incidents is still a form of othering, but it is an othering, in Trinh Minh-ha's (1991: 186) words, based on 'allowing the Other an apparent aura'. In contemporary Australia, then, Asians are no longer excluded (as they were during the White Australia policy), nor are they merely reluctantly included *despite* their 'difference', but *because* of it! What we have here is acceptance through difference, inclusion by virtue of otherness.

What, then, are the consequences of this pervasive ambivalence? How should we respond to it politically? For one thing, it is important that we recognize the very operation of ambivalence in our relations with each other. Jane Flax, using a Freudian perspective, defines ambivalence thus: 'Ambivalence refers to affective states in which intrinsically contradictory or mutually exclusive desires or ideas are each invested with intense emotional energy. Although one cannot have both simultaneously, one cannot abandon either of them' (1990b: 50). She goes on to note that such ambivalence is not necessarily a symptom of weakness or confusion but, on the contrary, 'a strength to resist collapsing complex and contradictory material into an orderly whole' (ibid.). In this sense, ambivalence is 'an appropriate response to an inherently conflictual situation' (ibid.: 11). Translating this to the situation in/of 'multicultural Australia', I would like to suggest that it is the *repression* of ambivalence that makes us unable to grasp the complexities and difficulties of 'living with difference', and the contradictions inherent in the very multicultural idea(l) itself. But if ambivalence is an appropriate response here, psychologically or emotionally, how can it be reckoned with in our political pursuits?

Several authors, mainly working within postcolonial and postmodern theory, have proposed that ambivalence itself is a political force of sorts. Bhabha (1990b), for example, has coined the space of ambivalence as 'the third space' – a space in between sameness and otherness, occupying the gap between equality and difference – and he is generally quite hopeful about the subversive potential of this liminal space of ambivalence, seeing it as the place from where one might go beyond the contained grid of fixed identities and binary oppositions through the production of hybrid cultural forms and meanings. Trinh (1991) also enunciates the productivity of liminal in-betweenness as a place from where the minority subject can become an unsettling agent:

> Not quite the Same, not quite the Other, she stands in that undetermined
> threshold place where she constantly drifts in and out. Undercutting the
> 'inside/outside' opposition, her intervention is necessarily that of both
> a deceptive insider and a deceptive outsider. She is this Inappropriate
> Other/Same who moves about with always at least two/four gestures:
> that of affirming 'I am like you' while persisting in her difference; and

that of reminding 'I am different' while unsettling every definition of otherness arrived at.

(ibid.: 74)

This insightful description of the positioning of the minority subject as more or less undecidable, as eluding the fixed identity conferred on her, relies on a recognition of ambivalence as a source of strength for those at the margins of the dominant symbolic order. In Bauman's (1991: 179) provocative words: 'Ambivalence is the limit to the power of the powerful. For the same reason, it is the freedom of the powerless.' But a romanticizing tendency in this valorization of the ambivalent hybrid is imminent, based not only on the assumption that the deconstruction of binary oppositions as such is politically subversive and desirable, but also, in my view, on an overstating of the unsettling power of the hybridized minority subject; that is, the power of ambivalence.

As my analysis shows, the discourse of multiculturalism itself is based on a structural ambivalence which, however, does not overturn the binary opposition between the (white) self and the (non-white) other, but reinscribes it in a different fashion, in which the very status of the other is now invested with ambivalence. To put it concretely, being 'Asian' in 'multicultural Australia' means being positioned in the grey area of inclusion and exclusion, in the ambivalent space of 'almost the same [as us], but not quite', to use Homi Bhabha's (1994: 86) phrase. In other words, the ambivalent position of inside/outside is not just of the minority subject's own making, as at least Trinh seems to suggest, but it is *imposed* on her by the multicultural ethos itself. In short, if the ambivalence of multicultural discourse creates a space, itself replete with ambivalence, in-between sameness and otherness, then it is a space in which minority subjects are both discursively confined and symbolically embraced. Ambivalence is not only a source of power but also a trap, a predicament.

From this perspective we should not just seize on the 'not quite' in terms of its indeterminacy (and therefore its opportunity for hybridity, for 'freedom'), but must also look at its functionality for the dominant discourse. That is, precisely the 'not quite' status of the 'Asian' in 'multicultural Australia' enables this sign to be filled with meanings of 'Asianness' which can operate as a function of Australia's nationalist desire. That is to say, 'we let you in despite/because of your difference' because, ultimately, 'we want your difference'. But, we must now add, not just any difference. To see this, let us return to the image of the 'Asian' woman on the government poster. While the state's preferred meaning of the poster is clearly that of benevolent inclusiveness – it effectively says, 'you can be part of our Australian family too' – a creeping ambivalence becomes apparent when we make explicit the tension unwittingly created by that last word 'too' and continue the sentence: not just 'you can be part of our Australian family *even though* you are/look Asian', but also 'please become a member of our Australian family *because* you are Asian'. Crucially, however, what the image represents is not just any 'Asian'. Most conspicuously, she is a (young) woman. Why? Why is the Australian image of the ideal (as well as ideal-typical) 'Asian' migrant more often than not feminized? To be sure, it should be clear that the appearance of an 'Asian' woman on the government poster should not just be seen as a feminist triumph, but as a symptom of the particular national desires invested in the image. The kind of 'Asian' desired in 'multicultural Australia' is evident from the selection of the official two millionth migrant in 1988. As Stephen Castles *et al.* (1990: 170) have observed, the choice fell on someone who 'fit the Prime Minister and staffer's bill as "a presentable, articulate Asian, and a woman"'.

I have to admit that I would probably fit the bill too. That is, I realize that, from the perspective of Australian multiculturalism, I am now positioned as a *desired* other, and that my femininity actually enhances that desirability, at least at the level of cultural representation (in social actuality, the most desired 'Asians' in Australia are more likely to be overseas Chinese business migrants, who are mainly male). The Asianness imagined and represented here is one which is useful and flattering for Australia's self-image and projected future: not quite the same, but almost. To put it differently, I am not a dispossessed refugee with no job and no proper linguistic skills living on welfare, but a westernized, highly educated professional whose English is *almost* fluent, a presentable and articulate Asian whose presence is arguably of economic and social benefit to the nation. That the image of the desired Asian other is feminized, however, might be precisely a sign that Asians, no matter how desired, can still *not quite* be imagined as integral to the national self. No matter how 'multicultural', Australian national identity still bears the traces of orientalism in a Eurocentric discourse renowned for its feminization of the 'Orient' despite all well-intentioned efforts to wipe them out. It is telling, for example, that one of the most popular books on 'Australian impressions of Asia' in the past decade bears the title *The Yellow Lady* (Broinowski 1992), thereby replicating (unconsciously, ambivalently) the very process of gendering/othering that the author had wished to criticize.

Some time ago I read a poem in my local community newspaper entitled 'Vietnamese girl'. I want to end with a brief description of this poem because both its textual ambivalence and the ambivalence in my own reading of it sum up what I have tried to argue. The poem was written by a mother of four and expresses the resentment many ordinary Australians must have felt when Asian migrants first came into the country in large numbers in the 1970s. The writer describes her feelings of rising hostility, hatred and panic as she drives in her car and sees so many strangers with 'dark skin and slanted eyes' on the footpath, in the buses. But then, in the poem's finale, comes the moment of reconciliation, of redemption:

> Dark skin and slanted eyes.
> Go home! We don't want you here!
> Then you look at me.
> You smile.
> My anger dissipates, and, so does my fear.
> (Read 1993)

Aware of my own 'dark skin and slanted eyes', I was hurt and angry by what I read as the unconscious racism of this poem, although I later recognized the courage of the poet to reveal her own feelings of resentment and vulnerability in the face of the unfamiliar, the strange, the different. In this sense, the poem reminds us of the fact, too often suppressed by the fantasy of easy harmony endorsed by the multicultural ideal, that the difficulties of 'living with difference' should not be underestimated.

Nevertheless, I identified with the 'Vietnamese girl', the writer's addressee and initial object of hatred. The moment of acceptance at the end – when the Vietnamese girl smiled – did not conciliate me. Are we accepted, or tolerated, only when we display our girly smile – the stereotypical submissive smile of the exotic oriental woman traditionally so enchanting and pleasing to Westerners? To put it more abstractly, must Asianness be feminized in order to be welcomed into Australian culture? If so, where does this leave the Vietnamese boy? The Vietnamese girl's key to acceptance – her smile – is simultaneously the metaphoric seal of her approval and the sign of her continued positioning as other in an Australia that has learned to be 'tolerant' and to enjoy and celebrate 'cultural diversity'.

However, my identification with the Vietnamese girl of the poem would be presumptuous and inappropriate if I did not also recognize the myriad possible differences between us in terms of class, education, language, and so on. There is no homogeneous entity of 'Asians' simply by virtue of our common 'dark skin and slanted eyes'; to suggest otherwise would be to collude with the very process of othering we are struggling with, and against, with so much difficulty. What she and I do seem to share, though, is the curse of the smile.

9

IDENTITY BLUES

Rescuing cosmopolitanism in the era of globalization

There is something distinctly idealistic, if not utopian, in the statement that identities are a matter of becoming rather than being, a question, as Stuart Hall (1996g: 4) puts it, not 'of "who we are" or "where we came from", so much as what we might become'. This idealism is tinged with a deep sense of historical and political urgency. In foregrounding the connection of 'identity' with the future, with what we might become, Hall's reflections on the meaning of cultural identity in contemporary life seek to provide a counter to the rampant tendency to use 'identity' as unfailingly chained to our real or imaginary past. Identity, says Hall, belongs to the future as much as to the past: 'Cultural identities come from somewhere, have histories. But, like everything which is historical, they undergo constant transformation. Far from being eternally fixed in some essentialised past, they are subject to the continuous "play" of history, culture and power' (Hall 1990: 225). Consequently, so is the implication, cultural identities may be the very subjective instruments, or discursive conduits, through which we may shape and construct our futures: they provide the 'stuff' that enables us to become political agents. Our role in the making of history depends on how we conceive of ourselves as active, changing subjects, in ways which generate meaningful links between 'how we have been represented and how that bears on how we might represent ourselves' (Hall 1996g: 4). By emphasizing the notion of becoming as central to our identities, Hall rescues the possibility for 'identity' – the way we represent ourselves to ourselves and to others – to be a resource of hope, the site of agency and attachment that energizes us to participate in the making of our own ongoing histories, the construction of our continuously unfolding worlds, now and in the future. It is in this implicit faith in the future that we can discern the idealism – in the non-philosophical, existential meaning of that word – of Hall's politics of identity. But how sustainable is this faith in these cynical times, when pessimism abounds and the future is envisaged by millions across the globe more with fear and dread than with hope and anticipation?

Against the background of a world-wide proliferation of particularist, exclusionary, and determinist modes of identity politics – both on the right and on the left, in the developed as well as in the developing world, in the West and the 'rest' alike – Hall has been at pains to foreground a double focus in his theoretical

150

approach. On the one hand, he highlights the inadequacy of conventional conceptions of 'identity', but on the other, he simultaneously affirms its irreducible political and cultural significance. We do not have to repeat here the well-known chorus of anti-essentialist, deconstructive and postmodern critiques which have stripped 'identity', as a concept, from its elevated status as the fundamental inner core of 'me' or 'us', representing the true, inalienable self of the subject, individual or collective. However, no matter how convinced we are, theoretically, that identities are constructed, not 'natural', invented not given, always in process and not fixed, at the level of experience and common sense identities are generally expressed, and mobilized politically, precisely because they *feel* natural and essential. Indeed, as Craig Calhoun (1994) has remarked, the constant emphasis on identity as construction in contemporary theoretical discourse (and, by implication, as somehow not 'real' and therefore not worth fighting for) 'fails to grapple with the real, present-day political and other reasons why essentialist identities continue to be invoked and often deeply felt' (ibid.: 14). 'For better *and* worse', James Clifford (1998: 369) has recently observed, 'claims to identity – articulations of ethnic, cultural, gender, and sexual distinction – have emerged as things people, across the globe and the social spectrum, care about.' The persistent gap between the imaginaries of everyday experience and the orthodoxies of contemporary theory points to the irreducibility of identity as an operative concept; in Hall's words, it is 'an idea which cannot be thought in the old way, but without which certain key questions cannot be thought at all' (1996g: 2). To put it differently, while we may have discarded 'identity' in theory, we cannot do away with cultural identities as real, social and symbolic forces in history and politics. In this context, according to Hall (ibid.: 16), we have fully and unambiguously to acknowledge 'both the necessity and the "impossibility" of identities'.

It is in the face of this double bind between necessity and impossibility that the idealistic move to highlight the possibility of future-oriented, open-ended identities acquires its understandable urgency. If we cannot do without identities, so the reasoning seems to go, then we'd better make sure that they are vehicles for progressive change! Indeed, the so-called new social movements that have emerged since the 1960s – feminism, gay and lesbian movements, anti-racist, ethnic and multicultural movements, various environmentalist, youth and counter-cultural movements, and so on – are often cited as forms of identity politics that have contributed to democratization and progressive change in many arenas of social life, especially in the rich Western world. However, Calhoun observes rightly that this idea of new social movements is problematic because

> [it] groups together what seem to the researchers relatively 'attractive' movements, vaguely on the left, but leaves out such other contemporary movements such as the new religious right and fundamentalism, the resistance of white ethnic communities against people of color, various versions of nationalism, and so forth.
>
> (1994: 22)

151

Yet, Calhoun pointedly adds, these are equally manifestations of identity politics. Indeed, there is a streak of romanticism in many critical intellectuals' identification of and with 'new social movements' as agents of progressive radicalism. As the twentieth century draws to a close, however, it is clear that modes of identity politics are proliferating across the globe with which most critical intellectuals would not be able or willing to identify, based on the articulation of identities we generally dismiss as conservative, right-wing, or simply *other*. How, then, can the pull of reactionary conservatism which is so manifest in so many assertions of collective identities in the late twentieth century be reconciled with the more hopeful association of identities with becoming, with an investment in a 'better future', however defined?

The conservative rhetoric of identity has permeated the cultural and political landscape everywhere in a time when old certainties – of place, of belonging, of economic and social security – are rapidly being eroded by the accelerating pace of globalization: the processes by which intensifying global flows of goods, money, people, technologies and information work to dissolve the real and imagined (relative) autonomy and 'authenticity' of local traditions and communities. The current salience of the discourse of identity signifies the level of resistance against the forces of globalization as they are experienced and perceived 'on the ground'. Indeed, Manuel Castells (1997), author of *The Power of Identity*, volume two of his three-volume analysis of the contemporary world economy, society and culture, opens his book with the dramatic statement that '[o]ur world, and our lives, are being shaped by the conflicting trends of globalization and identity' (ibid.: 1). He observes that 'we have experienced, in the last quarter of the century, the widespread surge of powerful expressions of collective identity that challenge globalization and cosmopolitanism on behalf of cultural singularity and people's control over their lives and environment' (Castells 1997: 2). In this scenario, globalization is constructed as an overpowering source of destruction, while identity is being launched not only as that which must be protected, but also, more defiantly, as that which will *provide* protection against the threat of dangerous global forces. In this sense, identity – together with its equally ubiquitous companion terms 'culture' and 'community' – become the key sites for people's righteous sense of self-worth and integrity, worth defending, perhaps even dying for, against the onslaught of 'globalization'. In this light, struggles for or on behalf of identity tend to be conservative, even reactionary movements, aimed at restoring or conserving established orders of things and existing ways of life, and keeping at bay the unsettling changes that a globalizing world brings about.

This is not the place to provide a substantial assessment of the complex, contradictory and multidimensional processes and forces which have come to be subsumed under the shorthand term 'globalization'. It is beyond doubt that the economic and cultural effects of diverse globalizing forces such as the creation of a more or less borderless world market, the virtual annihilation of time and space by the Internet, and the intensification of transnational migrations of people, are being increasingly felt everywhere, though unevenly and unequally. It is clear, too, that the world being remade by these forces is a deeply unjust and inequitable one, dominated by the economic might of transnational corporations, the elusive power of mobile finance capital and the ruthless logic of the market. Resistance, in this light, is completely legitimate and politically necessary. However, as this resistance is framed increasingly frequently through a downright oppositional stance against 'globalization' *per se*, as if it were the cause for almost all the world's economic, social, political, cultural and ecological problems, identities are being (re)asserted which achieve imaginary closure through an absolutization of a strictly localized, exclusionary 'us', and the symbolic warding off of everything and everyone that is associated with the invading 'outside'. The resurgence of ethnic nationalisms and absolutisms in many parts of the world is one of the most frequently cited examples of the increasing appeal of such fortress identities. It seems clear, however, that such embattled identities, in their quest for certainty, refuge and protection, can only represent a defensive resistance against the global disorder so relentlessly produced by the volatile forces of capitalist postmodernity. They are driven not by a positive hope for the future, or by a project to actively shape that future, but by what Meaghan Morris (1998b) calls 'future fear': a sense that things can only get worse. Ironically, perhaps it is precisely the presumed truth that the battle against the monster of 'globalization' is a virtually hopeless one that explains both the intensity and the tenacity of the defensive identities forged against it.

Here in Australia, the turbulences and uncertainties arising from the government's sustained and relentless pursuit of neo-liberal economic policies in the past two decades, arguably to restructure the nation so that it can take advantage with more gusto from the promise of wealth delivered by a rapidly globalizing economy, have been all too palpable in recent years. Importantly, this process of restructuring is not only an economic project but also a cultural one, designed to rework and redefine the nation's representation of itself, its national identity – all with the ultimate economic motive of improving the national marketing image, as Morris (1998b: 217) puts it, to 'make Australia "look better" to its trading partners'. Thus, as I have discussed in previous chapters, it was only a few years ago, in the first half of the 1990s, that Australian official culture could present this nation proudly, and rather superciliously, as a progressive, world-class 'multicultural nation' which has successfully discarded and left behind its shameful racist past, embodied by the infamous White Australia Policy. Under the flamboyant leadership of former Prime Minister Paul Keating (1992–96), Australians were interpellated to see themselves as an outward-looking, cosmopolitan and worldly nation, fully integrated and thriving in the global village and the new world order. But the failure of this globalist nationalist desire was rudely illuminated in the years after 1996, when it became clear that neither multiculturalism nor cosmopolitanism were universally embraced by the population at large.

Under the leadership of Pauline Hanson, who draws her charisma from an aggressively lower middle-class, anti-intellectual and anti-cosmopolitan populist nationalism, a vigorous grassroots political movement emerged of disenchanted, mostly white, rural and working-class people who revolted against what they saw as the disempowerment of their identities as 'ordinary Australians'. Hanson's popularity has given the lie to the progressive national image preferred by the major political leaders, the corporate world and the intellectual class. For Hanson, divorced mother of four, former small businesswoman and anti-establishment politician, the future can only be secure if a certain, old-fashioned kind of Australian identity is upheld: notionally white, culturally homogeneous, naturally parochial. Hanson's apocalyptic future fear, disguised under a thick dose of bad-tempered anger and aggression, made her turn against those she believed will rob her from her country: Aboriginal people and Asians, and their supporters in the intellectual and political elites. Not surprisingly, critics have routinely accused her of racism for her attacks on what she ungenerously calls 'the Aboriginal industry' and her infamous statement that Australia is being 'swamped by Asians'. But the moral(istic) critique of racism does not take account of the deeper, more pervasive sense of identity panic that underlies this call for the nation to retreat back into its insulated, isolated condition as a parochial island-continent, culturally and psychologically distant from the rest of the world, particularly 'Asia', the geographical region the country reluctantly, but inescapably finds itself in.

As the process of globalization in the past few decades has drawn Australia irrevocably into the global network, particularly with 'Asia' – through trade, travel and migration – many Australians, especially those who lack the social, cultural and educational capital to adjust to and survive in this brave new world, find themselves de-centred, devalued and marginalized from a national culture in which 'Australian identity' can no longer be securely anchored in a safely secluded, British-derived, white homogeneity but has become thoroughly unsettled and opened up by the everyday impact of social, cultural and racial heterogeneity, difference, flexibility, and hybridity. Against this background, Pauline Hanson's politics is exemplary of the kind of reactionary identity politics I have outlined above, the tragedy of which is that it contributes to its own continued self-disempowerment. The identity asserted here, as Phil Cohen (1999: 22) has remarked about the different but similar case of the old, white working class in East London, is 'by and large immobilised in a culture of nativist complaint' – the very terms in which they stake their claims to cultural entitlement and insiderdom, excludes them from the central sites of contemporary cultural *and* economic power in the globalized world, where cosmopolitan sophistication and ease with rapid change and multiple realities are the preferred, even necessary assets.

While Hanson's movement represents only a small (but significant) minority of disaffected Australians, it would be a mistake to underestimate its cultural significance as symptomatic of a much wider trend, not only in Australia but across the globe. For peoples who feel hard done by the rapid and unsettling changes brought about by globalization tend to mobilize essentialized, backward-looking conceptions of identity in an effort to find a magical solution to life in a world in which uncertainty is the name of the global game. Indeed, it may not be exaggerated to say, sociologically speaking, that whenever the discourse of identity is articulated today, the desire expressed in it has more to do with a nostalgic harking back to an imagined golden past – embodied in a selective memory of 'tradition' and 'heritage' – than with the visionary articulation of a new future. This use of 'identity' is clearly in sharp contradistinction to Hall's buoyant association of cultural identities with becoming rather than being, with the confident embrace of the open-endedness of history and destiny. On the contrary, here 'identity' is firmly conjoined with the very antithesis of change, with some core, immutable essence that needs to be cherished and protected, precisely because recourse to the discourse of identity has become a key mechanism to alleviate the fear of the terrifying future associated with 'globalization'. Absent, in this perspective, is a sense of identities as the dynamic repositories or channels of historical agency: clinging to (an imagined) past inheritance and to the idea of conservation. Identity here is a sign not of the active making of history, but of being the passive prisoner of it.

I have invoked the Australian situation here in order to expose the partiality of my own theoretical predilections. As a relatively recent immigrant into Australia and a person of 'Asian' background, I had (and have) a personal cultural stake in the redefinition of 'Australian identity' as an open space of diverse influences, traditions and trajectories and as the intersection of a multiplicity of global cultural flows – of Australia as a 'transnation' (Appadurai 1996a). Such a postmodern, transnational nation would be more rather than less prepared than others in the world to feel comfortable in the globalized world of the twenty-first century. It would be a future-oriented nation which is not just capable of change but actively desires change, turning necessity into opportunity in times of altered economic and geopolitical circumstances (Turner 1997). Indeed, as a migrant who was eager to find my place in this society I was excited to notice, in the early 1990s, that a new Australian nationalism could so elegantly, and with such apparent ease, shift its identificatory allegiance from being a racially and culturally exclusionary 'White Australia' to an inclusive and cosmopolitan 'multicultural Australia in Asia'. There was no lack of rationale for this triumphant national self-understanding. After all, Australia is a relatively new, settler nation mostly populated by waves of immigrants (the persistent significance of its indigenous people notwithstanding), and as such, so the theory goes, much less weighed down by historical establishment, with an identity based much more on invention, improvisation and borrowing than on an entrenched sense of primordial givenness. Indeed, what seemed at stake in the new Australian nationalism was identity construction rather than identity expression, the sense that 'what we might become' is more important than 'who we are'. In this sense, Australian national identity could arguably be imagined as the perfect embodiment of Hall's preferred association of identity with becoming rather than with being, with the future as much as the past.

A quiet euphoria took hold of me when I found that my status as a well-educated Asian migrant added significantly to my cultural capital in early 1990s' Australia. 'Asia' had become, however ambiguously and not without harsh controversy, the sign of success, of Australia's becoming – Asia was Australia's fantasmatic passport to a prosperous and affluent future in a globalized world. This sense of euphoria was not unlike Stuart Hall's (1993b) exhilarated realization, as a West Indian migrant in England, to find himself 'centred at last' in the postmodern culture of multiracial London in the late twentieth century, precisely when many (white) British themselves, in Hall's observation, had started to 'feel just marginally "marginal"'.

On the other side of the world, I could similarly indulge in the feeling of being on the right side of history, as it were, on the side of the future not the past, of change rather than stasis, of becoming rather than being. I never thought I could ever experience my migrant identity as an asset rather than a liability, but this was made possible in the cultural ideological configuration of 1990s' Australia – a configuration which, in global terms, is part of 'that immense process of historical relativization' which has seen the 'Rest' creeping into the 'West' (Hall 1993b: 138). My euphoria was reassuringly validated by the assertion in much recent cultural and postcolonial theorizing, from Iain Chambers to Salman Rushdie, from Trinh Minh-ha to Julia Kristeva, from John Berger to Paul Carter, that 'the migrant' embodies *par excellence* the values and practices of cosmopolitanism, worldliness and multiple identifications that the new, multicultural and globalizing Australia was supposed to have embraced. This imagined Australia was a postmodern and postcolonial, transnational Australia in which my own subject position would be, well, perhaps not quite socially centred, but certainly symbolically central – central to some desired imaginary future of Australia as 'part of Asia', not separate and aloof from it.

Of course, my self-interested euphoria, always easily disrupted and marred by distrust anyway, turned out to be premature and short-lived, as the eruption of Pauline Hanson's movement made it all too painfully clear. People like Hanson had obviously started to feel more than just marginally marginal, and resisted virulently that felt marginalization. Worse, she has pointed the finger in the direction of those who, from her point of view, are the progenitors of her marginalization and decentralization: all those who are the representatives and promoters of the forces of 'globalization'. As Peter Cochrane (1996: 9) has noted, 'Hanson represents the grief that goes with the loss of cultural centrality and the loss of identity that happens when a cosmopolished (Anglo) elite lines up with the new ethnic forces on the block.' This means, logically and emotionally, that I represent all that Hanson is fighting against! Yet it is far too facile, in this context, to play the anti-racism card. As Meaghan Morris remarks:

> When the overwhelming majority of poor, economically 'redundant', and culturally 'uncompetitive' people in a nation are white, [Pauline Hanson's voice] is very easily redeemed as that of the oppressed – white victims of history silenced by the new, cosmopolitan, multicultural elites.
>
> (1998b: 221)

Against this background, how should the well-educated, Asian migrant and critical intellectual, a card-carrying member of the 'new, cosmopolitan, multicultural elites', respond?

What I have evoked in this chapter is a confrontation of the past and the future, a tussle between 'identity' as essential being, locked in (an image of) the past, and 'identity' as open-ended becoming, invested in a future that remains to be struggled over. But it is clear that the confrontation has to be negotiated, worked over: the very prominence and appeal of reactionary identity politics among those who feel left out and disempowered as we are about to enter the twenty-first century betoken that we cannot simply dismiss their fears, anxieties and grievances. We cannot discard them simply as irrational, senseless or illegitimate. To put it differently, what is called for now is active negotiation within the *present*, a present in which, for better and worse, conflicting cultural identities share the same (national) space and cannot but relate to one another: as long as democracy prevails, these differences will have to be sorted out in some way, whether we like it or not. In this respect, the very relegation of the Hanson phenomenon to 'the past' by the self-declared guardians of 'the future' is part of the problem rather than the solution, unless we declare that those often denigrated as 'white trash' have no place in the present world and simply write them off for the future.[1] I, for one, do not believe such a politics of exclusion is an option.

Meaghan Morris asks the hard, awkward questions this way:

> What sort of unity can be projected for a free-trading nation at the mercy of world economic forces that no government can control? For a society unable effectively to legitimize its norms with reference to a common culture, yet with large numbers of citizens yearning to do so?
>
> (1998b: 208)

For Morris, these are political questions that require pragmatic answers, not principled ones: the national, in this light, is not to be defined primarily in terms of 'identity' at all, but as a problematic *process*, not in terms of the formulation of a positive 'common culture' or 'cohesive community' but as the unending, day-to-day hard work of managing and negotiating differences, the practical working out of shared procedures and codes for co-existence, conciliation and mutual recognition.

As an Asian migrant and arguably as a member of the cosmopolitan, multicultural elites, I have nothing in common with the white, underprivileged, xenophobic Hanson supporter living in rural or suburban Australia. Yet as we share the territorial and symbolic space of the nation, there is an involuntary relationship between us which I cannot simply extract myself from. In this situation it is the struggle over the ways in which this relationship is made to mean which matters: it can mean either an absolute antagonism, as has been the dominant tendency on both sides, e.g. global versus local, privileged versus marginalized, progressive versus reactionary, or it can be conceived in more negotiated, conciliatory, exploratory terms, terms in which no singular antagonism is allowed to saturate the entire significance of the relationship. How this relationship is made to mean is not predetermined, but is open to active intervention at diverse levels of political practice, including the often overlooked micro-politics of everyday life, where the concrete, practical implications of globalization are most keenly and intimately felt.

In this respect, we should take seriously the Hansonites' fear that they might become 'strangers in their own land', which is another way of saying that they fear that 'others' will 'take over' the country. Even if these fears may be motivated by 'irrational' xenophobic impulses, they are still real, and need to be addressed as such. I myself, as a representative of the 'others', of the threat of 'globalization', am often deeply aware of these fears as I participate in the most mundane social interactions. I am aware, for example, that many white locals in my neighbourhood feel very uneasy about the large influx of Chinese, Vietnamese and other non-whites in recent years, which has qualitatively changed the streetscape, the social mix, the language one tends to overhear, and the range of services available in the neighbourhood.

A fierce local protest against the establishment of a Chinese temple in the neighbourhood, on the grounds that it ran against the area's 'heritage', made it clear that more established inhabitants have been feeling dislocated as they saw the area change beyond recognition and be 'appropriated' by newcomers. A reactionary sense of loss, a nostalgic longing for the old days, and a notion of progressive decline is an all too common response among those who do not possess the cultural (and other) capital to benefit from these changes.[2] In response, Doreen Massey (1994: 151) remarks wisely that '[t]here is a need to face up to – rather than simply deny – people's need for attachment of some sort, whether through place or anything else'. At the same time, as there is no going back to the old days, we need to find ways of working towards 'an adequately progressive sense of place, one which would fit in with the current global-local times and the feelings and relations they give rise to' (Massey 1994: 151–2).

Precisely as a member of the cosmopolitan, multicultural elites, I take it as my responsibility to take seriously not just the pleasures, but the difficulties associated with the construction of such a progressive sense of place, not only in my neigh-bourhood but nationally and internationally, what Massey (1994) calls a 'global sense of place'. Self-reflexivity requires me to be aware of my own relative cultural empowerment *vis-à-vis* those much more restricted in their mobility, both physical and cultural, than I am, even as my 'Asianness' remains an at best ambivalent signifier for my (lack of) ability to belong, to feel at home in Australia.

As a critical intellectual and an academic, I can write books such as this one, which attempts to understand the fears of cultural loss and exclusion rather than simply dismiss them as irrelevant or illegitimate. But in daily life as a citizen and co-resident of this country I can also try to help alleviate these fears in more practical, modest ways, by establishing cross-cultural rapport and a sense of social sharing on an everyday basis, however fleeting, in shops, at the train station, and so on. I make it a point, for example, to use my cultural capital to act as a translator between different regimes of culture and knowledge in order to facilitate the creation of a sense of shared reality, a togetherness in difference. I make it a point, that is, that I am working to be a *part* of the 'local community' as much as I lead the globalized existence of a cosmopolitan and multicultural diasporic intellectual, simply by talking to people and sharing our experiences (about which fish to buy or the quality and the origins of the fruit in the fruit market, figuring out how to translate certain words, the state of the real estate market in the neighbourhood, and so on).

What such mundane local interactions can contribute to, I believe, is the incremental and dialogic construction of lived identities which slowly dissolve the boundaries between the past and the future, between 'where we come from' and 'what we might become', between being and becoming. Being is enhanced by becoming, and becoming is never possible without a solid grounding in being. As subjects from multiple backgrounds negotiate their social co-existence and their mutual entanglement, the contradictory necessity and impossibility of identities are played out in the messiness of everyday life, as the global and the local interpenetrate each other. This gradual hacking away at the absolutist antagonism between 'identity' and 'globalization' in practice is never guaranteed – it is an ongoing process bound to have its ups and downs in its own right. But it is a form of micro-politics of everyday life informed by the pragmatic faith in the capacity for cultural identities to change, not through the imposition of some grandiose vision for the future, but slowly and unsensationally, by elaborating 'the practical means . . . that enable deep and lasting social change' (Morris 1998b: 209). In this way, a cosmopolitan ethos can be fostered from below, based not on a separation between 'elites' and 'the people', but on their mutual intermingling, and ultimately, on an effort to break down this very divide.

Part III

BEYOND IDENTITY
Living Hybridities

10

LOCAL/GLOBAL NEGOTIATIONS

Doing cultural studies at the crossroads

The spatial metaphor of the crossroads signals for me a heightened sense of paradox in the contemporary practice of cultural studies. Cultural studies is often described as a practice of the crossroads, practised at the crossroads of various discourses, the busy and vibrant 'meeting point in between different centres, disciplines and intellectual movements', as the brochure for the first Crossroads in Cultural Studies conference, held in Tampere, Finland, in 1996, put it. According to the organizers of this conference, 'the vitality of cultural studies depends on a continuous traffic through this crossroads'. Indeed, the (self-)legitimacy of cultural studies – as an increasingly global, transdisciplinary intellectual practice – depends *par excellence* on an ethics (and a politics) of the encounter: on the claimed productivity of dialogue across disciplinary, geographical and cultural boundaries, on a committed desire to reach out to 'the other', and on a refusal to homogenize plurality and heterogeneity as a way to resist, subvert or evade hegemonic forms of power. All these avowedly 'postmodern' ideals have become virtual articles of faith in cultural studies today. All well and good, but what does all this mean in practice? What do we do once we arrive at the crossroads? How are the encounters we enter into at the crossroads supposed to inspire, enrich, or stimulate us? How, that is, can the myriad, different and distinct projects we are all engaged in in our own peculiar contexts be meaningfully articulated into a larger, transnational and transdisciplinary, yet coherent intellectual formation? While preparing this chapter, these questions put me in a mood of serious doubt, even a serious crisis about what it means to be doing cultural studies in a global(izing) context. This is not necessarily a bad thing. After all, as Gayatri Spivak (1990: 139) once pointedly remarked, 'crisis management is [just] another name for life' – an observation of particular resonance within the stressful societies of advanced postmodern capitalism. But let me share with you what this sense of crisis is, and how I think we can try, not so much to overcome it, as I don't think it is possible to overcome it, but to live with it.

The importance of an ethics of the encounter is reflected in the current popularity within cultural studies of a notion closely related to that of the crossroads, that of the borderlands, aptly described by Henry Giroux (1992: 209) as a space 'crisscrossed with a variety of languages, experiences, and voices'. For Giroux, such borderlands are analytically and politically productive because the experiences and voices coming together in them 'intermingle with the weight of particular histories that will not fit into the master narrative of a monolithic culture' (ibid.). Giroux talks here about the voices and experiences of students in the context of the teaching of cultural studies, but it seems fair to say that these ideas are axiomatic more generally for cultural studies as an academic practice. As cultural studies routinely conceives of itself as a borderland formation, an open-ended and multivocal discursive formation with a commitment to what Stuart Hall refers to as 'going on theorizing' (in Grossberg 1996c: 150), there is a clear inclination in this theorizing to value, if not celebrate and romanticize notions of the borderland, the 'third space', the liminal in-between, and so on as the symbolic spaces where fixed and unitary identities are hybridized, sharp demarcations between self and other are unsettled, singular and absolute truths are ruptured, and so on. That is, the borderlands tend to be imagined as a utopian site of transgressive intermixture, hybridity and multiplicity, the supposed political radicalness of which mostly remains largely unquestioned.[1]

This utopian vision of the borderlands strikes me, ironically, as a postmodern version of the modernist Habermassian notion of the 'ideal speech situation', where everybody can participate equally and freely in unrestrained rational conversation and communication (Habermas 1984). Habermas' vision has rightly been criticized for its universalist oversight of the power relations which over-determine the differential communicative capacities and opportunities of inescapably embodied speakers. But postmodern celebrations of the borderlands, too, are often infused by a desire to wish away – or at least overcome – the operation of power and by a claim to the possibility of transcendence. They tend to nurture a poetic vision of the borderlands as a site of radical openness where the 'resistive' forces of dialogic excess triumph over the dominant forces of discursive closure, where the disorderly contaminations of the margins subvert the orderly impositions of the centre, where, as Hall states in his essay 'For Allon White', 'the fluidity of heteroglossia' dislocates and displaces 'language's apparently "finished" character' (1996b: 297).

Thus for the Chicana feminist poet Gloria Anzaldúa, author of the influential and widely acclaimed *Borderlands/La Frontera: The New Mestiza*, the borderlands, 'that juncture where the mestiza stands', is the site 'where the possibility of uniting all that is separate occurs' (1987: 79). As she says in her preface, 'the Borderlands are physically present wherever two or more cultures edge each other, where people of different races occupy the same territory, where under, lower, middle and upper classes touch, where the space between two individuals shrinks with intimacy' (ibid.: np). The hybrid creature of the mestiza is, for Anzaldúa, the inhabitant *par excellence* of the borderlands. The mestiza 'operates in a pluralistic mode – nothing is thrust out, the good the bad and the ugly, nothing rejected, nothing abandoned' (ibid.), giving birth to 'a new consciousness': 'though it is a source of intense pain, its energy comes from continual creative motion that keeps breaking down the unitary aspect of each new paradigm' (ibid.: 80). Drawing on her own experience of living on the traumatizing cultural border zone between Mexico and the United

States, Anzaldúa celebrates the 'new consciousness' that has grown in her. 'To survive the Borderlands', she exclaims, 'you must live *sin fronteras*, be a crossroads' (ibid.. 195).

Writing from an entirely different socio-spatial positionality, Iain Chambers (1994) also emphasizes the transgressive and redemptive cultural effects of crossing borders. Entering the cultural borderlands, as he eloquently describes:

> I perhaps learn to tread lightly along the limits of where I am speaking from. I begin to comprehend that where there are limits, there also exist other voices, bodies, worlds, on the other side, beyond my particular boundaries. In the pursuit of my desires across such frontiers I am paradoxically forced to face my confines, together with that excess to sustain the dialogues across them. Transported some way into this border country, I look into a potentially further space: the possibility of another place, another world, another future.
>
> (Chambers 1994: 5)

Yet we all know that traffic through a crossroads – and the borderlands can be described as a space where the condition of crossroads traffic is normalized – is never free-flowing and uncontrolled: there are traffic lights, road signs and rules which all road users are supposed to obey, and those who approach the crossroads from a minor road are supposed to give way to those passing through from the main road. Consequently, borderlands are generally heavily policed and patrolled, and it depends on your identity card, your credentials, what you own, or simply the way you look, and in the intellectual borderlands of cultural studies: which theorists you have read, how you are treated, whether you are searched, whether you are let in and out, and so on. In other words, these interstitial spaces are pervaded by power structures of their own. As the Mexican performance artist Guillermo Gómez-Peña notes, referring as does Anzaldúa to the Mexican/US border, 'Crossing the border from North to South has very different implications than crossing the same border from South to North; the border cannot possibly mean the same to a tourist as it does to an undocumented worker' (1996: 9). Indeed, it is precisely because the borderlands are a site for potentially conflictive juxta-positionings and collisions between incompatible or irregular types that the operation of regulatory and classificatory powers is intensified here. In this sense, the voluntaristic desire for dialogues with 'the other side' in the border country expressed by Chambers may be a luxury pursuit possible only from a position of relative, arguably Eurocentric privilege. As Gómez-Peña pointedly reminds us, 'People with social, racial, or economic privilege have an easier time crossing physical borders, but they have a much harder time negotiating the invisible borders of culture and race' (ibid.). In other words, it matters who you are in border encounters, as it does matter *which* borders, both physical and symbolic, are being crossed. Chambers, in fact, does not present his discourse as context-neutral: the historical experiences which made him reflect on the necessity of 'border dialogues' are the influx of North-African immigrants into Italy, where Chambers, himself an immigrant from England, lives and works.[2] Yet while Chambers celebrates the borderlands for the opportunity it affords him to be enriched by encounters with others and to be made aware of his own boundaries (which conjures the assumption that away from the border zone he can live with a 'normal' – if perhaps staid – sense of unitary self and identity), for Anzaldúa inhabiting (and celebrating) the borderlands as the site where the mestiza's plural personality is forged is not a matter of desire, but one of survival.

I am invoking these divergent political and cultural meanings of borderland existence to make the point that if doing cultural studies implies entering a borderlands of sorts – the transdisciplinary, translocal, transcultural borderlands of critical intellectualism in the globalized world on the cusp of the twenty-first century – then this shouldn't be mythologized simply as a liberating space for the democratic expression and articulation of multiple perpectives, partial truths and positioned identities, the space for the emergence of a happy (and radical) hetero-glossia of narratives, experiences and voices. Inhabiting the borderlands not only entails political empowerment and transcultural enrichment, but poses its own, distinctive difficulties, which we cannot capture through the abstract embrace of what Arif Dirlik (1994b) calls 'borderland radicalism'. While I do not share all of Dirlik's dismissive attack on authors such as Anzaldúa, there is much validity in his complaint that the notion of the borderlands appears too often in cultural studies and postcolonial theory 'in ahistorical and metaphorical guise' (ibid.: 97). Indeed, as Caren Kaplan (1996) has noted, one of the problems in much cultural studies writing these days is the extent to which interrelated spatial notions such as border-crossing, travel, migrancy, exile, deterritorialization, and so on have taken on the status of abstract metaphors, severed from their historical grounding in concrete, specific and particular contexts. But didn't the strength of cultural studies lie precisely in its attention to context, in the rigorously anti-reductionist theoretical and methodological assumption that relations between people, culture and power – to capture in a catchphrase what cultural studies is 'about' – can only be grasped in their concrete, particular and specific contexts?

I can clarify now why the metaphor of the crossroads signals a heightened sense of paradox and crisis for me. The paradox, it seems to me, is that the very self-reiteration of cultural studies as a transdisciplinary, transnational borderland, an intellectual crossroads of people and ideas coming from different locations and encompassing a wide range of focal concerns, approaches and interests, may have contributed to the increasing prominence of metaphorical thinking in its theoretical discourses. If the crisscrossing of a variety of languages, experiences and voices is characteristic of the discursive world of cultural studies, how does one make oneself not only heard, but also listened to? How, put simply, does one communicate in a heterogeneous world? This, to an extent, is a question of what is commonly called 'intercultural communication'. But if the problematic this refers to – how differently positioned subjects can make themselves understood and construct shared understandings across cultural boundaries – is a central one for social life in our increasingly multicultural world, both nationally and globally, isn't it, or shouldn't it be, equally central in the borderland world of cultural studies?

How, say, would Gloria Anzaldúa and Iain Chambers, coming from such contrasting gender, racial, geographical and cultural backgrounds that they do, be able to enter into a dialogue with each other and have a meaningful conversation? Such questions are not often asked in cultural studies; instead, differential position-alities and discursive (in)commensurabilities are glossed over precisely through the use, for example, of metaphors. The use of metaphors may give us a sense of communicative satisfaction precisely because they work to condense complex and contradictory meanings into handsome, manageable symbols. Thus the common use of 'borderlands' as a metaphor for the experience of the blurring of cultural boundaries that both Anzaldúa and Chambers thematize in their work may establish a shared discursive territory, but it may also obscure the very different trajectories each has travelled to arrive at that common ground, the distinctive histories and experiences which have informed their respective conceptualizations and experiences of the 'borderlands'. One consequence is that Anzaldúa's specific reference to the physical Mexican/US border and her particular Chicana perspective tends to be ignored as her work is taken up as representing the borderlands in general, while Chambers' reference to the Italian/North African interface remains unspecified in favour of an abstract appreciation of the notion of 'border dialogues' as such. At worst, then, the metaphorization of the notion of the borderlands can have the effect of foreclosing rather than stimulating the going on theorizing through ongoing contextualization that cultural studies purports to be committed to.

It is this paradox which I find myself in need of coming to terms with in thinking about my own work in doing cultural studies as/at the crossroads, which is a central intellectual preoccupation behind the main focus of this book. After all, 'living between Asia and the West' is itself a complex borderland experience, made up of multiple crossings of peoples, traditions, knowledges, histories . . . I have not, in this book, aimed to do justice to all the disparate 'local' trajectories of this borderland experience, many of which are of course entirely incomparable to my own. Instead, my own biography has served here as the starting point for my reflections on the mutual entanglement of 'Asia' and 'the West', inflected by the historical formation of overseas Chinese diaspora, on the one hand, and by the oblique Australian experience of being part of the West, on the other. Admission of positionality – and (self-)reflection upon it – have become a recognized analytical strategy in cultural studies, generating an awareness of the inevitable situatedness of discursive knowledge (as I have highlighted in juxtaposing Azaldúa and Chambers above), but it does not resolve the problem of communication at the crossroads; indeed, it complicates it.

This is because more often than not, meetings at a crossroads, for example in the global, transdisciplinary cultural studies borderlands represented by conferences, and so on, are not just brief encounters; they are seemingly decontextualized, fleeting moments of incidental and transient linkage after which we all go our separate ways – on to our individual destinations back in our own countries, institutions, disciplinary enclaves, and specialist fields of interest. If the conference is a meeting place for such a diverse range of people to share their ideas under the common banner of 'cultural studies', what can that sharing consist of? Or better, how can we make sure that that sharing takes place, that the brief encounters we make here will have more long-standing effects? Of course, brief encounters are by no means necessarily inconsequential – we all know that they are not! – but for them to have life-changing impacts, so to speak, there would need to be some pretty powerful and effective communicative exchange going on. And just as in advertising, effective communication in the heterogeneous field of cultural studies also depends on the right rhetorical strategies.

Let me give you a concrete example to clarify what kind of difficulties I have in mind. In recent years, I have been engaged in a research project with a highly localized and historically specific focus, entitled 'Reimagining Asians in Multicultural Australia'.[3] How could I speak about this project without losing some of my readers – many of whom may be neither familiar with nor interested in such a topic – along the way? How could I avoid risk sinking into a discourse of conjunctural idiosyncracy which may fail to connect and intersect with other concerns, other interests, other knowledges? Somehow it would seem much easier, in a global cultural context at least, to evoke the concepts of race, ethnicity and nation, for example, or those of migrancy, hybridity and diaspora – the globally trendy theoretical concepts framing my particular object of study – *without* rather than *with* a particular reference to the uncommon specificities of the Australian context.

The paradox, then, is that while cultural studies has staked so much on the irreducible significance of context, on the importance of specificity and particularity and on the articulation of historical conjuncture, the valorization of crossroads encounters in the borderlands can actually have the effect of discouraging us from grounding our discourse in the uncompromising contingencies of local partic- ularities and specificities, as it would necessitate the tedious explanation of a wealth of more or less rarified descriptive nuances which might not resonate with the curiosity and the interests of our interlocutors on the crossroads. In such a situation the metalanguage of metaphor and theory – the stylish abstractions of which can be picked up and recycled without the inhibiting interference of particularizing context – would be much more instantly gratifying for its apparent communicative achievement. Thus, it is probably much more likely for an Australian and a Finnish conference delegate quickly to find common ground, say, in a discussion about the figure of the migrant as a metaphor for the prototypical postmodern subject – an ontological discourse able to be globalized as if it were context-neutral – than in a sustained and more time-consuming cross-cultural exchange about the history of Aboriginal politics in Australia, on the one hand, and that of Sami politics in Finland, on the other, even though a superficial similarity can be found in the trans-specific, globally salient category of 'indigenous peoples'. Of course, as Stuart Hall, Larry Grossberg and many other cultural studies theorists have repeatedly argued, cultural studies can only proceed through a 'detour through theory' – for no understanding can be reached without an appropriate level of theoretical abstraction – but there is a danger, as the cultural studies borderlands becomes increasingly globalized, to never return from the detour, to turn the detour into a never-ending trip in itself. The comparison I made a while ago with the world of advertising is not entirely gratuitous in this respect. Precisely because theory 'travels' more easily across cultural and national borders, it is also more amenable to global marketing, as any academic publisher would tell you. As Meaghan Morris and Stephen Muecke (1995: 1) remark in their editorial statement to the new Australian cultural studies journal the *UTS Review*, 'as publishers want cultural studies from all over the world to be written for an international market', what tends to be favoured is a 'socially groundless, history-free genre of "Theory" that cannot engage with the cultural differences it endlessly evokes'. Decontextualized theory sells precisely because its abstractions allow it to be appropriated by a wide range of audiences, while localized studies and knowledges are always in danger of being ghettoized in their own field of particularity.[4]

This is not, of course, a call for the abandonment of the ethics of the encounter, and for a return to the illusory security of the confines of home disciplines, local cultures and bounded communities. On the contrary, precisely to counter the ghettoization of localized knowledges we need more, not less encounters between disparate local knowledges; that is, we need to *increase* traffic through the crossroads – not least, as I will elaborate below, in order to destabilize the closures involved in establishing the localness of local knowledges. We need to take the challenge of living in the borderlands more, not less seriously, because, frankly, I think we have no choice. In this increasingly interconnected and interdependent globalized world we can all be said to live, indeed, in metaphorical if not literal borderlands, although of course not all in the same borderlands, as we have seen with Anzaldúa and Chambers. Within a transnationally dispersed cultural studies, itself a symptom and an effect of this globalized postmodern condition which both subsumes and fragments us all, this means that we need to work through and with the paradox I have just outlined; the paradox, that is, which is produced by the simultaneous operation of the pull toward abstraction and decontextualization, on the one hand, and the need to concretize, historicize and contextualize, on the other (Stratton and Ang 1996).

The cultural studies borderlands, then, are not a power-free site for unrestrained and heteroglossic dialogue and exchange, but a contested terrain where concrete, differentially positioned subjects have to forge particular strategies to speak and to be heard. At play here is a politics of (mis)communication where the transfer of meaning cannot be taken for granted. Take, for example, my research topic 'Re-imagining Asians in Multicultural Australia'. How can I speak about this topic in such a way that it doesn't compromise the historical and political specificities involved, while still being understood by and of interest to an international cultural studies audience who may not be particularly interested in either Asians or Australia, or in multiculturalism for that matter? While the intellectual and political import of my project, as represented in its title, would in all likelihood strike a chord quite immediately with those who are more than superficially familiar with contemporary Australian culture and society, I cannot assume such a thing from those who are not. Further, in presenting the project in an international forum – as in the publication of this book – in taking my localized object of study into the transnational cultural studies borderlands, I have to be aware that language does not elicit unitary meanings; aware, that is, of the multiaccentuality of the sign. I would have to be especially aware, for example, that certain signs already circulate in cultural studies with powerful meanings attached to it, mostly, to be sure, originating in corners of the world which dominate the global intellectual scene, i.e. Britain and the United States.[5]

We pay far too little attention to the historical and cultural traces carried by our seemingly most abstract or general theoretical concepts and metaphors. As Dirlik (1994b: 97) remarks: 'Borderlands may appear on the surface as locations of equal cultural exchange, but they are products of historical inequalities, and their historical legacy continues to haunt them.' Thus, it is interesting to note that in metaphoric renderings of 'the borderlands' in cultural studies it is precisely the US/Mexican border looming large as the 'real' but tacit reference point, thanks of course to the pioneering work of Anzaldúa and others, and not, say, the North/South Korean border, the Russian/Finnish border or, for that matter, the (real and imagined) border zone that separates Australia and 'Asia'.[6] Another example is the elevation and repetitive evocation of Los Angeles as the quintessential 'postmodern city' (e.g. Soja 1996). More directly relevant to my project, the term 'race', too, has a heavy connotative loading within cultural studies discourse which almost inevitably associates it with the African diaspora in the United States and Britain. It is mainly due to the very important and innovative theorizations of 'blackness' on both sides of the Atlantic that 'race' has acquired its current conceptual prominence in cultural studies. Anyone doing work on 'race' today will have to take account of the pathbreaking work of Paul Gilroy (1987; 1993a; 2000), Kobena Mercer (1994), Henry Louis Gates (1986), bell hooks (1990; 1992), and Cornel West (1994), to name a few – at least, anyone who wants to join and be taken seriously in the ongoing intellectual conversation on the politics of 'race' in transnational cultural studies. At the same time this work, while constituting a prerequisite reference point, cannot just be a neutral template for engagements with 'race' in other geo-cultural and political-historical contexts. Thus, the category 'black' in Australia refers to Aboriginal people, whose history of dispossession and genocide and whose resistive indigenous attachment to 'the land' have nothing in common with the African diasporic history of forced transatlantic movement as symbolized by the slave ship (Gilroy 1993a). In discussing the politics of 'race' in Australia, I cannot afford to overlook such vast differences in political and cultural inflection: indeed, I am aware that when I am addressing an international readership, I can only make myself understandable by taking on a self-consciously comparative perspective.

My project, however, does not focus on 'blacks' but on 'Asians' – a category positioned very differently in the politics of 'race' and, in general, for various reasons

I cannot elaborate on here, rather less talked about in transnational cultural studies.[7] First of all, I would need to problematize the category itself and take into account that the term 'Asian' has different referents in different contexts, depending on very particular historical, geographical and demographic factors. Thus in Britain 'Asians' are most routinely and unthinkingly associated with people from what is known as 'South Asia', comprising the modern nation–states of India, Pakistan and Bangladesh, reflecting, of course, Britain's long-standing post-imperial entanglement with its former 'Jewel in the Crown', colonial India. In Australia, by contrast, the generic 'Asian' in popular consciousness would traditionally be Chinese, going back to the nineteenth-century history of Chinese migration to the then British settler colony as goldmines were opened up in Victoria and Western Australia.[8] In today's Australia, however, 'Asian' has become the signifier for a much more pluralized signified, but still mostly associated with people from East and South-East Asia and much less with South Asians, as is the case in Britain.

The anomaly becomes apparent, for example, when I read David Parker's book *Through Different Eyes* (1995), a pioneering ethnographic analysis of the cultural identities of young Chinese people in Britain. In Parker's terminology, 'Chinese' are decidedly separated out from the two key categories for racialized and ethnicized people in the British context, 'blacks' and 'Asians', and his study is therefore a valuable contribution to rescue the marginalized Chinese presence in Britain from its previously complete invisibility in British cultural studies. In the Australian context, such a political intervention would be misdirected because in the Australian discursive configuration, not only are the 'Chinese' – itself, as discussed in Part I of this book, an uncertain, shifting category with multiple meanings – the most prominent 'Asians', it is also the case that the category 'Asian' has historically operated as one of the two key markers for processes of racialization in Australia, the other being, of course, the category of 'Aboriginal'. To explain to you why and how this is the case would take me into a long exposition on the political history of Australian national identity construction, on the ideological and strategic specifics of the infamous White Australia Policy which was only abolished in the early 1970s, and how all this affected the complex social and cultural positioning of 'Asians' in Australia, past and present. Furthermore, it would also be essential to discuss the particular meaning of 'multiculturalism', as this now very fashionable term has very specific inflections in the Australian context, where talk about Australia as a multicultural nation is official discourse launched by the state, in a way very different from the much more internationally renowned US furore over multi-culturalism as a form of oppositional politics mostly limited to the field of higher education and more directly related to 'identity politics'. In other words, I would have to clarify how in Australia multiculturalism is part of an expansive yet not uncontested dominant discourse, not that of a radical fringe, as it has been positioned in the USA. Only then, after having discussed all these over-determining contextualizations, could I begin to get across to you with any necessary subtlety what the intricate and multifaceted intellectual and political import of *re-imagining*

'Asians' in 'multicultural Australia' would be in the current historical and geo-political conjuncture. These are only some of the points I would feel obliged to address in presenting this peculiar national problematic to an international audience, as I have done in Part II of this book.

The difficulties I am alluding to here are suggestive of the multifaceted complexity of questions of 'cross-cultural' or 'intercultural' communication. Overcoming them necessitates the strategic enunciation of a narrative on my part which negotiates the gap between 'the particular' and 'the universal', the 'specific' and the 'general', or to put it in another register, between 'the local' and 'the global'. Far from being easily transcended when we enter the borderlands through some magical process of discursive blending which 'resolves the tension between two [or more] cultures . . . in a dialectical play of "recognition"' (Bhabha 1994: 114), these gaps become the discursive sites where the full extent of the irreducibility of inter/cultural, inter/local tension becomes clear. The borderlands represent what Bhabha (1994) calls a 'disjunctive present', where this tension is not only endemic, but *constitutive* of our crossroads encounters. And if we want these encounters to be meaningful at all, then we have no choice but to occupy this space of tension, and enunciate a speaking position from within this interstitial space. How, to put it concretely, to speak about the 'particular', the 'specific', the 'local' in a way which doesn't subsume and absorb these into the abstractions of the 'universal', the 'general' and the 'global', while at the same time not succumbing to the conservative and essentialist notion of complete untranslatability of cultures? How can I discuss the re-imagining of Asians in multicultural Australia without representing it as either a unique 'local' case or as just a version of a singular 'global' model?

Of course, the binary logic through which this space of tension is often made sense of – the 'local' *versus* the 'global' – needs to be displaced. Indeed, recent theorizing about the relation between 'the local' and 'the global' emphasizes the interpenetration, the intertwining of the two, in an ardent deconstructive attempt to overcome seeing them in terms of a binary opposition (e.g. Appadurai 1996a; Grossberg 1996b: 176; Wilson and Dissayanake 1996). And indeed, in these postmodern times and this globalized world it is no longer possible to isolate any 'local' which does not, in some way or other, depend on extra-local forces and influences for the construction of its identity. Cultural geographer Doreen Massey puts it this way in relation to our definition of 'place', which we most commonly associate with 'the local':

> Instead . . . of thinking of places as areas with boundaries around, they can be imagined as articulated moments in networks of social relations and understandings, but where a large proportion of those relations, experiences and understandings are constructed on a far larger scale than what we happen to define for that moment as the place itself, whether that be a street, or a region, or even a continent.
>
> (1994: 154)

It is worth noting that Massey's redefinition of 'place' here involves its theoretical rearticulation precisely as a borderland, that is, a space where the boundaries between inside and outside are blurred, a space characterized by a multiplicity of criss-crossing forces rather than by some singular and unique, internally originated 'local' identity. Massey's attempt to redefine 'place' in terms which does away with the need to draw boundaries around it is an attempt, not just to deconstruct the binary oppositioning of 'the local' and 'the global', but to build the 'global' into the very definition of 'the local', to allow 'a sense of place which is extroverted, which includes a consciousness of its links with the wider world, which integrates in a positive way the global and the local' (ibid.: 155). 'Definition', says Massey, 'does not have to be through simple counterposition to the outside; it can come, in part, precisely through the particularity of linkage to that "outside" which is therefore itself part of what constitutes the place' (ibid.). We can see here how Massey shares a preference for mixture and hybridity, interconnectivity and the destabilization of identities, with the borderland romantics we encountered earlier. And indeed, there is no doubt that to see a 'place' – whether a neighbourhood, a nation or a whole continent – as an 'articulated moment in networks of social relations and understandings' rather than a bounded area defined through a counter-position to what is outside that area makes a lot of sense, not only theoretically but also politically. As Massey says, defining a place through its particular linkages to the 'outside' 'helps get away from the common association between penetrability and vulnerability' (ibid.), and thus would help break down a fundamental mechanism of the production of xenophobia.

There is a famous characterization of Australia – the 'place' I wanted to speak about here – as a 'multicultural nation in Asia', coined by former Prime Minister Paul Keating. Those familiar with Australian debates will know that this much-contested phrase represented a discursive strategy, central to Keating's political project, to dislocate the old, inward-looking, and defensive manner in which the white settler state defined itself as a far-flung European outpost in an alien region, and to relocate it in an integrative relation to and directly within the geographical region it finds itself in. To be sure, this very geo-cultural reorientation in the identification of the Australian nation in more 'cosmopolitan' terms forms an important backdrop for my interest in 'reimagining Asians in multicultural Australia'. Will the (partial) 'Asianization' and multiculturalization of Australian national identity open up a space for less antagonistic 'race relations' between 'Asians' and 'non-Asians' in Australia? This is a complicated and quite singular political question the historical and cultural contradictions, ironies and ambivalences of which I have discussed in previous chapters. Suffice it to say here that the theoretical rearticulation of 'place' or 'the local' as traversed and produced by non-local, translocal and global forces – in Stuart Hall's words, a 'tricky version of "the local" which operates within, and has been thoroughly reshaped by "the global"' (1993a: 354) – does enable us to theorize local identity not in its binary oppositioning to some external global monster but as always-already a crossroads, an intersection of global/local linkage, shaped by what Wilson and Dissanayake (1996: 5) call 'the counterlogic of the both/and'.

There is another paradox lurking here, however, a paradox which will lead me back to the problematic of trans-local, cross-cultural communication in the borderlands. The paradox is that the direct political usefulness of globalizing the imaginary construction of a particular local identity, say, that of 'Australia', remains circumscribed within the framework of cultural politics in that particular locality itself: that is, it is in the first instance only within Australia itself that the renegotiation of and struggle over Australian national identity will be meaningful and consequential. To put it bluntly, I am interested in it because I live here, and because it affects the conditions of my daily existence. I don't think it would be reasonable or realistic to expect cultural studies practitioners from elsewhere, each of them involved in their own 'local' practices and interventions, to be interested (in the full, political sense of that word) in the peculiarities of these Australian negotiations other than for purely scholarly or informational reasons. In this sense the popular slogan, 'Think globally, act locally' harbours an often unrecognized contradiction: while it encourages all of us to think of what unites us, it simulta-neously fragments us by its encouragement to focus our political practice on each of our immediate local surroundings. Indeed, it is well recognized that the very intensification of globalization has led to an increased felt necessity and desire to elaborate 'an intensified vision of the local situation' (Wilson and Dissanayake 1996: 5), a new localism which, precisely because of its awareness of the power of globalizing forces, is ever more motivated to guard its distinctive identity (Featherstone 1996; Castells 1997).

Paradoxically, then, the project of reconstructing 'the local' in terms of 'the cross-border linkages and synergies at the global/local interface' (Wilson and Dissanayake 1996: 6) depends for its affective and political engagement precisely on the continued existence of that 'local' as a 'real' locality, a materially existing geographical, social and cultural location for situated living and working. For all the hype about the increasing deterritorialization of life in capitalist post-modernity (as exemplified by cyberspace), most of us still depend for our everyday reproduction on the here-and-nowness of (a) 'home', however defined. For all the attempts by Keating and others to re-imagine 'Australia' so that it embraces rather than closes itself off from 'Asia'/'Asians', Australia remains, for both historical and geographical reasons, a locality distinctly set apart from Asia, experienced as such by its inhabitants and fought for as such, by many of those inhabitants, against the increasing intensity of global flows (of capital, people, culture) traversing and entering Australian territory, mostly originating in Asian sites. In short, while the dichotomy between the 'local' and the 'global' may have been sophisticatedly put under erasure in theory, the sturdy intransigence of 'the local' tends to continually reassert itself in practice, in everyday life, in public discourses such as the news, in political struggles, and, as I have indicated, in international cultural studies meetings. While we know now, thanks to both poststructuralist cultural theory and postmodern late capitalism, that the local/global dichotomy is not ontologically real but a discursive construct, this does not mean that as a discursive construct it no longer operates as a social and cultural reality. While transnational capital and information technology are increasingly creating a 'borderless world' (Myoshi 1996), the symbolic importance of borders remains a constitutive element in the formation of identity, community and affiliation. As Hall puts it:

> The concepts of ambivalence, hybridity, interdependence, which . . . began to disrupt and transgress the stability of the hierarchical ordering of the cultural field into high and low [and, we may add, inside and outside, us and them, here and there, local and global], *do not destroy the force of the operation of the hierarchical principle in culture.*
>
> (1996b: 302, emphasis in original)

We should not, in short, underestimate or deny the continued operation of dichotomizing and separating forces in any encounter, any transcultural interaction in the borderlands, as well as the forces of exchange, sharing, and mutual recognition.

What is at stake here then is not a fetishization of the local which, as Grossberg (1996b) has noted, often accompanies the call for specification and particularization within cultural studies. My problematic here is the opposite one: how can we, in recognition of the inescapable situatedness of all intellectual production, translate localized, specific knowledges onto the translocal, transspecific register of the 'global', transnational borderlands? As Bruce Robbins (1993: 183) puts it: 'How far can this metaphor of locality be reconciled with the expansive awareness or worldliness that we also aspire to?' To return to my own case, how can I speak about 're-imagining Asians in multicultural Australia' without descending into an unproductive, conversation-stopping particularism which would merely confirm the intransigence of the local and the relativity and incommensurability of all knowledge? How would it be possible for me to tell this story not just as one with 'local' points of departure, but as one with 'global', or at least translocal, transspecific destinations and effects?

As I have already suggested, an explicitly comparative perspective is called for here, as the strategy of comparison implies an awareness of difference as its epistemological stimulus while at the same time, in its very requirement of juxtaposing at least two realities, being a guard against exaggerated notions of uniqueness and incommensurability. Thus, we should expect as much as we can, say, from a dialogue between Gloria Anzaldúa and Iain Chambers; and put as much effort as we can in the substantiation and specification of the metaphors and concepts we use to establish our common grounds. This is not altogether different from the ideal of cosmopolitanism, embraced by Bruce Robbins not, in his words, 'as a false universal' but 'as an impulse to knowledge that is shared with others, a striving to transcend partiality that is itself partial, but no more so than the similar cognitive strivings of many diverse peoples' (ibid.: 194). This, of course, returns us straight to the borderlands, the arena where the sharing of partial perspectives and knowledges are supposed to take place, in what Robbins (ibid.: 196) calls 'a long-term process of translocal connecting'. What I have tried to emphasize in this chapter, however, is the practical fact that there are limits to the sharing we can do, that there is only so much (or so little) that we can share. Indeed, I think we could only stand to gain from the recognition that any process of 'translocal connecting' not only needs hard work, but, more importantly, can only be partial also. I would even suggest that our crossroads encounters would be more productive if we recognize the moments of actual disconnection rather than hold on to the abstract utopian ideal of connection so bound up with celebrations of the borderlands. For it is in the realization and problematization of such moments of actual disconnection – that is, moments when the act of meaningful comparison and communication reaches its limits – that the material consequences of difference, of the irreducible and unrepresentable specificity and particularity of 'the local' are most bluntly exposed, but always-already within the translocal context within which that 'local' is distinctively constituted.

In short, it is at moments when comprehending my local-specific narrative becomes problematic to you, my reader, when such comprehension seems muted because I do not seem to speak in familiar discourse, that the malleability of general theoretical concepts such as 'race', 'nation' and 'identity', not to mention metaphors such as the 'borderlands' and the 'crossroads', becomes evident. It is the ways in which we both do and do *not* share these (and many other) concepts and metaphors across local/particular/specific boundaries that we should begin to interrogate and highlight.

11

I'M A FEMINIST BUT . . .

'Other' women and postnational identities

In the last few decades of the twentieth century, the problematic of race and ethnicity has erupted as one of the most hotly debated and politically sensitive issues in Western societies, especially in those countries with increasingly multiracial populations as a consequence of large-scale immigration from non-European parts of the world. In these countries, the politicization of race and ethnicity was an effect of the increased political consciousness and activism of those who have found themselves marginalized and discriminated against on the basis of their 'race' – people who have come to be represented and represent themselves – variously as 'blacks', 'people of colour', 'visible minorities' or 'ethnic minorities'. The issue of racism – experienced at both structural and personal levels – and the desire to struggle against it became a passionate point of identification for many, and as such it has become an unavoidable one for society at large to deal with. This is especially the case for self-declared progressive movements: from the labour movement to the feminist movement, it became impossible for these powerful political agents for social justice and equality to ignore the calls for 'anti-racist' politics. This is especially the case for feminism, which since the 1970s has been one of the most influential political discourses and forces of cultural change in the postmodern Western world. Feminism, after all, is itself a movement which derives its political energy from a desire to struggle against discrimination and oppression on the basis of a collective marker of identification: gender. It is safe to say that with the rising to prominence of the problematic of race and ethnicity, feminism has been thrown into a crisis – a not unproductive crisis.

I am implicated in this crisis. As a woman of Chinese descent living in the West and who has been a (marginally) committed feminist since the emergence of the second wave women's movement in the 1970s, I found myself increasingly, as the politics of race and ethnicity gained momentum, in a position in which I can turn my racial/ethnic 'difference' into intellectual and political capital, where 'white' feminists invite me to raise my 'voice', *qua* a non-white woman, and make myself heard. This became an increasingly insistent appeal in the 1990s. Anna Yeatman (1995), in a thoughtful article aptly titled 'Interlocking oppressions', suggests that voices such as mine are needed to contest and correct the old exclusions of the established feminist order, and that they will win non-white women

177

BEYOND IDENTITIES: LIVING HYBRIDITIES

authorship and authority within a renewed, less exclusionary feminism. In this sense, feminism acts like a nation; just like Australia, it no longer subscribes to a policy of assimilation but wants to be multicultural.

In many respects, this is a laudable aim: the politics of multiculturalism, as I have argued throughout this book and especially in the chapters about Australia in Part II, is not without problems, but it can be said to be a necessary governmental strategy for the harmonization and management of racially and ethnically diverse nations in an increasingly plural, globalizing world. Isn't it more than understandable, then, that feminism, too, wishes to embrace the multicultural ideal? Isn't it necessary for the feminist movement to bring women from 'other' races and ethnicities into its fold, if only in their own interests as women?

In this chapter, I want to complicate this scenario by looking at the *problems* of what we can term 'multicultural desire' in feminism. Rather than positively representing a 'Chinese' or 'Asian' contribution to Australian feminism, which would only risk reinforcing the objectification and fetishization of 'Asianness', I want to argue that the very attempt to construct a voice for self-presentation in a context already firmly established and inhabited by a powerful formation – the formation of what is now commonly called, rather unreflexively, 'white/Western feminism' – is necessarily fraught with difficulty. To me, non-white, non-Western women in 'white/Western' societies can only begin to speak with a hesitating 'I'm a feminist, but . . .', in which the meaning and substance of feminism itself become problematized. Where does this leave feminism? Feminism, I argue, must stop conceiving itself as a nation, a 'natural' political destination for all women, no matter how multicultural. Rather than adopting a politics of inclusion, which is always ultimately based on a notion of commonality and community, it would do better to develop a self-conscious politics of partiality, and imagine itself as a *limited* political home, which does not absorb difference within a pre-given and predefined space but leaves room for ambivalence and ambiguity. In the uneven, conjunctural terrain so created, white/Western feminists too will have to detotalize their feminist identities and be compelled to say: 'I'm a feminist, but . . .'.

The politics of difference and its limits

In the early days of the second wave, feminist theory and practice were predicated on the assumptions of women's common identity *as* women, and of a united global sisterhood. It was the universalization of white, middle-class women's lives as representative of *the* female experience which made it possible for modern Western feminism to gather momentum and become such an important social movement. In this sense feminism, like any other political philosophy, is an 'interested universalism' (Yeatman 1993), based on the postulate that women have common experiences and share common interests *qua* women.

By the 1980s, it was precisely this homogenizing idea of sisterhood which came under increasing attack within feminism itself. After all, not all women share the same experience of 'being a woman', nor is shared gender enough to guarantee a commonality in social positioning. As Elizabeth Spelman (1988: 14) rightly stated, 'even if we say all women are oppressed by sexism we cannot automatically conclude that the sexism all women experience is the same'. This is an important realization which has undermined any reductionist, essentializing definition of 'women's oppression' as a universal female experience. It also means the end of the authority of the category of 'women' as the 'natural' binding factor for feminist politics. Instead, as Judith Butler (1990: 3) has noted, '*women* has become a troublesome term, a site of contest, a cause for anxiety'.

It is now widely acknowledged that differences between women undermine the homogeneity and continuity of 'women' as a social category: differences produced by the intersections of class, race, ethnicity, nationality, and so on. So by the 1990s 'difference' has become an obligatory tenet in feminist discourse, and feminism's ability to 'deal with it' is often mentioned as a condition for its survival as a move-ment for social change. The so-called politics of difference recognizes the need to go beyond the notion of an encompassing sisterhood, and acknowledges that feminism needs to take account of the fact that not all women are white, Western and middle-class and take into consideration the experiences of 'other' women as well.[1]

What does it mean, however, to 'deal with difference'? Australian feminist theorist Jan Jindy Pettman (1992: 158) suggests among other things that it means 'recognising unequal power and conflicting interests while not giving up on community or solidarity or sisterhood'. But this sounds all too deceptively easy, a formula of containment that wants to have it both ways, as if differences among women could unproblematically be turned into a 'unity in diversity' once they are 'recognized' properly. Yeatman (1993: 241) suggests that the politics of difference should encourage 'the complexity of dialogue' between differently situated feminists (e.g. Aboriginal and Anglo-Australian women) who are not positioned as mutually exclusive selves versus others, but 'who understand themselves to be complexly like and different from each other'. However, isn't 'women' being surreptitiously smuggled back in here as the essential way in which the interlocutors are assumed to resemble each other?

The way difference should be 'dealt with', then, is typically imagined by the feminist establishment through such benevolent terms as 'recognition', 'under-standing' and 'dialogue'. The problem with such terms is first of all that they reveal an over-confident faith in the power and possibility of open and honest communication to 'overcome' or 'settle' differences, of a power-free speech situation without interference by entrenched presumptions, sensitivities and preconceived ideas. It is a faith in our (limitless?) capacity not only to speak, but, more importantly, to listen and hear. Spelman, speaking to fellow white feminists, relentlessly questions the (white) feminist ability to listen in this regard:

> Is the reason we haven't heard from them before that they haven't spoken, or that we haven't listened? . . . Are we really willing to hear anything and everything that they might have to say, or only what we don't find too

disturbing? Are we prepared to hear what they say, even if it requires learning concepts or whole languages that we don't yet understand?

(1988: 163)

Spelman's very phrasing brings to bear a deep and disturbing gulf between 'us' and 'them' (i.e. 'other' women). This suggests that 'difference' cannot be 'dealt with' easily, and can certainly not just be 'overcome'.

Therefore, I want to stress here the *difficulties* of 'dealing with difference'. These difficulties cannot be resolved through communication, no matter how complex the dialogue. Indeed, the very overwhelming desire to resolve them in the first place could result in a premature glossing-over of the social irreducibility and inescapability of certain differences and the way they affect women's lives. To focus on *resolving* differences between women as the ultimate aim of 'dealing with difference' would mean their containment in an inclusive, encompassing structure which itself remains uninterrogated; it would mean that 'these differences must comply with feminism's . . . essentialising frame' (Kirby 1993: 29). In such a case, difference is 'dealt with' by absorbing it into an already existing feminist community without challenging the naturalized legitimacy and status of that community *as* a community. By dealing with difference in this way, feminism resembles the multicultural nation – the nation that, faced with cultural differences within its borders, simultaneously recognizes and controls those differences among its population by containing them in a grid of pluralist diversity (Bhabha 1990b). However, reducing difference to diversity in this manner is tantamount to a more sophisticated and complex form of assimilation. As Chandra Talpade Mohanty puts it:

> The central issue . . . is not one of merely *acknowledging* difference; rather, the more difficult question concerns the kind of difference that is acknowledged and engaged. Difference seen as benign variation (diversity), for instance, rather than as conflict, struggle, or the threat of disruption, bypasses power as well as history to suggest a harmonious, empty pluralism. On the other hand, difference defined as asymmetrical and incommensurate cultural spheres situated within hierarchies of domination and resistance cannot be accommodated within a discourse of 'harmony in diversity'.
>
> (1989: 181)

To take difference seriously, then, we need to examine the sources and effects of the threat of disruption Mohanty talks about. Concretely, it would mean a focus on how the gulf between mainstream feminism and 'other' women is constructed and reproduced, and paying attention to, rather turning our gaze away from, those painful moments at which communication seems unavoidably to *fail*.[2] Rather than assuming that ultimately a common ground can be found for women to form a community – on the *a priori* assumption that successful communication can be achieved – we might do better to start from point zero and realize that there may be moments at which no common ground exists whatsoever, and when any communicative event would be nothing more than a case of speaking past one another. I want to suggest, moreover, that these moments of ultimate failure of communication should not be encountered with regret, but rather should be accepted as the starting point for a more modest feminism, one which is predicated on the fundamental *limits* to the very idea of sisterhood (and thus of the potency and salience of the category 'women' to anchor feminist community) and on the necessary partiality of the project of feminism as such.

In other words, I suggest that we would gain more from acknowledging and confronting the stubborn solidity of 'communication barriers' than from rushing to break them down in the name of an idealized unity. Such an idealized unity is a central motif behind a politics of difference which confines itself to repairing the friction between white women and 'other' women. The trouble is that such reparation strategies often end up appropriating the other rather than fully confronting the incommensurability of the difference involved. This is the case, for example, in well-intentioned but eventually only therapeutic attempts on the part of white women to overcome 'our own racism' through consciousness-raising, a tendency particularly strong in some strands of American liberal feminism. White feminists worried about their own race privilege typically set out to overcome their feelings of guilt by identifying with the oppressed other. Thus, Ann Russo (1991: 308) claims that her ability to 'connect with women of color' is greater when she faces the ways in which she herself has been oppressed in her own life as a white, middle-class woman. She would be less able to empathize, she says, if she would see herself 'as only privileged' and 'as only an oppressor', because then she would see herself as 'too different' from 'women of color'. In other words, the white woman can become a 'politically correct' anti-racist by disavowing the specificity of the experience of being a racialized 'other', reducing it to an instance of oppression which is essentially the same as her own, gender-based oppression. This form of appropriation only reinforces the security of the white point of view as the point of reference from which the other is made same, a symbolic annihilation of otherness which is all the more pernicious precisely because it occurs in the context of a claimed solidarity with the other. The very presumption that race-based oppression can be understood by paralleling it with gender-based oppression results in a move to reinstate white hegemony. Such a move represses consideration of the cultural repercussions of the structural ineluctability of white hegemony in Western societies. (I have used the terms 'white' and 'Western' in an over-generalizing manner here, but will specify them later.)

Of course, the most powerful agents of white/Western hegemony are white middle-class males,[3] but white middle-class females too are the bearers of whiteness which, because of its taken for grantedness, is 'a privilege enjoyed but not acknowl-edged, a reality lived in but unknown', as one of Ruth Frankenberg's informants says in her pathbreaking study *White Women, Race Matters* (Frankenberg 1993). To her credit, Russo is aware of the possible ramifications of this shared whiteness.

As she admits: 'While white feminists have directed our anger at white men for their sexual (and other) atrocities, there remains a common historical and cultural heritage which carries with it a certain familiarity and even subconscious loyalty to our skin and class privilege' (1991: 308). These comments elucidate the fact that white privilege does not have to do necessarily with overt or explicit forms of racism, but with a much more normalized and insidious set of assumptions which disremember the structural advantage of being white, and which generalize specifically white cultural practices and ways of seeing and being in the world as normal (Frankenberg 1993).

The extent to which this white self-exnomination permeates mainstream feminism should not be underestimated. It is a core, if unconscious, aspect of (white/Western) feminism, which appears unaware that even some of its apparently most straightforward ideas and beliefs reveal its embeddedness in particular orientations and tendencies derived from 'white/Western' culture. For example, the well-known maxim 'When a woman says no, she means no!' to articulate the feminist stance on rape and sexual harassment invokes an image of the ideal feminist woman as assertive, determined, plain-speaking and confrontational. The slogan does not just speak to men (who are commanded to take no for an answer), but also implicitly summons women to take up these feministically approved qualities and mean no when they say it. However, these qualities are far from culturally neutral: they belong to a repertoire of rules for social interaction which prizes individualism, conversational explicitness, directness and efficiency – all Western cultural values which may not be available or appeal to 'other' women.

Many Asian women, for example, may well deal with male dominance in culturally very different, more circuitous (and not necessarily less effective) ways. A rather painful instance of this is staged in Dennis O'Rourke's controversial documentary film *The Good Woman from Bangkok* (1992), in which the Thai prostitute Aoi, with whom the white Australian filmmaker has an affair, simultaneously gives in to and evades his chivalrous advances. The film drew a storm of criticism, especially from white/Western feminists who saw the film as exploitative of Aoi, the Asian woman. In the process Aoi's own subjective, culturally specific way of dealing with O'Rourke tends to be discredited or overlooked as feminists prefer to see her as representing the passive, victimized other.[4] Viewing the (making of the) film from Aoi's point of view, however, we can witness the obvious power and strength with which she handles her white male predator/suitor, not through militant rejection but through the ambiguous tactics of subterfuge. She did not say 'no' in any straightforward manner, but that doesn't mean she simply surrendered to patriarchal power . . .

In other words, far from being culturally universal, 'When a woman says no, she means no!' implies a feminist subject position and style of personal politics that are meaningful and empowering chiefly for those women who have the 'correct' cultural resources. I am not saying that the maxim itself is ethnocentric; what is ethnocentric is the assumption that it represents all women's experiences and interests in sexual relations – arguably it doesn't even represent those of all 'white/Western' women. Even more perniciously, this universalist feminist assumption implicitly finds wanting all women who do not have these cultural resources. As a result, these different women are, as Mohanty says about Third World women, 'stripped of their existence as concrete historical subjects living, working, acting and fighting in particular societal circumstances, and are objectified as a generalised, always-already oppressed "other woman" (e.g. the veiled woman, the chaste virgin)' (1984: 353), against whom Western women become elevated as the self-professed avant-garde of liberated womanhood (see also e.g. Jolly 1991; Mohanty *et al.* 1991; Kirby 1993; Ong 1988).

In acknowledgement of the need to deconstruct such universalizing assumptions of white/Western feminism, feminist theorists have concerned themselves increasingly with the issue of representation, of 'who is permitted to speak on behalf of whom'. If speaking in the name of the other is no longer politically acceptable, how, then, should the other be represented? Or should white feminists refrain from representing 'other' women at all? Would the problem be gradually solved if more 'other' women start raising their voices and presenting 'their' points of view? Here again, the implicit assumption is that a diversification of discourse would eventually lead to a broader, more inclusive representation of 'all' women. However, what implications the resulting contesting discourses can and should have for feminist politics remain glaringly unresolved. In other words, where does the emanating 'complexity of dialogue' lead us?

Let me address this question through an example, again derived (mainly) from American feminist criticism. As is well known, there has been much controversy in the academy about the cultural and sexual politics of the pop singer Madonna. Her many white feminist defenders see her as a postmodern proto-feminist heroine, a woman who manages to create a cultural space where she can invent and play with daring representations of feminine sexuality while remaining in control and in charge (see Schwichtenberg 1993). While white critics have generally appreciated Madonna in terms of her clever subversion of male dominance,[5] however, black feminist critic bell hooks has argued that Madonna's gender politics can only be interpreted as liberating from a 'white' perspective:

> In part, many black women who are disgusted by Madonna's flaunting of sexual experience are enraged because the very image of sexual agency that she is able to project and affirm with material gain has been the stick this society has used to justify its continued beating and assault on the black female body.
>
> (1992: 159–60)

According to hooks, what Madonna's white feminist fans applaud her for, namely, her power to act in sexually rebellious ways without being punished, cannot be experienced as liberating by the vast majority of black women in the USA, as dominant myths of black females as sexually 'fallen' force them to be 'more concerned with projecting images of respectability than with the idea of female sexual agency and transgression' (ibid.: 160). In other words, hooks contends, Madonna's status as a feminist heroine makes sense only from a white woman's perspective, and any deletion of this specification only slights the black woman's perspective.

The point I want to make is not that the white feminist interpretation is wrong or even racist, or that hooks's view represents a better feminism, but that we see juxtaposed here two different points of view, constructed from two distinct speaking positions, each articulating concerns and preoccupations which make sense and are pertinent within its own reality. The meaning of Madonna, in other words, depends on the cultural, racially marked context in which her image circulates, at least in the USA. Nor can either view be considered the definitive white or black take on Madonna; after all, any interpretation can only be provisional and is indefinitely contestable, forcing us to acknowledge its inexorable situatedness (Haraway 1988). Nevertheless, a reconciliation between these points of view is difficult to imagine. And this is not a matter of 'communication barriers' that need to be overcome, of differences that need to be 'recognized'. What we see exemplified here is a fundamental *incommensurability* between two competing feminist knowledges, dramatically exposing an irreparable chasm between a white and a black feminist truth. No harmonious compromise or negotiated consensus is possible here.

This example illuminates the limits of a politics of difference focused on representation. The voice of the 'other', once raised and taken seriously in its distinctiveness and specificity, cannot be assimilated into a new, more totalized feminist truth. The otherness of 'other' women, once they come into self-representation, works to disrupt the unity of 'women' as the foundation for feminism. This is the logic of Butler's (1990: 15) claim that '[i]t would be wrong to assume in advance that there is a category of "women" that simply needs to be filled in with various components of race, class, age, ethnicity, and sexuality in order to become complete'. That is, there are situations in which 'women' as signifier for commonality would serve more to impede the self-presentation of particular groups of female persons, in this case African-American women struggling against racist myths of black female sexuality, than to enhance them. White women and black women have little in common in this respect. Teresa de Lauretis (1988: 135) has put it this way: 'the experience of racism changes the experience of gender, so that a white woman would be no closer than a Black man to comprehending a Black woman's experience'. So we can talk with each other, we can enter into dialogue – there is nothing wrong with learning about the other's point of view – provided only that we do not impose a premature sense of unity or consensus as the desired outcome of such an exchange.

Considering white/Western hegemony

But there is more. It is clear that, while white critical discourse could afford to be silent about the racial dimension of the cultural meaning(s) of Madonna and could assume a stance of seeming racial neutrality,[6] hooks (1992) is only too aware of the marginal situatedness of her own point of view. She does not share the sense of entitlement which empowers white women to imagine a world in which they are 'on top', as it were, successfully turning the tables on men (white and black). Yet this is the quintessence of the all-powerful fantasy Madonna seems to offer white women. Black women like hooks operate in the certainty that they will *never* acquire the power to rule the world; they know that this world – white-dominated, Western, capitalist modernity – is quite simply *not theirs*, and can never be. This fundamental sense of permanent dislocation, this feeling of always being a foreigner in a world that doesn't belong to you (cf. Kristeva 1991) is what all those who are 'othered' – racialized or ethnicized – in relation to white/Western hegemony share.

It is important to emphasize, at this point, that white/Western hegemony is not a random psychological aberration but the systemic consequence of a global historical development over the last 500 years – the expansion of European capitalist modernity throughout the world, resulting in the subsumption of all 'other' peoples to its economic, political and ideological logic and mode of operation. Whiteness and Westernness are closely interconnected; they are two sides of the same coin. Westernness is the sign of white hegemony at the international level, where non-white, non-Western nations are by definition subordinated to white, Western ones (despite occasionally erupting fantasies of powerful Asian countries such as Japan and China that they might once overtake the West). It is the globalization of capitalist modernity which ensures the structural insurmountability of the white/non-white and Western/non-Western divide, as it is cast in the very infrastructure – institutional, political, economic – of the modern world (Wallerstein 1974). In other words, whether we like it or not, the contemporary world system is a *product* of white/Western hegemony, and we are all, in our differential subjectivities and positionings, implicated in it and constituted by it.

We are not speaking here, then, of an *ontological* binary opposition between white/Western women and 'other' women. Nor is it the case that white feminists are always-already 'guilty' – another psychologizing gesture which can only paralyse. But the fracturing of the category of 'women' is historically and structurally entrenched, and cannot be magically obliterated by (white) feminism through sheer political will or strategy. As a consequence, in the words of de Lauretis (1988: 136):

> the feminist subject, which was initially defined purely by its status as colonised subject or victim of oppression, becomes redefined as much less pure [and] as indeed ideologically complicitous with 'the oppressor' whose position it may occupy in certain sociosexual relations (though not others), on one or another axis.

Complicity, in other words, is a structural inevitability which we can only come to terms with by recognizing it as determining the *limits* of political possibilities, not as something that we can work to undo (by consciousness-raising, for example).

185

In other words, it is important to realize that the white/'other' divide is a historically and systemically imposed structure which cannot yet, if ever, be superseded.

Until now I have deliberately used the term 'other' to encompass all the disparate categories conjured up to classify these 'others': for example, 'black women', 'women of colour', 'Third World women', 'migrant women', 'ethnic minority women', or, a specifically Australian term circulating in official multicultural discourse, 'NESB (non-English-speaking-background) women'. Of course these different categories, themselves labels with unstable and shifting content and pasting over a multitude of differences, cannot be lumped together in any concrete, historically and culturally specific sense. In structural terms, however, they occupy the same space insofar as they are all, from a white perspective, relegated to the realm of racialized or ethnicized 'otherness', a normalizing mechanism which is precisely constitutive of white/Western hegemony. As we have seen, feminism in Australia and elsewhere is not exempt from such hegemonizing processes: in most feminist theory, too, whiteness is the unmarked norm against which all 'others' have to be specified in order to be represented. Spelman (1988: 169) points this out astutely: 'Black women's being Black somehow calls into question their counting as straightforward examples of "women," but white women's being white does not.'

What difference can a politics of difference make in the face of this fundamental, binary asymmetry? Sneja Gunew (1993: 1) claims that '[t]he dismantling of hegemonic categories is facilitated by the proliferation of difference rather than the setting up of binary oppositions that can merely be reversed, leaving structures of power intact'. This postmodern celebration of a 'proliferation of difference' as a utopian weapon in the destruction of hegemonic structures of power is also proposed by Jane Flax, as in this oft-quoted statement:

> Feminist theories, like other forms of postmodernism, should encourage us to tolerate and interpret ambivalence, ambiguity, and multiplicity as well as expose the roots of our needs for imposing order and structure no matter how arbitrary and oppressive these needs may be. If we do our work well, reality will appear even more unstable, complex and disorderly than it does now.
>
> (Flax 1990a: 56–7)

For reasons which will become clear, I am generally sympathetic to Flax's emphasis on ambivalence, ambiguity and multiplicity as theoretical principles in our approach to 'reality'. But she surreptitiously displays another form of psychological reductionism when she ascribes the imposition of order and structure to the obscurity of 'our needs', and suggests that we should learn to 'tolerate' ambivalence, ambiguity and multiplicity. To be sure, the consequence of Flax's postmodern equation of 'doing our work well' with making reality 'appear even more unstable, complex and disorderly' amounts to an underestimating of the historical tenacity and material longevity of oppressive orders and structures, such as those entailing sedimented consequences of white/Western hegemony. This postmodern optimism, I suspect, can only be expressed from a position which does not have to cope with being on the receiving end of those orders and structures. Flax's 'we', therefore, can be read as a white 'we': it is white needs for order and structure which she implicitly refers to and whose roots she wants to expose (and, by implication, do away with), and it is only from a white perspective that 'tolerating' ambivalence and disorder would be a 'progressive', deuniversalizing step. The problem is, of course, that the order and structure of white/Western hegemony cannot be eliminated by giving up the 'need' for it, simply because its persistence is not a matter of 'needs'. From the perspective of 'other' women (and men), then, there is no illusion that white/Western hegemony will wither away in any substantial sense, at least not in the foreseeable future. The nature of global capitalist modernity is such that these 'other' peoples are left with two options: either enter the game or be excluded. At the national level, either integrate/assimilate or remain an outsider; at the international level, either 'Westernize' or be ostracized from the 'world community', the 'family of nations'. This ensures that the position of the non-white in a white-dominated world and the non-Western in a Western-dominated world is always necessarily and inescapably an 'impure' position, always dependent on and defined *in relation to* the white/Western dominant.[7] Any resistance to this overwhelming hegemony can therefore only ever take place from a position always-already 'contaminated' by white/Western practices, and can therefore only hope to carve out spaces of relative autonomy and freedom within the interstices of the white/Western hegemonic world itself.

It is in this historical sense that the hierarchical binary divide between white/non-white and Western/non-Western should be taken account of as a master-grid framing the potentialities of, and setting limits to, all subjectivities and all struggles. Feminists and others need to be aware of this systemic inescapability when 'dealing with difference'. This is where I find Flax's insistence on ambivalence, ambiguity and multiplicity useful, not to celebrate 'difference' as a sign of positive post-modern chaos, but to describe the *necessary condition of existence* of those who are positioned, in varying ways, as peripheral others to the white/Western core. There is no pure, uncontaminated identity outside of the system generated by this hegemonic force. Despite hooks's largely autonomist stance on the African-American political struggle and counter-hegemonic practice (see for example, her essays in hooks 1990), it is clear that the very construction of Black identity in the USA is intimately bound up with the history of slavery and segregation, just as contemporary Aboriginal 'identity' in Australia cannot erase the effects of 200 years of contact and conflict with European colonizers (see Attwood 1989; Collishaw 1999), and the 'identity' of Third World nations, mostly postcolonial, cannot be defined outside the parameters of the international order put in place by the unravelling of European colonial and imperial history. The irony is that while all these 'identities' are effected by the objectification of 'others' by white/Western subjects, they have become the necessary and inescapable points of identification from which these 'others' can take charge of their own destinies in a world not of their own making. Ambivalence, ambiguity and multiplicity thus signal the unfinished and ongoing, contradictory, and eternally unresolved nature of this double-edged process of simultaneous objectification/subjectification. Seen this way, the politics of difference, while bitterly necessary now that 'other' voices are becoming increasingly insistent, has not resulted in a new feminist consensus and never will. There will always be a tension between difference as benign diversity and difference as conflict, disruption, dissension.

Australian whiteness, the postcolonial and the multicultural

I have used the terms 'white' and 'Western' rather indiscriminately so far. This is problematic, especially given the rapidity with which these terms have become 'boo-words' in certain circles, signifying irredeemable political incorrectness. To counter such sloganeering and to clarify my argument, I should stress that I have used these concepts first of all as generalizing categories which describe *a position in a structural, hierarchical interrelationship* rather than a precise set of cultural identities. Thus, being white in Australia is not the same as being white in Britain, France or the United States, as whiteness does not acquire meanings outside of a distinctive and over-determined network of concrete social relations within which it is embedded. Even who counts as white is not stable and unchanging. We should not forget, for example, that in the post-war period there was official doubt about the whiteness of Southern European immigrants to Australia (Italians, Greeks), as well as that of the Jews, signifying anxiety among proponents of the White Australia Policy about the (un)suitability of these groups as new migrants into the country! (Stratton 2000, Chapter 7). Whiteness, then, is not a biological category but a political one: to be 'white' signifies a position of power and respectability, of belonging and entitlement, but who is admitted to this position of global privilege is historically variable. Some peoples have *become* white over time as their status and power have risen (such as the Irish and the Jews in the USA) (Ignatiev 1996; Brodkin 1999), while others have been known for their *desire* to be white or at least be treated as white (such as the Japanese in the early twentieth century, when they managed to be recognized by the European powers as 'honorary whites') (Tanaka 1993; Brawley 1995). These historical complexities suggest that we need to go beyond the generalizations of generic whiteness and undifferentiated Westernness if we are to understand the specific cultural dynamics in which these interrelationships are played out in any particular context. In other words, analysing and interrogating the culturally specific ways in which whiteness, including white femininity, has been historically constructed and inflected is a necessary condition if feminism is to effectively deuniversalize the experience of white women in feminist theory and practice.[8]

Australia is implicated in the global configuration of white/Western hegemony in ways which are particular to its history – of European settlement and Aboriginal genocide, of the White Australia policy, official multiculturalism, and the current 'push toward Asia'. Despite this, Australia remains predominantly populated by

Anglo-Celtic people (making up about 75 per cent of the population according to the 1996 Census), who inhabit ex-nominated whiteness in this country. Its main social institutions and basic cultural orientations are identifiably Western with solid British moorings, and as a nation it is categorized in the international order as a part of 'the West'. Yet it is important to note that Australian whiteness is itself relatively marginal in relation to world-hegemonic whiteness. The fact that Australia itself is on the periphery of the Euro-American core of 'the West' (and as such is often forgotten or ignored by that core), produces a sense of non-metropolitan, postcolonial whiteness whose structures of feeling remain to be explored. Meaghan Morris (1992) has begun to capture the distinctive ambiguities of Australian whiteness with the term 'white settler subjectivity', a subject position which, Morris notes, oscillates uneasily between identities as colonizer and colonized. This tallies empirically with what Susanne Schech and Jane Haggis (2000) have found in their interviews with young Anglo-Australians, from which they teased out a persistent incoherence of white Australians' sense of self in the late twentieth century: on the one hand, many of them passionately wanted to see Australia as a multicultural society in which everyone 'could be themselves', but on the other hand they kept stressing anxiously that 'we should be one country'. In this light, Australian whiteness proves to be steeped in a deep sense of the ambivalence, ambiguity and multiplicity so valued by Flax. Here again, however, it doesn't get us very far to celebrate these conditions as inherently positive principles. Rather, they signal a historically specific cultural predicament which has led Morris (1992: 471) to describe the Australian social formation as both 'dubiously postcolonial' and 'prematurely postmodern'. I want to suggest that the precariousness and fragility of this antipodean whiteness, so different from (post-)imperial British whiteness or messianic, superpower American whiteness, inscribe and affect the way in which white Australia relates to its non-white 'others'. I will finish this chapter then, by sketching briefly how Australian feminism is implicated in this.

Being Asian in Australia necessarily implies a problematic subject positioning. Earlier in this book I have described at length how the White Australia policy effectively excluded Asian peoples from settling in the country, because Australia wanted to be a 'white nation', a far-flung outpost of Europe, the West. Since the abandonment of this policy, however, 'we' Asians are allowed in. And the rhetoric of multiculturalism even encourages us to contribute to the cultural diversity of Australia. Still, the presence of Asians is not naturalized. A while ago I bumped into a middle-aged white woman in the supermarket. Such small accidents happen all the time; they are part of the everyday experience of sharing a space, including national space. But she was annoyed and started calling me names. 'Why don't you go back to your own country!' she shouted. I am familiar with this exhortation: it is a declaration of exclusion racialized and ethnicized people have to put up with all the time. But what does such a comment mean in Australia? I want to suggest that, placed in the larger context of Australian cultural history, in the context of the racial/spatial anxiety I discussed in Chapter 7, the racism expressed here is not just ordinary prejudice. Indeed, prejudice is never ordinary, never culturally neutral:

it is always infused by peculiar cultural assumptions and affectations. There was a notable measure of anxious spite in the insistence with which this white woman proclaimed Australia as her 'home' while emphatically denying me the right to do the same thing. It shocked me, because I thought this kind of thing was possible in Europe, not in a settler society such as Australia where everyone, after all, except from the original inhabitants, comes from somewhere else. In declaring herself, like Pauline Hanson, to be a native threatened by alien immigrants, she displays a historical amnesia of (British) colonialism which actively erases the history of Aboriginal dispossession of the land. In other words, in her claim that Asians don't belong in this country, she simultaneously reproduces, in a single appropriative gesture, the exclusion of Aboriginal people. A disturbing bunker mentality is expressed in this peculiar double-edgedness of white Australian ethnocentrism, a mentality of tenaciously holding on to what one has which, I suggest, is sourced precisely in the precariousness and fragility, the moot legitimacy and lack of historical density of white settler subjectivity.[9]

Australian feminism has to take into account this two-sided antagonism, in which white Australia constitutes and asserts itself by demarcating itself from the immigrant on the one hand and the indigene on the other by racializing and/or ethnicizing both, naturalizing its own claim to nativeness in the process. It is clear that an Australian feminist politics of difference needs to dismantle and deconstruct the hierarchical relations involved in this complex and contradictory, three-pronged structure of mutual exclusivism, in which 'white' is the constitutive centre. This quotation from anthropologist Margaret Jolly typifies the problematic as it is currently seen through white feminist eyes:

> There is the general problem of white feminists dealing with Australian women of colour, the rainbow spectrum of ethnic identities resulting from a long process of migration. *But the problem is more acute* with indigenous women because they identify us not so much as Anglo-inhabitants of Australia, but as the white invaders of their land. There is a strong and persistent sense of racial difference and conflict born out of the history of colonialism in our region.
>
> (1991: 56; emphasis added)

My quarrel with this comment is that it reinstates the white feminist subject as the main actor, for whom the Aboriginal other and the migrant other are two competing interlocutors, kept utterly separate from each other. One result of this is that the differing relations between indigenous peoples and various groups of settlers remain unaddressed, and that the Anglo centre – *its* problems and concerns pertaining to identity and difference – remains the main focus of attention. In intellectual terms, this amounts to a non-dialogue between the postcolonial and the multicultural problematic, the serial juxtapositioning of the two conditional entirely upon the distributive power of the hegemonic Anglo centre. From a white (Anglo) perspective, it may be understandable that priority be given to Anglo-

Aboriginal relations (as Jolly suggests), as it is this relation which marks the original sin foundational to Australian white settler subjectivity, which can now no longer be repressed. However, this intense investment in the postcolonial problematic, which is the locus of the distinctively Australian quandary of 'white guilt', may be one important reason why there is so little feminist engagement with the challenge of constructing a 'multicultural Australia'. 'Migrant women', lumped together in homogenizing and objectifying categories such as NESB, are still mostly talked about, not spoken with and heard (see Martin 1991); they remain within the particularist ghetto of ethnicity and are not allowed an active, constitutive role in the ongoing construction of 'Australia' (see, for example, Curthoys 1993). Multiculturalism remains, as Gunew (1993: 54) complains, 'the daggy cousin of radical chic postcolonialism'.

It is this context which makes it problematic to construct an 'Asian' voice in Australian feminism. Despite the increasingly regular presence of Asians in contemporary Australia and despite the recurrent official rhetoric that Australia is becoming 'part of Asia', Asianness remains solidly defined as external to the symbolic space of Australianness, in contrast with Aboriginality, which has now been accepted by white Australia, albeit reluctantly, as occupying an undeniable place, however fraught by the injustices of history, in the heart of Australian national identity. To define myself as Asian, however, unavoidably and logically means writing myself out of the bounds of that identity and into the margins of a pre-given, firmly established Australian imagined community, the boundaries of which 'are still Eurocentric, cemented together around a core of white traditions' (Schech and Haggis 2000: 236). The only escape from this marginalization, from this perspective, would be the creation of a symbolic space no longer bounded by the idea(l) of national identity; a space, that is, where 'Australia' no longer has to precede and contain, in the last instance, the unequal differences occurring within it. Of course, such a space is utopian, given the fact that 'Australia' is not a floating signifier but the name for an historically sedimented nation–state. Yet the imagination of such a space – a space without borders, a giant, limitless borderlands of sorts where differences exist and intertwine without predetermined categorization (see Chapter 9) – is necessary to appreciate the permanent sense of displacement experienced by all racialized and ethnicized people living in the West, including, I want to stress, indigenous peoples.[10]

What does this tell us, finally, about the feminist politics of difference? As I have already said, too often the need to deal with difference is seen in light of the greater need to save, expand, improve or enrich feminism as a political home which would ideally represent all women. In this way, the ultimate rationale of the politics of difference is cast in terms of an overall politics of *inclusion*: the desire for an overarching feminism to construct a pluralist sisterhood which can accommodate all differences and inequalities between women. It should come as no surprise that such a desire is being expressed largely by white, Western, middle-class women, whom Yeatman (1993) calls the 'custodians of the established order' of contemporary feminism. Theirs is a defensive position, characterized by a reluctance to question the status of feminism *itself* as a political home for all women, just as Australia will not – and cannot, in its existence as a legislative state – question its status as a nation, even 'one nation', despite its embrace of multiculturalism. Yeatman herself, for example, considers the politics of difference as an 'internal politics of emancipation *within* feminism' (1993: 230, emphasis added). In this conception, difference can only be taken into consideration insofar as it does not challenge the rightfulness of feminism as such. Feminism functions as a nation which 'other' women are invited to join without disrupting the ultimate integrity of the nation. But this politics of inclusion is born of a liberal pluralism which can only be entertained by those who have the *power* to include, as pointed out poignantly by Spelman (1988: 163): 'Welcoming someone into one's own home doesn't represent an attempt to undermine privilege; it expresses it.'

Taking difference seriously necessitates the adoption of a politics of *partiality* rather than a politics of inclusion. A politics of partiality implies that feminism must emphasize and consciously construct the limits of its own field of political intervention. While a politics of inclusion is driven by the ambition for universal representation (of all women's interests), a politics of partiality does away with that ambition and accepts the principle that feminism can never ever be an encompassing political home for all women, not just because different groups of women have different and sometimes conflicting interests, but, more radically, because for many groups of 'other' women other interests, other identifications are sometimes more important and more politically pressing than, or even incompatible with, those related to their being women.

Yeatman (1993: 228) acknowledges the necessary partiality of the feminist project when she points to the incommensurability of its insistence on the primacy of gender oppression with the political foci of movements against other forms of social subordination. It is this structural incommensurability that feminists need to come to terms with and accept as drawing the unavoidable limits of feminism as a political project. In short, because all female persons 'do not inhabit the same sociohistorical spaces' (Chow 1991: 93), (white/Western) feminism's assumption of a '"master discourse" position' (ibid.: 98) can only be interpreted as an act of symbolic violence which disguises the fundamental structural divisions created by historical processes such as colonialism, imperialism and nationalism. As Butler (1990: 4) puts it, 'the premature insistence on a stable subject of feminism, understood as a seamless category of women, inevitably generates multiple refusals to accept the category'. It compels us to say, 'I'm a feminist, but . . .', in the same way that I could ever only say, 'I am Australian but . . .'

12

CONCLUSION

Together-in-difference
(The uses and abuses of hybridity)

One of the most urgent predicaments of our time can be described in deceptively simple terms: how are we to live together in this new century? 'We' and 'together' are the key sites of contestation here. In this postmodern world of multiplying claims to particularist identities, any overarching sense of 'we' has become fundamentally problematic and contentious. The emergence of what Cornel West (1990) has called 'the new cultural politics of difference' has bred a profound suspicion of any homogenizing representation of 'us', especially among those who used to be silenced or rendered invisible by such universalizing claims to 'humanity'. In this climate, the very idea of living 'together' becomes hugely daunting. Can togetherness be more than a coincidental and involuntary aggregation of groups being thrust into the same time and space, an uneasy and reluctant juxtapositioning of different bodies and identities forced to share a single world even if their respective imaginative worlds are worlds apart? What are the possibilities of constructing transcultural imagined communities in this era of rampant cultural differentiation and fragmentation? How, in short, can we live together-in-difference?

This book is a contribution to our thinking about these difficult but urgent questions, focusing – in broad terms – on the entrenched dichotomy between 'Asia' and 'the West', as well as the internal divisions within each of these categories. Throughout, I have argued for the importance of hybridity as a means of bridging and blurring the multiple boundaries which constitute 'Asian' and 'Western' identities as mutually exclusive and incommensurable. Theories of hybridity, however problematic, are crucial in our attempts to overcome what Rita Felski (1997) has termed 'the doxa of difference'. As she puts it:

> Metaphors of hybridity and the like not only recognize differences *within* the subject, fracturing and complicating holistic notions of identity, but also addresss connections *between* subjects by recognizing affiliations, cross-pollinations, echoes and repetitions, thereby unseating difference from a position of absolute privilege. Instead of endorsing a drift towards ever greater atomization of identity, such metaphors allow us to conceive of multiple, interconnecting axes of affiliation and differentiation.
>
> (ibid.: 12)

In other words, by recognizing the inescapable impurity of all cultures and the porousness of all cultural boundaries in an irrevocably globalized, interconnected and interdependent world, we may be able to conceive of our living together in terms of complicated entanglement, not in terms of the apartheid of insurmountable differences. If I were to apply this notion of complicated entanglement to my own personal situation, I would describe myself as suspended in-between: neither truly Western nor authentically Asian; embedded in the West yet always partially disengaged from it; disembedded from Asia yet somehow enduringly attached to it emotionally and historically. I wish to hold onto this hybrid in-betweenness not because it is a comfortable position to be in, but because its very ambivalence is a source of cultural permeability and vulnerability which, in my view, is a necessary condition for living together-in-difference.

As Robert Young (1995: 27) puts it, hybridity 'is a key term in that wherever it emerges it suggests the impossibility of essentialism'. Hybridity – simply defined, the production of things composed of elements of different or incongruous kind – instigates the emergence of new, combinatory identities, not the mere assertion of old, given identities, as would seem to be the case in ultimately essentialist formulations of identity politics, even in their new-fangled, apparently transgressive guises of 'diaspora' or 'multiculturalism'. However, we shouldn't extol uncritically the value of hybridity without carefully understanding its complexity and its contradictions. Indeed, too often hybridity is taken simply as the easy antidote to the social divisions produced by the proliferation of difference. In this way, the term loses its political edge and becomes simply a mechanism for *overcoming* difference rather than living with and through it.

Take, for example, the cover of the 1996 Australia Day Edition of *The Bulletin*, Australia's premier current affairs magazine. We see an eye-catching group photo of about twenty men, women and children of a variety of 'races' (Caucasian, Asian, Aboriginal), all stripped down to underpants and with their arms crossed in front of their chests. This mixed group is supposed to represent 'the new Australian race'. As *The Bulletin* writes:

> Australia is slowly turning into a nation of hybrids. By the turn of the century, more than 40% of Australia's population will be ethnically mixed as a result of intermarriage between Anglo-Celtic Australians and migrants, or between people from the different ethnic groups.
>
> (Kyriakopoulos 1996)

Far from a mixed blessing, this purported hybridization of the Australian population is presented by *The Bulletin* as a straightforwardly good thing. A demographer is quoted as saying that the high rate of 'inter-cultural marriage' provides 'Australia's best protection against becoming a battleground of "warring tribes"' (ibid.).

The unqualified desire for hybridity expressed in this discourse is in fact quite progressive, certainly in light of the massive unease about miscegenation and racial interbreeding which pervaded Western societies earlier. As Young (1995: 25) observes, 'anxiety about hybridity reflected the desire to keep races separate', to maintain a clear-cut racial hierarchy which would be disturbed by the mixed-race offspring resulting from inter-racial sexual intercourse. In nineteenth-century Western racial theory the proliferation of 'half-castes' was accompanied by forewarnings about the degeneration and decay which would be the result of an emerging 'raceless chaos'. Young describes these hybrids as the 'living legacies that abrupt, casual, often coerced, unions had left behind' (ibid.), a description which implicitly connects hybridity with rape (mostly, of coloured, colonized women by white, colonizing men) and conjures up the deeply exploitative and hierarchical colonial context in which nineteenth-century miscegenation generally took place. This situation, of course, differs considerably from the relative commonness of voluntary cross-racial or cross-ethnic marital unions in the globalized, transnational and multicultural world of the late twentieth century. Does this mean then that hybridity has now become normalized, and that as a result old racist divisions have been overcome?

According to *The Bulletin*, 'intermarriage is by definition a force of social cohesion' (Kyriakopoulos 1996: 17). It becomes clear then that hybridity is constructed here as the imaginary solution for the real and potential interethnic friction within the boundaries of the multiracial and multicultural nation–state. That is, if keeping non-white others out (as in the White Australia policy) can no longer be pursued, and if managerial multiculturalism threatens to keep ethnic groups apart in their separate boxes, then, so it seems, the opposite strategy becomes attractive: intermixture and amalgamation. So hybridity operates in this discourse as a promise for multicultural, multiracial, multi-ethnic harmony: hybridity as, in Nicholas Thomas's (1996: 11) words, 'a smooth process of synthesis or fusion'. In this model, differences may not be completely erased, but made harmless, domesticated, amalgamated into a variegated yet comfortable whole. To be sure, promoting and popularizing the image of Australia as a 'hybrid nation' – as a nation of endlessly mixed-up differences and samenesses, does seem like an exceedingly progressive alternative in the face of resurgent exclusionary white nationalisms of the Pauline Hanson kind. The problem is, however, that the very equation of hybridity with harmonious fusion or synthesis – which we may characterize as 'liberal hybridism', simplifies matters significantly and produces power effects of its own, which reveal some of the problems with an uncritical use of the idea of hybridity.

To illuminate the stakes in this conceptual tussle, we can contrast the rosy melting-pot vision of liberal hybridism with that of Ian Anderson's (1995) militant refusal to call himself a 'hybrid'. Anderson, a Tasmanian Aboriginal descendant of Truganini[1] and thus one of the living legacies of enforced miscegenation which has littered Australian colonial history, stresses the political and psychological importance of affirming his indigenous identity in a context in which non-indigenous Australians often pressure people like him to acknowledge their white ancestry. In response, Anderson articulates his resistance against the disempowerment ensuing from being categorized as 'hybrids' who 'have lost their culture, and have no past other than being the dupes of white Australian history'. 'I am no hybrid', Anderson says:

> I do not experience my body as a fragmented entity of black and white compartments. Even though I sense its transformative potential, and its internal contradictions and conflicts, it is one entity. My body is an Aboriginal body, and could not be otherwise – unless someone cared to dismember my historical consciousness, my experience of family, my experience of being treated as an Aboriginal, and acting in a particular manner because of who I am.
>
> (1995: 38)

The strategic essentialism – or rather, strategic anti-anti-essentialism – involved in this assertion of a coherent, unambiguously Aboriginal identity is founded on a political claim of historical continuity and memory, not on biology. For Anderson, the traumatic history of indigenous dispossession and genocide in Tasmania is more important in shaping his sense of identity than his biological origins as a mixed-race child born of that very violent colonial encounter. So when queried, 'Why do you people deny your white ancestry?', Anderson (1995: 35) replies:

> Our families have been born out of horrific violence. Some of our white ancestors were direct perpetrators to that. . . . I do see the evidence of British colonialism – every day. *But Britain may as well be on the moon. . . . How can Britain as a place or society hold any special significance?* I fail to feel positive about this British cultural tradition. Nor do I see it as mine. I simply acknowledge its impact.
>
> (italics in original)

Anderson's active disidentification with the 'white' contribution to his existence enables the construction of an Aboriginal identity that counters the dominant denomination of Truganini's descendants as the 'hybrid children of a dead race'. It is clear, then, that for Anderson, hybridity does not stand for happy fusion but for 'racial' disappearance, for the fatal completeness of genocide and the impossibility of Aboriginal survival. In other words, Anderson's determination to essentialize Aboriginality stems from a desire to maintain an indubitable position of resistance through the radical affirmation of an insurgent counter-identity.

From the progressivist perspective of white liberal hybridism Anderson's militant refusal of hybridity in favour of an affirmation of an unambigously oppositional identity can only be dismissed as a retrograde clinging to the past. As Nicholas Thomas (1996: 10–11) remarks in his critique of the popularity of the concept of hybridity in contemporary art and cultural theory, '[i]f fusion is [conceived as] the highest stage of cultural evolution, those still preoccupied with anticolonialism or nativism . . . can only be disparaged'. In other words, while in an earlier period hybridity (in the sense of miscegenation) served as a sign of degeneration and, ultimately, the extinction of indigenous populations, today an uncritically cele-bratory endorsement of hybridity serves prematurely to undercut contemporary indigenous identity politics. In this light, the question, 'Why do you people deny your white ancestry?' thrown at Anderson can be read as an aggressive attempt to delegitimize the assertion of Aboriginal identity in the name of an appropriative, assimilatory hybridity, born of impatience with the insistence of indigenous people on maintaining their distinctive status and their unwillingness to go along with a benign and convenient model of interracial harmony and 'reconciliation', of happy hybridity.

And yet it has to be said that the political need to mobilize an essentialized Aboriginal identity, as articulated by Anderson, has arisen precisely in a context in which the condition of hybridity has become an integral part of social and cultural life in contemporary society. After all, Aboriginal people's lives today are on the whole shaped and moulded, unavoidably and ongoingly, within the economic, political and ideological parameters set by the European settler nation–state, whose coming into hegemony has instigated the very construction of 'the Aborigines' as a residual category on the margins of the white Australian nation (Attwood 1989). In other words, the essentializing strategy of Aboriginal self-identification and self-representation can be seen as a political corollary of being marginalized in a thoroughly and irrevocably hybridized world, a world of necessary interdepen-dencies, interconnections and intercultural entanglements. In this sense, the postmodern condition of hybridity can ironically be seen as *constitutive* of Aboriginality as identification point for indigenous Australians today.

This is to suggest, then, that while the rhetoric of hybridity can easily be put to political abuse if it is co-opted in a discourse of easy multicultural and multiracial harmony, we cannot, in fact, escape the predicament of hybridity as a real, powerful and pervasive force in a world in which togetherness-in-difference is the order of the day. Indeed, it has become commonplace in contemporary cultural studies to claim that all cultures in modernity are always-already hybrid, always the impure products of intersecting influences and flows. But this does not mean that as a result, all cultures inhabit the same symbolic and historical space and are equivalent and equal to each other. Indeed, liberal-pluralist calls for harmonious amalgamation are generally conveniently neglectful of the specific power relations and historical conditions configuring the interactions and encounters which induce forced and unforced processes of hybridization. As Ella Shohat (1992: 100) has remarked, '[a]s a descriptive catch all term, "hybridity" *per se* fails to discriminate between diverse modalities of hybridity, for example, forced assimilation, internalised self-rejection, political co-optation, social conformism, cultural mimicry, and creative transcendence'. What we need to question, then, is not so much hybridity as such, which would be a futile enterprise, but the depoliticization involved in the reduction of hybridity to happy fusion and synthesis. I would argue that it is the *ambivalence* which is immanent to hybridity that needs to be highlighted, as we also need to examine the *specific contexts and conditions* in which hybridity operates – in Annie Coombes' (1994) words, the how and who of it.

For postcolonial cultural theorists such as Stuart Hall, Paul Gilroy, Trinh Minh-ha, Homi Bhabha and others, hybridity has an explicitly critical political purchase. They see the hybrid as a critical force that undermines or subverts, from inside out, dominant formations through the interstitial insinuation of the 'different', the 'other' or the 'marginalized' into the very fabric of the dominant. Hall and Gilroy, for example, insist on enunciating a hybrid speaking position they call 'Black British' – a mode of self-representation designed to interrogate hegemonic 'white' definitions of British national identity by interjecting it with blackness (see Ang and Stratton 1995b). This procedure results, in Hall's words, in 'a kind of hybridisation' of the English, 'whether they like it or not' (quoted in Mercer 1994: 24). The politics of hybridity here, then, is one of active intervention, involving both a disarticulation of exclusionary conceptions of Britishness as essentially 'white' and its rearticulation as a necessarily impure and plural formation which can no longer suppress the black other within. In this sense, hybridity is, as Coombes (1994: 90) puts it, 'an important cultural strategy for the political project of decolonisation'. It destabilizes established cultural power relations between white and black, colonizer and colonized, centre and periphery, the 'West' and the 'rest', not through a mere inversion of these hierarchical dualisms, but by throwing into question these very binaries through a process of boundary-blurring transculturation.

Here we have a positive valuation, if not celebration of hybridity, but for reasons virtually opposed to that of liberal hybridism. While the latter, as we have seen, is fuelled by hybridity's perceived potential to absorb difference into a new consensual culture of fusion and synthesis, for postcolonial migrants such as Hall and Gilroy no such consensual culture comes out of hybridity. Indeed, for them any apparent consensus or fusion can be revealed as partial, incomplete, and ultimately impossible, because the ideological closure on which it depends will always be destabilized by that difference that is too difficult to absorb or assimilate. In other words, any intercultural exchange will always face its moment of incommensurability, which disrupts the smooth creation of a wholesome synthesis (see Ang 1997). 'Consensus', as David Scott has argued in his essay 'The permanence of pluralism':

> has now to be seen not as a final destination, a distant horizon, but as one moment in a larger relation permanently open to contestation, open to the moment when difference contests sites of normalized identity and demands a rearrangement of the terms, and perhaps even the very *idiom*, of consensus.
>
> (2000: 298)

Hybridity here has interrogative effects, it is a sign of challenge and altercation, not of congenial amalgamation or merger. To refer to the Australian context, the vision of an 'Asianization' of Australia provides a clear example of how uncomfortable and threatening the idea of a hybrid future can be for some: hybridity, in this case, does not stand for a new national harmony but for cross-cultural anxiety, fear of the undigestible difference – 'Asianness' – which would transform Australia as a whole.

198

If there is an overall theoretical thread in this book, then it is the deployment of this postcolonial concept of hybridity to problematize the concept of *ethnicity* which underlies the dominant discourses of both 'diaspora' and 'multiculturalism' Ethnicity, as Arjun Appadurai (1996a: 13) has noted, is 'the idea of naturalized group identity', and both diaspora and multiculturalism ultimately rely on the 'ethnic group' as their main constituent or building block. But as I have argued in my reflections on Chineseness and Chinese identity, the very consciousness of the 'ethnic group' in and for itself, say, 'the Chinese' or any combinatory, hyphenated specification of it, is not the result of some spontaneous, primordial idea of kinship. As Appadurai (ibid.) points out, ethnic consciousness depends on the active mobilization of certain differences to *articulate* group identity. Both 'diaspora' and 'multiculturalism' are profoundly implicated in this very process of cultural mobilization of difference in the interest of (ethnic) identity: diaspora by globalizing the 'ethnic group', thus emphasizing 'sameness in dispersal', and multiculturalism by subsuming it as a neatly delimited box, one among many, within the bounded container of the pluralistic nation–state, what I have described as 'living apart together'. There is a tension between the two insofar as diaspora tends to pull ethnic identification out of the circumscribed space of the nation–state, while multiculturalism desperately attempts to contain ethnic group formation within the nation–state's boundaries. But both logically operate as conceptual brakes on the idea of hybridity because in the end, they cannot exist without a reification of ethnicity, and therefore of identitarian essentialism and closure.

To be sure, ethnicity is a very powerful mode of collective identification in the globalizing world of today. Ethnic categories exert their influence either as bureaucratic fictions – as in official policies of multiculturalism – or as imagined communities constructed from below, by 'ethnics' themselves, as a means of accentuating 'our' difference in a context of fluid co-existence with many heterogeneous others. Diasporas are the globalized embodiments of such ethnicized imagined communities. The very ubiquity of ethnic claims today points to the apparent paradox of ethnicity's mobilizing power in a thoroughly hybridized world. In this context, as Pnina Werbner (1997a: 22) points out, 'we have to recognise the differential interests social groups have in sustaining boundaries'. She considers the question (ibid.: 4) 'why borders, boundaries and "pure" identities remain so important, the subject of defensive and essentialising actions and reflections, and why such essentialisms are so awfully difficult to transcend'. Indeed, in arguing *for* hybridity I am not denying the cultural and political significance of ethnic identifications today; nor do I wish to essentialize essentialism by suggesting that all (self-)essentializing strategies are the same and necessarily 'bad'. After all, as the example of Aboriginal identity shows, essentialism can operate as 'a political weapon in a public struggle for state resources, citizenship rights or a universal morality' (Werbner 1997b: 249). However, while the politics of ethnicity – either in diaspora or in multiculturalism – can be enormously empowering, its broader effects are not always benign or beneficial, on the contrary. As Werbner (ibid.: 229) remarks: 'Policy decisions, state fund allocations, racial murders, ethnic cleansing, anti-racist struggles, nationalist conflicts or revivals, even genocide, follow on essentialist constructions of unitary, organic cultural collectivities.' In other words, identity politics is never innocent.

It is in this light that the importance of hybridity needs to be stressed. Gregor McLennan (1995: 90) has commented that the problem with hybridity is that it 'does not easily produce a *people*'. This is true, but I would argue that we need to lay stress on the unsettling horizon of hybridization precisely because essentializing and divisive claims to ethnicity, the assertion of distinct and separate 'peoples', are so rampant. The sheer force of identity politics gives us a sense of 'why [cultural hybridity] is experienced as dangerous, difficult or revitalising despite its quotidian normalcy' (Werbner 1997a: 4). We live in the paradoxical situation, then, that hybridity is still seen as a problem or an anomaly despite the fact that it is every-where, because it is identity that has been privileged as the naturalized principle for social order. Therefore, it is the very preoccupation with demarcating the line between 'Chinese' and 'non-Chinese', 'Asian' and 'Western' – that is, the preoccu-pation with boundary-setting and boundary-maintenance – that I have wanted to problematize in this book. Against such essentializing moves, I wish to hold up the non-Chinese-speaking figure of the banana – 'yellow outside, white inside' – to stress the porousness of identities and, more importantly, the fact that they evolve and take shape through multiple interrelationships with myriad, differently positioned others. These interrelationships, whether economic, political, professional, cultural or personal, are never power-free, but they cannot be avoided, they have to be continually negotiated and engaged with somehow. More, these interrelationships are by definition *constitutive* of contemporary social life. This, of course, is what togetherness-in-difference is all about: it is about co-existence in a single world.

To conclude then, rather than seeing hybridity as a synonym for an easy multicultural harmony, or as an instrument for the achievement thereof, I want to suggest that the concept of hybridity should be mobilized to address and analyse the fundamental *uneasiness* inherent in our global condition of togetherness-in-difference. This unease has been historically produced, in that we are still overwhelmingly captured by the dominant habit of thinking about ourselves and the world in terms of identity, ethnic, national and otherwise. As a result, mixture is still often inevitably thought of and felt as a contamination, a breach of purity, an infringement of 'identity'. In fact, even in its celebration of interethnic marriage as the creative generator of the happy hybrid nation, *The Bulletin* has to admit that all is not that simple. A marriage consultant is quoted as saying: 'The fact of intermixing tells us little about the adaptation and adjustments couples and their children are required to make, and the processes which occur when values are in conflict' (Kyriakopoulos 1996). In short, hybridity is not only about fusion and synthesis, but also about friction and tension, about ambivalence and incom-mensurability, about the contestations and interrogations that go hand in hand with the heterogeneity, diversity and multiplicity we have to deal with as we live together-in-difference. Robert Young (1995) describes the situation succinctly:

Hybridity thus makes difference into sameness, and sameness into difference, but in a way that makes the same no longer the same, the different no longer simply different. In that sense, it operates according to the form of logic that Derrida isolates in the term 'brisure', a breaking and a joining at the same time, in the same place: difference and sameness in an apparently impossible simultaneity.

(1995: 36)

In the hybrid cultural predicament, as McLennan (1995: 90) puts it, we have to learn 'how to live awkwardly (but also wisely and critically)' in a world in which we no longer have the secure capacity to draw the line between 'us' and 'them' – in which difference and sameness are inextricably intertwined in complicated entanglement.

Let me close with these eloquent words from Edward Said, arguably one of the most influential postcolonial intellectuals in the world today:

No one today is purely *one* thing. Labels like Indian, or woman, or Muslim, or American are no more than starting points, which if followed into actual experience for only a moment are quickly left behind. Imperialism consolidated the mixture of cultures and identities on a global scale. But its worst and most paradoxical gift was to allow people to believe that they were only, mainly, exclusively, white, or black, or Western, or Oriental. Yet just as human beings make their own history, they also make their cultures and ethnic identities. No one can deny the persisting continuities of long traditions, sustained habitations, national languages, and cultural geographies, but there seems no reason except fear and prejudice to keep insisting on their separation and distinctiveness, as if that was all human life was about. Survival in fact is about the connections between things; in Eliot's phrase, reality cannot be deprived of the 'other echoes [that] inhabit the garden'. It is more rewarding – and more difficult – to think concretely and sympathetically, contrapuntally, about others than only about 'us'. But this also means not trying to rule others, not trying to classify them or put them in hierarchies, above all, not constantly reiterating how 'our' culture or country is number one (or *not* number one, for that matter). For the intellectual there is quite enough of value to do without *that*.

(1993: 407–8)

201

NOTES

INTRODUCTION

1 For a diversity of popular accounts, see e.g. Schlosstein (1989); Gibney (1992); Chu (1995); Naisbitt (1997).

2 Of course, not all of Asia is considered 'modern' by Western standards. Indeed, large parts of Asia, mostly 'less developed' regions and countries (such as rural China and large parts of Indochina) are still conveniently treated as backward, even by other, more modern Asians such as the Japanese and the Taiwanese (see e.g. Iwabuchi, forthcoming).

3 In a famous row, former Australian Prime Minister Paul Keating dismissed his Malaysian colleague, Mahathir Mohammad, as 'recalcitrant' when the latter refused to attend a meeting of the fledgling Asia Pacific Economic Forum (APEC) in Seattle in 1993, on the grounds that the organization was too dominated by Western powers such as the USA and Australia.

4 The assertion of this symbolic equality is never more spectacularly displayed than at photo sessions of APEC summits. All leaders wear the same outfit, vaguely derived from the national cultural tradition of the host nation. There is something truly ironic and poignant about the line of leaders all wearing a batik shirt, as during the summit in Jakarta (1994): the sheer economic, social and political diversity of the nation–states comprising this regional forum is suppressed by a symbolic declaration of sameness expressed in the uniform costume.

5 For a recent discussion of assimilationism in the United States in relation to the Jews, see Stratton (2000), Chapter 9.

6 Paul Gilroy, in his otherwise admirably anti-essentialist treatment of the Black diaspora in his influential study *The Black Atlantic* (1993a), nevertheless gestures towards this internal coherence and unity of the diaspora through his concept of the 'changing same'.

7 In this respect, there is the real issue of Asians' relative collective success in advancing themselves within Western societies compared with other racial minority groups, such as African Americans and Hispanics in the USA and indigenous people and people of Middle Eastern backgrounds in Australia. Such differences in success in 'integration' highlight the complexity of the politics of race and ethnicity in the postmodern, heterogeneous West.

1 ON NOT SPEAKING CHINESE

1 How the 'Tiananmen Massacre' (as it has come to be known in the West) should be judged is a complex issue, too easily schematized in the complacent West in terms of good and bad, heroic students versus a villainous communist dictatorship – a

202

schematization that only enhances feel-good smugness, not nuanced analysis. This is not an issue I would like to go into, but see e.g. the articles in Wasserstrom and Perry (1992) and Rey Chow's critical essay, 'Violence in the Other Country: China as Crisis, Spectacle and Woman' in Chow (1993). For an engaging and discerning, anti-reductionist account of the politics of the 1989 Beijing uprising, based on anthropological participant obsevation, see Chiu (1991).

2 See for a good example of the use of the autobiographic method for cultural theorizing, Steedman (1986). In his review of this book Joseph Bristow (1991: 118–19) states that 'Steedman's work, making . . . observations about how the self is situated within the devices of reading and writing, has a fascination with those moments of interpretation (or identification) that may, for example, move us to anger or to tears.' In more general terms this kind of project draws on Raymond Williams's concept of 'structure of feeling': 'specifically affective elements of consciousness and relationships: not feeling against thought, but thought as felt and feeling as thought: practical consciousness of a present kind, in a living and interrelating continuity' (Williams 1977: 132).

3 The term *peranakan* meaning 'children of', is derived from the Indonesian word for child, *anak*, which is also the root of, for example, *beranak*, to give birth. Other terms used to designate members of this community are *baba* (for the males), *nyonya* (married female) and *nona* (unmarried female). Significantly, these are all Malay/ Indonesian terms, which are also in use in Malaysia and Singapore.

4 *Totok* is an Indonesian term meaning 'pure blood foreigner'. The *peranakans* used the term *singkeh* to designate this category of Chinese, meaning 'new guests'.

5 It should be noted that the practices of the Dutch colonizers were particularly oppressive in this respect. A fundamental principle of British colonialism, universal equality before the law, was conspicuously absent in the Dutch system. Singapore Chinese under British rule, for example, were not burdened with hated pass and zoning systems (Williams 1960: 43). Such historical specificities make it impossible to generalize over all *peranakans* in the South-East Asian region: the differential Western colonialisms have played a central role in forming and forging specific *peranakan* cultures.

6 This transnational political unification of overseas Chinese, a powerful precursor of contemporary diaspora politics, is not unproblematic. For its unfortunate implications for later generations of Indonesian Chinese, see Chapter 3; for its effects on the construction of Chineseness in postcolonial South-East Asia more generally, see Chapter 4.

7 This view was expressed, for example, by the Partai Tionghoa Indonesia (the Indonesian Chinese Party), founded in 1932, which was Indonesia-oriented and identified itself with Indonesia rather than China or the Netherlands. Suryadinata (1975) does not say how popular this position was.

8 Of course, the constitution of the modern nation–state of Israel is based on this scenario.

9 See for a discussion of the paradox between the increasing appeal of nationalism on the one hand, and the decline of the significance of the nation–state on the other, Hobsbawm (1990), Chapter 6.

10 In Chapter 4 I will make the more radical argument to 'undo' the notion of (Chinese) diaspora itself.

11 I appropriate this crucial distinction from Sollors (1986).

2 CAN ONE SAY NO TO CHINESENESS?

1 See Stuart Hall's similar critique of the notion of the 'essential black subject', e.g. in his essays 'New Ethnicities' (1996d) and 'What is this "Black" in Black Popular Culture?' (1996e).

2 The emergence of a discourse on 'cultural China', as launched by Tu, is closely related to the growing prominence of the discourse of 'Greater China'. The latter is the most commonly used term, in English at least, for 'the system of interactions among mainland China, Hong Kong, Taiwan and people of Chinese descent around the world' (Harding 1993: 683). Harding (1993) distinguishes three key themes in the contemporary discourse of Greater China: the rise of a transnational Chinese economy; the (prospect of a) reunification of a Chinese state; and the emergence of a global Chinese culture, to which Tu's (1994c) discussion of 'cultural China' is a key contribution.

3 It should be noted that Tu's paper first appeared in 1991, only two years after the crushing of pro-democracy demonstrators at Tiananman Square in June 1989 by the People's Liberation Army. This event has had a massive impact on the fate of representations of 'Chineseness' in the contemporary world, and has been of major significance in the emergence of the dissident discourse of 'cultural China'.

4 It is ironic, however, that by the beginning of the twenty-first century the Western world has largely abandoned its moral preoccupation with human rights issues in China in favour of strengthening economic relations with the largest country in the world, which is opening up its economy to global capitalist market forces at breakneck speed.

5 Gilroy explicitly and passionately rejects Africa-centred discourses of the black diaspora, which are highly influential among some African-American intellectuals in the USA (as in the idea of Africentricity).

6 Thus, Suryadinata mentions a survey which reveals that most South-East Asian Chinese capitalists who have invested in mainland China are mainly those who are 'culturally Chinese'. *Peranakan* Chinese have by and large been prevented from this 'return' for economic purposes because 'having lost their command of Chinese, [they] are unable to communicate with the mainland Chinese' (Suryadinata 1997: 16).

7 For a discussion of Chinese conceptions of race, see Dikötter (1992).

8 Yang's book *Sadness* (which was originally presented as a one-man slide show) alternately traces two stories of his life – one around his Chinese family and the other of his gay community in Sydney.

3 INDONESIA ON MY MIND

1 This was an anti-communist pogrom, not an anti-Chinese one, although press accounts during the 1998 unrest sometimes gloss over the difference. The association of communism with the People's Republic of China did create an atmosphere of suspicion among the Chinese, but according to one historian, 'killings of the Chinese because they were Chinese were more sporadic and less systematic' (Coppel 1983: 58). Most anti-Chinese violence after the 1965 coup, according to Coppel, did not take the form physical harm (including killing) but of damage of property, looting, and burning of shops and houses. This pattern was largely repeated in the 1998 anti-Chinese riots, although many did get killed in the process. A disturbing new feature of the 1998 riots was the occurrence of rape, often gang rape, of ethnic Chinese women by the rioters.

2 In his book *Culture and Society*, Williams (1961: 289) argued that 'masses' are illusory totalities: there no masses, 'only ways of seeing people as masses'.

3 For historical accounts of the position of the Chinese minority in the Indonesian nation–state, see e.g. Mackie (1976); Suryadinata (1975; 1979); Coppel (1983).

4 It should be pointed out that who 'the Chinese' are in Indonesia is not a question with a straightforward, objective answer. Those of Chinese ancestry who live in the country are a very diverse group: an important distinction stemming from colonial times is often made between the the more locally-rooted *peranakan* Chinese and the more

recently arrived, 'purely Chinese' *totok* Chinese. A more recent distinction is that between those Chinese who are Indonesian citizens and those who are not. While the latter distinction has been crucial for both government policy and for Indonesian Chinese leaders, society at large generally does not use passport identities as markers of difference. Coppel (1983: 5) therefore includes in his definition of Indonesian Chinese those 'who are regarded as Chinese by indigenous Indonesians (at least in some circumstances) and given special treatment as a consequence'. This definition thus includes people who regard themselves as Indonesians and have refused to identify themselves in any sense with 'Chineseness', but whose Chinese characteristics (mostly physical appearance) still allow them to be labelled and treated as 'Chinese'. Thus, the borderline between 'Chinese' and 'non-Chinese' is not always clear; 'the Indonesian Chinese' are neither an internally homogeneous nor a securely bounded category of people.

5 Ariel Heryanto (1998b; 1999) has objected to the designation of this event as 'anti-Chinese riots' because it suggests, unfairly in his view, that the violence erupted spontaneously and that the culprits were ordinary people motivated by racial prejudice. He wants to emphasize the clear evidence that sections of the military had an active hand in fuelling the 'riots' and uses the term 'racialized state terrorism' to describe the May 1998 violence.

6 Personal email correspondence with Dan Tse, April 1998.

7 I am especially referring here to the 'News & Politics' section of the site's Bulletin Board. Since the launch of the site in February 1998 this was the most heavily frequented electronic discussion space on the site, especially at the height of the Indonesian Chinese crisis and its immediate aftermath. All quotations from the Bulletin Board in the rest of this chapter are taken from this corner of cyberspace.

8 The word *pribumi* to refer to indigenous Indonesians was introduced during Suharto's New Order era in replacement of the older word *asli*, which was used in the 1945 constitution. Both words carry the meaning 'indigenous', but in contrast to *asli*, *pribumi* does not connote 'genuine' or 'authentic'. According to Coppel (1983: 158), this discursive shift can be read as an attempt to soften the loadedness of the distinction between 'indigenous' and 'non-indigenous' in the designation of Indonesians, against which Chinese have protested. At the same time, however, the government sanctioned the use of the derogatory word *Cina* to refer to 'Chinese', over and above the word *Tionghoa*, which is preferred by the Chinese themselves.

9 Unlike Kwok's family, who presumably is of *totok* Chinese background (given that she refers to Chinese schools and a Chinese-speaking father), my family, who is of *peranakan* background, has never been in active pursuit of Chinese cultural heritage. Even though I grew up in Indonesia in a time when Chinese schools were not banned yet, I was sent to a Christian school run by Dutch nuns. There were some (wealthy) *pribumi* children in this school. According to Coppel (1983: 162), Christian schools attract a very high proportion of Chinese students and children from wealthy *pribumi* families. He comments that in this respect Chinese schools play a role in 'assimilating the Chinese into a particular sector of upper and middle-class Indonesian society'.

10 For the theoretical formulation of the economic as determinant in the first, not last, instance, see Hall (1996b).

11 The Chinese demand to be granted the formal status of Europeans was inspired by the fact that the Japanese had managed to acquire such a privileged status in 1899.

12 In colonial times all inhabitants of the colony were 'Dutch subjects', with no citizenship rights in the modern, nationalist sense of that word.

13 It is of course difficult to acquire 'objective' information about the exact damage done by the riots, but an independent Human Rights Commission in Indonesia has estimated that the number of victims killed was around 1,200. It should be stressed that many of these were not Chinese.

14 In the first four months of its existence (from February 1998), there were some 100,000 visits to the site. However, this number increased exponentially in the wake of the crisis. The rapid rise in Huaren's popularity in this respect can be compared with that of CNN in 1989, when the 24-hour global news network provided non-stop up-to-date news about the fall of the Berlin Wall and the Tiananmen Square student protests and its violent suppression on 4 June. Major crises have launched these new global communications media – satellite TV in the late 1980s, the Internet in the late 1990s – into the mainstream.

15 B.J. Habibie, President Suharto's immediate successor, issued a decree that the distinction *pribumi*/non-*pribumi* must no longer be used. Under President Wahid, elected in 1999, bans on the expression of Chinese cultural traditions (e.g. Chinese New Year celebrations) were slowly removed.

16 As mentioned earlier, separatist movements are particularly strong in Aceh and in West Papua. And of course, the East Timorese, whom Indonesia attempted to incorporate in its national imagined community, voted overwhelmingly for their independence in 1999.

4 UNDOING DIASPORA

1 The journal was first published by Oxford University Press, later by Toronto University Press.

2 The World Chinese Entrepreneurs Convention was an initiative of the Singaporean Chinese Chamber of Commerce and Industry. It holds biannual international conventions to facilitate global networking for Chinese entrepreneurs worldwide. Its inaugural convention was held in Singapore, where Senior Minister Lee Kuan Yew delivered the keynote address; since then there have been conventions in Hong Kong (1993), Bangkok (1995), Vancouver (1997) and Melbourne (1999). The 2001 convention was held in Nanjing, China, in June 2001.

3 An exception is Singapore, the only nation–state outside Greater China with a diasporic Chinese majority, where there has been a long history of government-sanctioned resinicization policies such as the Speak Mandarin Campaign.

4 Lynn Pan has made the astute remark that the very quest for ethnic self-discovery and identity is a mark of Americanness, not Chineseness: 'To the villagers in Toishan, the Chinese American who returns to rediscover his origins is doing a very American thing, for the last thing *they* feel is the need for roots' (1990: 295). Pan informs us that Toishan village has taken advantage of this diasporic longing by tapping into the 'roots business' in the USA, offering tours to ancestral villages and wooing investments by returning local sons. Here, diaspora consciousness is expressly encouraged by the homeland because it is economically profitable.

5 A comparative analysis with other diasporic formations would enable us to assess to which extent the core/periphery divide is a general characteristic of all diasporic formations, and in which ways they are variably imagined in particular diasporas.

6 This does not mean, of course, that there are no forces of exclusion at work in the global city, on the contrary. Exclusionary and divisive processes based especially on class and race (and to a lesser extent gender) tend to carve the space of the city up into particular 'enclaves' or 'ghettos' where certain groups are more or less welcome. Unlike in the case of diasporas, however, such exclusionary mechanisms are not essentialized nor predetermined; for example, a previously white neighbourhood can over time become multiracial or even predominantly black or Asian (as is the case in some major cities in North America and Australia).

7 This ethnographic story comes from fieldwork among the East Timorese diaspora in Sydney by my PhD student Amanda Wise.

206

5 MULTICULTURALISM IN CRISIS

1 The Liberal Party and the Labor Party are the two main political parties in Australia. The conservative Liberal Party, which draws its support mainly from the cities, is in an ongoing coalition with the much smaller National Party, which mainly represents the interests of farmers, graziers, and the 'bush' more generally.

2 Full texts of Pauline Hanson's parliamentary speeches can be browsed at http://www.gwb.com.au/onenation/ Her early speeches, including her infamous Maiden Speech, were reprinted in a book which included material by some of her supporters but published under her name, entitled *The Truth* (Hanson, 1997a).

3 At the height of her popularity in the first half of 1997, Hanson and her newly established political party, One Nation, could attract more than 10% of national support, according to one opinion poll, while another poll suggested that one in four voters were prepared to back the new party (see Rothwell 1997). In the 1998 election Hanson lost her parliamentary seat, but remained the highly visible President and charismatic leader of her party. One Nation went on to attract significant support during a number of state elections, especially in her home state Queensland. By 2001 the One Nation party looks set to have become a more or less permanent minor force in Australian politics, representing the small people who feel left out by the rapid social transformations elicited by globalization.

4 We owe the phrase 'white panic' to Meaghan Morris (1998a).

5 Howard has persistently argued that it is better to ignore Pauline Hanson than to pay attention to her and comment on her views. This politics of evasion has generally been criticized as weak leadership on Howard's part, not suitable for someone holding the powerful position of Prime Minister. A more important reason why Howard has found it so difficult to distance himself from Hanson, however, is that he shares some of Hanson's sentiments about the state of Australia in the 1990s, if not the political remedies she proposes.

6 A look at Howard's personal views and attitudes, however, clearly reveals his unease with the growing ethnic and cultural diversification of Australia in the past few decades. In interviews he has repeatedly expressed his fond memories of his young life in a Sydney suburb in the 1950s, where everybody was supposedly 'the same'. For an astute analysis see Fiona Allon (1997).

7 One reason for the confusion around what 'multiculturalism' actually means is the lack of discussion about it in the public sphere. While there has been considerable intellectual and theoretical engagement with multiculturalism at policy level, where it has evolved from being discussed in liberal terms of representation (Ten 1993) to ethical terms of social justice (Theophanous 1995), and while there has generally been a shift from emphasizing diversity to emphasizing the common values which enable that diversity to be practised, lay people's understanding of multiculturalism is confined simply to a mere recognition of ethnic difference and its superficial cultural expression (e.g. food, language, customs).

8 This issue has been the object of major political and moral soul-searching in the late 1990s. One of the main recommendations of the National Inquiry into the Separation of Aboriginal and Torres Strait Islander Children from their Families (1997) was that the government issue a national apology to the victims of this policy, which some have equated with a case of 'genocide'. Significantly, Prime Minister John Howard has always refused to express such a formal apology on behalf of the nation.

9 It should be pointed out that Australia was one of the last Western nations to scrap racially discriminatory immigration laws. In both Canada and the United States this change took place in the 1960s.

10 For example, prior to the early 1970s liberal intellectuals, such as members of the

Immigration Reform Group (1962; 1975) advocated a gradualist policy of multi-racialism. After the early 1970s, no one talked about multiracialism on either side of politics – a decisive discursive shift.

6 ASIANS IN AUSTRALIA

1 Over the years, the Hanson phenomenon has come to be interpreted in official political circles mainly as the expression of discontent among rural and regional communities, who were left behind by the rapid economic changes caused by globalization. Hence, the masive attention paid by the major political parties to the plight of rural and regional Australia in the year 2000. Interestingly, however, this emphasis served to downplay the racial dimension of the fear of globalization which has been a persistent part of the Hansonite worldview.
2 While Ms Hanson lost her seat in parliament at the 1998 Federal Elections, the fact that her party received around 8 per cent of the primary vote during these elections indicates that what she represents to the nation will not simply go away.
3 For a concise history of Australian immigration, see e.g. Jupp (1991).
4 For a theoretical elaboration of the concept of (dis)articulation as used here, see Laclau and Mouffe (1983) and Slack (1996).
5 For two centuries, the European occupation of Australia was legitimized through the invention of the principle of *terra nullius*, the notion that the land was not inhabited before the Europeans came. In 1992, this colonial principle was officially overturned (in the so-called Mabo decision) as the High Court recognized that the land was never 'empty' and acknowledged the right to 'native title' for Aboriginal and Torres Strait Islander groups throughout the country. Needless to say, this recognition was received with great apprehension in many parts of white Australia, especially those who felt that it damaged their material interests in the land such as mining companies and farmers.

7 RACIAL/SPATIAL ANXIETY

1 This *Sydney Morning Herald* article (Phelan 1997) reports on an AGB McNair survey which found that at least one-third of people overestimate boat arrivals by 11 times, believing that more than 4,000 arrived annually, while the true 1996 figure was 376. The 'boat people' hysteria re-emerged in 2000 when the number of intercepted boats increased dramatically, often containing 'illligal immigrants' from Afghanistan, Iraq, and so on who were seduced by organized people smugglers. Australia has become a preferred destination for many refugees from war-torn or otherwise inflicted Third World countries willing to risk their lives in this way, but their total numbers are still much lower than in other parts of the Western world in Europe and North America.

9 IDENTITY BLUES

1 Pauline Hanson was reportedly very hurt, and cried, when she was called white trash by anti-racist protesters. For a look at the cultural politics of 'white trash' in the USA, see Wray and Newitz (1997).
2 Such responses are empirically manifest internationally. See e.g. May (1996).

10 LOCAL/GLOBAL NEGOTIATIONS

1 For a recent, quite comprehensive articulation and discussion of this theoretical perspective, see Soja (1996).
2 See also Chambers (1991), which is a book written from the site of the British/Italian borderlands.

3 The project, with co-researcher Jon Stratton, was funded by an Australian Research Council Large Grant.

4 It is notable that the transnational, if not global popularity of so-called 'French theory' has been predicated on a suppression of its origins in the French context, just as the global hegemony of Hollywood has been predicated on an ideological universalization (and therefore decontextualization) of its rootedness in American sensibilities.

5 I should add here that the relative visibility of *Australian* cultural studies in the international cultural studies scene (see e.g. Turner 1993; Frow and Morris 1993) is also due to the hegemony of English as the global language for theory and scholarship. It is significant, for example, that journals such as the *European Journal for Cultural Studies* and *Inter-Asia Cultural Studies* have to be published in English, most likely not the primary language of most of its authors. The politics of the linguistic power relations this situation gives rise to has hardly been addressed. See Ang (1992).

6 As Australia is an island-continent surrounded by sea, the absence of 'real', physical borders with neighbouring nation-states has been a major influence on the sense of geographical isolation and cultural insularity on the Australian psyche. One recurrent border dispute is with Indonesian fishermen, who allegedly regularly illegally enter Australian territorial waters to the north of the country. Whenever these people get caught, they are sent back to where they came from and their boats get confiscated. The constructed 'unrealness' of borders in the Australian imagination is also exemplified by the relegation of refugee detention centres (where illegal Asian 'boat people' are locked behind barbed wire) to the very remote Northwestern far end of the country, away from the 'civilized', modern and densely populated South, especially the Southeast (where cities such as Sydney, Canberra and Melbourne are located). See Neilson (1996) and Hage (1998) on 'ethnic caging'.

7 The dominant contemporary tendency to associate 'race' with 'blackness' needs to be interrogated; even the term 'people of color', used in the United States to design an inclusive category for all racialized people, cannot account for modes of racialization which do not depend on colour signifiers (as in the important case of the Jews). See Stratton (2000).

8 For historical accounts of the Australian colonial construction of the Chinese as an unwanted 'race' see e.g. Markus (1979), Cronin (1982).

11 I'M A FEMINIST BUT . . .

1 In Australian feminism, this trend was evidenced in important publications such as *Intersexions: Gender/Class/Culture/Ethnicity* (Bottomley *et al.* 1991), *Living in the Margins: Racism, Sexism and Feminism in Australia* (Pettman 1992) and *Feminism and the Politics of Difference* (Gunew and Yeatman 1993). Significantly, they all appeared in the early 1990s.

2 On the theoretical importance of emphasizing failure rather than success in communication, see Ang (1996), Chapter 10.

3 For a historical analysis of the construction of this hegemonic male identity in imperial Britain, see C. Hall (1992).

4 A compilation of the international debate on *The Good Woman of Bangkok*, see Berry *et al.* (1997).

5 While most white feminist critics have come out as Madonna enthusiasts, there are exceptions, see, for example, Bordo (1993).

6 See, however, Patton (1993).

7 It should be added that 'whiteness', too, is a structurally impure position, deriving its very meaning from suppressing and othering that which is not white. But while the centre, by virtue of its being the centre, can subsequently repress the marginalized

other in its sense of identity, the margin(alized) always has to live under the shadow of the centre and be constantly reminded of its own marginality.

8 For this kind of interrogation by white feminists in Britain and the USA, see Ware (1992) and Frankenberg (1993).

9 I would suggest that it is for this reason that the scare campaign against indigenous native title relied so much on a populist hysteria focused on the absurd assertion that if indigenous people gain land rights, 'people's backyards' would no longer be safe.

10 In this sense, the theme of 'reconciliation' is more important to the peace of mind of white Australians than to Aboriginal people, for whom reconciliation will never compensate for their permanent displacement from their land. Indeed, the very notion of reconciliation – and the willingness of Aborigines to engage in it – signal their recognition of the permanent presence of white Other on their land.

12 CONCLUSION

1 In white Australian mythology, Truganini was 'the last Tasmanian Aborigine'. Her death in Hobart in 1876 was a source of the commonly held ideological belief that the Aborigines as a people were inevitably doomed to extinction.

BIBLIOGRAPHY

Ahmad, Aijaz (1992) *In Theory: Classes, Nations, Literatures.* London: Verso.

Allon, Fiona (1997) 'Home as Cultural Translation: John Howard's Earlwood', in Ien Ang and Michael Symonds (eds), *Home, Displacement, Belonging.* Communal/Plural 5. Sydney: Research Centre in Intercommunal Studies.

Anderson, Benedict (1991) *Imagined Communities.* 2nd edn, London: Verso.

—— (1998) 'Nationalism, Identity and the World-in-Motion: On the Logics of Seriality', in Pheng Cheah and Bruce Robbins (eds), *Cosmopolitics.* Minneapolis: University of Minnesota Press, pp. 117–133.

Anderson, Ian (1995) 'Re-Claiming TRU-GER-NAN-NER: Decolonising the Symbol', in Penny van Toorn and David English (eds) *Speaking Positions. Aboriginality, Gender and Ethnicity in Australian Cultural Studies.* Melbourne: Victoria University of Technology, pp. 31–42.

Ang, Ien (1996) *Living Room Wars: Rethinking Media Audiences for a Postmodern World.* London: Routledge.

—— (1992) 'Dismantling "Cultural Studies"', *Cultural Studies,* 6 (3): 311–321.

—— (1997) 'Comment on Felski's "The Doxa of Difference: The Uses of Incommensurability', *Signs,* 23 (1): 57–63.

—— (1998) 'Eurocentric Reluctance: Notes Towards a Cultural Studies of "the new Europe"', in Kuan-Hsing Chen (ed.) *Trajectories: Inter-Asia Cultural Studies.* London: Routledge, pp. 87–108.

—— (2001 forthcoming) 'Trapped in Ambivalence: Chinese Indonesians, Victimhood, and the Debris of History', in *Traces: A Multilingual Journal for Cultural Theory,* 2.

Ang, Ien, Chalmers, Sharon, Law, Lisa and Thomas, Mandy (eds) (2000) *Alter/Asians: Asian Australian Identities in Art, Media and Popular Culture.* Sydney: Pluto Press.

Ang, Ien and Stratton, Jon (1995a) 'The Singapore Way of Multiculturalism: Western Concepts/Asian Cultures', in *Sojourn: Journal of Social Issues in Southeast Asia,* 10 (1): 65–89.

—— (1995b) 'Speaking (as) Black British: Race, Nation and Cultural Studies in Britain', in Penny van Toorn and David English (eds), *Speaking Positions: Aboriginality, Gender and Ethnicity in Australian Cultural Studies.* Melbourne: Victoria University of Technology, pp. 14–30.

—— (1996) 'Asianing Australia: Notes Towards a Critical Transnationalism in Cultural Studies', *Cultural Studies,* 6 (3): 16–36.

Anthias, Floya and Yuval-Davis, Nira (1992) *Racialized Boundaries: Race, Nation, Gender, Colour and Class and the Anti-Racist Struggle.* London and New York: Routledge.

211

Anwar Ibrahim (1996) *The Asian Renaissance*. Singapore and Kuala Lumpur: Times Books International.

Appadurai, Arjun (1996a) *Modernity at Large*. Minneapolis: University of Minnesota Press.

—— (1996b) 'Sovereignty without Territoriality: Notes for a Postnational Geography', in Patricia Yaeger (ed.) *The Geography of Identity*. Ann Arbor, MI: The University of Michigan Press, pp. 40–58.

Arnold, Wayne (1998) 'Chinese Diaspora Using Internet to Aid Plight of Brethren Abroad', *Wall Street Journal*, 23 July (reproduced in www.huaren.org).

Anzaldúa, Gloria (1987) *Borderlands/La Frontera: The New Mestiza*. San Francisco: Aunt Lute Books.

Attwood, Bain (1989) *The Making of Aborigines*. Sydney: Allen & Unwin.

Balibar, Etienne (1991) 'The Nation Form: History and Ideology', in Etienne Balibar and Immanuel Wallerstein, *Race, Nation, Class: Ambiguous Identities*. London: Verso.

Bauman, Zygmunt (1991) *Modernity and Ambivalence*. Cambridge: Polity Press.

—— (1993) *Postmodern Ethics*. Oxford: Blackwell.

Benjamin, Geoffrey (1976) 'The Cultural Logic of Singapore's Multiracialism', in R. Hassan (ed.) *Singapore: Society in Transition*. Kuala Lumpur: Oxford University Press.

Bennett, David (ed.) (1998) *Multicultural States*. London and New York: Routledge.

Berry, Chris, Hamilton, Annette and Jayamanne, Laleen (eds) (1997) *The Filmmaker and the Prostitute*. Sydney: Power Publications.

Bhabha, Homi (1990a) *Nation and Narration*. London: Routledge.

—— (1990b) 'The Third Space', in J. Rutherford (ed.) *Identity*. London: Lawrence & Wishart, pp. 207–221.

—— (1994) *The Location of Culture*. London and New York: Routledge.

Blussé, Leonard (1989) *Tribuut aan China*. Amsterdam: Cramwinckel.

Bordo, Susan (1993) '"Material Girl": The Effacements of Postmodern Culture', in Cathy Schwichtenberg (ed.) *The Madonna Connection*. Sydney: Allen & Unwin, pp. 265–290.

Bottomley, Gillian *et al.* (eds) (1991) *Intersexions: Gender/Class/Culture/Ethnicity*. Sydney: Allen & Unwin.

Brah, Avtar (1996) *Cartographies of Diaspora*. London: Routledge.

Brawley, Sean (1995) *The White Peril: Foreign Relations and Asian Immigration to Australasia and North America*. Sydney: University of New South Wales Press.

Brett, Judith (1997) 'The Politics of Grievance', *Australian Review of Books*, May.

Bristow, Joseph (1991) 'Life Stories: Carolyn Steedman's History Writing', *New Formations*, 13 (Spring): 113–131.

Brodkin, Karen (1999) *How Jews Became White Folks and What That Says About America*. New Brunswick, NJ: Rutgers University Press.

Broinowski, Alison (1992) *The Yellow Lady: Australian Impressions of Asia*. Melbourne: University of Oxford Press.

Buci-Glucksmann, Christine (1982) 'Hegemony and Consent', in Anne Showstack Sassoon (ed.) *Approaches to Gramsci*. London: Writers and Readers Publishing Cooperative Society.

Burrell, Steve (1999) 'Forget Recovery: This is an Asian Renaissance', *Sydney Morning Herald*, 14 May.

Butler, Judith (1990) *Gender Trouble: Feminism and the Subversion of Identity*. New York and London: Routledge.

Calhoun, Craig (1994) 'Social Theory and the Politics of Identity', in C. Calhoun (ed.) *Social Theory and the Politics of Identity*. Oxford: Blackwell, pp. 9–36.

Carruthers, Fiona (1997) 'Elusive M-Word Highlights PM's Personal Time Warp', *The Australian*, 12 December.

Castells, Manuel (1997) *The Power of Identity*. Oxford. Blackwell (volume II of *The Information Age: Economy, Society and Culture*).

Castles, Stephen, Kalantzis, Mary, Cope, Bill and Morrissey, Michael (1990) *Mistaken Identity: Multiculturalism and the Demise of Nationalism in Australia*. 2nd edn. Sydney: Pluto Press.

Chambers, Iain (1991) *Border Dialogues*. London: Routledge.

—— (1994) *Migrancy, Culture, Identity*. London: Routledge.

Chambers, Iain and Curti, Lidia (eds) (1996) *The Post-Colonial Question: Common Skies, Divided Horizons*. London: Routledge.

Chan Kwok Bun (ed.) (2000) *Chinese Business Networks: State, Economy and Culture*. Singapore. Prentice-Hall.

Cheah, Pheng (1998) 'Given Culture: Rethinking Cosmopolitical Freedom in Trans nationalism', in Pheng Cheah and Bruce Robbins (eds) *Cosmopolitics*. Minneapolis: University of Minnesota Press, pp. 290–328.

Cheah, Pheng and Robbins, Bruce (eds) (1998) *Cosmopolitics: Thinking and Feeling Beyond the Nation*. Minneapolis: University of Minnesota Press.

Chirot, Daniel (1997) 'Conflicting Identities and the Dangers of Communalism', in Daniel Chirot and Anthony Reid (eds) *Essential Outsiders*. Seattle and London: University of Washington Press, pp. 3–32.

Chirot, Daniel and Reid, Anthony (eds) (1997) *Essential Outsiders: Chinese and Jews in the Modern Transformation of Southeast Asia and Central Europe*. Seattle and London: University of Washington Press.

Chiu, Fred Y.L. (1991) 'The Specificity of the Political on Tiananmen Square, Or a Poetics of the Popular Resistance in Beijing', *Dialectical Anthropology*, 16: 333–347.

Chow, Rey (1991) *Woman and Chinese Modernity*. Minneapolis: University of Minnesota Press.

—— (1993) *Writing Diaspora: Tactics of Intervention in Contemporary Cultural Studies*. Bloomington: Indiana University Press.

—— (1997) 'Can One Say No to China?', *New Literary History*, 28 (1): 147–151.

—— (1998a) 'King Kong in Hong Kong: Watching the "Handover" from the USA', *Social Text*, 55, 16 (2): 93–108.

—— (1998b) 'Introduction: On Chineseness as a Theoretical Problem', *boundary 2*, 25 (3): 1–24.

Chu, Chin-Ning (1995) *The Asian Mind Game: A Westerner's Survival Manual*. Crows Nest: Stealth Productions.

Chua, Beng-Huat (1995) *Communitarian Ideology and Democracy in Singapore*. London: Routledge.

Chun, Allen (1996) 'Fuck Chineseness: On the Ambiguities of Ethnicity as Culture as Identity', *boundary 2*, 23 (2): 111–138.

—— (2001) 'Diasporas of Mind, or Why There Ain't No Black Atlantic in Cultural China', *Communal/Plural: Journal for Transnational and Crosscultural Studies*, 9 (1): 95–110

Clammer, John (1985) *Singapore: Ideology, Society and Culture*. Singapore: Chopman Publishers.

Clifford, James (1992) 'Travelling Cultures', in L. Grossberg, C. Nelson and P. Treichler (eds) *Cultural Studies*, New York: Routledge, pp. 96–111.

—— (1997) *Routes: Travel and Translation in the Late Twentieth Century.* Cambridge, MA: Harvard University Press.

—— (1998) 'Mixed Feelings', in Pheng Cheah and Bruce Robbins (eds), *Cosmopolitics.* Minneapolis: University of Minnesota Press, pp. 362–370.

Cochrane, Peter (1996) 'Race Memory', *Australian Review of Books*, November.

Cohen, Phil (1999) 'In Visible Cities', *Communal/Plural: Journal for Transnational and Crosscultural Studies*, 7 (1): 9–28.

Cohen, Robin (1997) *Global Diasporas: An Introduction.* Seattle: University of Washington Press.

Collishaw, Gillian (1999) *Rednecks, Eggheads and Blackfellas.* Sydney: Allen & Unwin.

Commonwealth of Australia (1999) *A New Agenda for Multicultural Australia*, Canberra: Commonwealth of Australia, December.

Coombes, Annie E. (1994) 'The Recalcitrant Object: Culture Contact and the Question of Hybridity', in Francis Barker, Peter Hulme and Margaret Iversen (eds) *Colonial Discourse/Postcolonial Theory.* Manchester: Manchester University Press, pp. 89–114

Coppel, Charles (1983) *Indonesian Chinese in Crisis.* Kuala Lumpur: Oxford University Press.

Coughlan, James E. and McNamara, Deborah J. (eds) (1997) *Asians in Australia: Patterns of Migration and Settlement.* South Melbourne: Macmillan Education

Cribb, Robert (2000) 'Political Structures and Chinese Business Connections in the Malay World: A Historical Perspective', in Chan Kwok Bun (ed.) *Chinese Business Networks.* Singapore: Prentice-Hall, pp. 176–192.

Cronin, K. (1982) *Colonial Casualties: Chinese in Early Victoria.* Melbourne: Melbourne University Press.

Curthoys, Ann (1993) 'Feminism, Citizenship and National Identity', *Feminist Review*, 44: 19–38.

—— (1999) 'Whose Home? Expulsion, Exodus and Exile in White Australian Historical Mythology', *Journal of Australian Studies*, 16: 1–18.

Curthoys, Ann and Johnson, Carol (1998) 'Articulating the Future and the Past: Gender, Race and Globalisation in One Nation Discourse', *Hecate*, 24 (2): 97–114.

Curthoys, Ann and Markus, Andrew (eds) (1978) *Who Are Our Enemies? Racism and the Australian Working Class.* Neutral Bay: Hale & Iremonger.

Davidson, Alistair (1997) *From Subject to Citizen.* Cambridge: Cambridge University Press.

De Lauretis, Teresa (1988) 'Displacing Hegemonic Discourses: Reflections on Feminist Theory in the 1980s', *Inscriptions*, 3–4: 127–144.

De Lepervanche, Marie (1980), 'From Race to Ethnicity', *Australian and New Zealand Journal of Sociology*, 16 (1).

Dijkink, Gertjan (1996) *National Identity and Geopolitical Visions.* London: Routledge.

Dikötter, Frank (1992) *The Discourse of Race in Modern China.* Stanford, CA: Stanford University Press.

Dirlik, Arif (1994a) 'The Postcolonial Aura: Third World Criticism in the Age of Global Capitalism', *Critical Inquiry*, 20 (2): 328–356.

—— (1994b) *After the Revolution: Waking to Global Capitalism.* Hanover, NH: Wesleyan University Press.

Donald, James and Rattansi, Ali (eds) (1992) *'Race', Culture and Difference.* London: Sage.

Duara, P. (1997) 'Nationalists Among Transnationals: Overseas Chinese and the Idea of China, 1900–1911', in Aihwa Ong and Donald Nonini (eds) *Ungrounded Empires: The Cultural Politics of Modern Chinese Transnationalism.* New York: Routledge.

Ebo, Bosah (ed.) (1998) *Cyberghetto or Cybertopia? Race, Class, and Gender on the Internet*. Westport, CT and London: Praeger.

Evans, Raymond, Moore, Clive, Saunders, Kay and Jamison, Bryan (1997) *1901. Our Future's Past*. Sydney: Macmillan.

Fanon, Frantz (1970) *Black Skin White Masks*. London: Paladin.

Featherstone, M. (1996) 'Localism, Globalism, and Cultural Identity', in R. Wilson and W. Dissanayake (eds) *Global/Local*. Durham, NC: Duke University Press, pp. 46–77.

Felski, Rita (1997) 'The Doxa of Difference', *Signs*, 23 (1): 1–22.

FitzGerald, Stephen (1975) *China and the Overseas Chinese*. Cambridge: Cambridge University Press.

—— (1997) *Is Australia an Asian Country?* Sydney: Allen & Unwin.

Fitzpatrick, John (1997) 'European Settler Colonialism and National Security Ideologies in Australian History', in Richard Leaver and Dave Cox (eds) *Middling, Meddling, Muddling: Issues in Australian Foreign Policy*. St Leonards: Allen & Unwin, pp. 91–119.

Flax, Jane (1990a) 'Postmodernism and Gender Relations in Feminist Theory', in Linda Nicholson (ed.) *Feminism/Postmodernism*. New York: Routledge, pp. 39–62.

—— (1990b) *Thinking Fragments: Psychoanalysis, Feminism and Postmodernism in the Contemporary West*. Berkeley, CA: University of California Press.

Frankenberg, Ruth (1993) *White Women, Race Matters: The Social Construction of Whiteness*. Minneapolis: University of Minnesota Press.

Freeman, Gary P. and James Jupp (eds) (1992) *Nations of Immigrants: Australia, the United States and International Migration*. Melbourne: Oxford University Press.

Friedman, Jonathan (1997) 'Global Crises, the Struggle for Cultural Identity and Intellectual Porkbarrelling: Cosmopolitans versus Locals, Ethnics and Nationals in an Era of De-hegemonisation', in Pnina Werbner and Tariq Modood (eds) *Debating Cultural Hybridity*. London: Zed Books, pp. 70–89.

Frow, John (1995) *Cultural Studies and Cultural Value*. Oxford: Oxford University Press.

Frow, John and Morris, Meaghan (eds) (1993) *Australian Cultural Studies: A Reader*. St Leonards: Allen & Unwin.

Fukuyama, Francis (1998) 'Asian Values and the Asian Crisis', *Commentary*, February.

Garcia Canclini, Nestor (1995) *Hybrid Cultures*. Minneapolis: University of Minnesota Press.

—— (2000) 'The State of War and the State of Hybridisation', in P. Gilroy, L. Grossberg and A. McRobbie (eds) *Without Guarantees: In Honour of Stuart Hall*. London: Verso, pp. 38–52.

Garnaut, R.G. (1989) *Australia and The Northeast Asian Ascendancy*. Canberra: Australian Government Publishing Service.

Gates, Henry Louis (ed.) (1986) *'Race', Writing, Difference*. Chicago: University of Chicago Press.

Geertz, Clifford (1988) *Works and Lives: The Anthropologist as Author*. Cambridge: Polity Press.

Gibney, Frank (1992) *The Pacific Century: America and Asia in a Changing World*. New York: Charles Scribner's Sons.

Gilroy, Paul (1987) *There Ain't No Black in the Union Jack*. London: Hutchinson.

—— (1990/1) '"It Ain't Where You're From, It's Where Your're At . . .": The Dialectics of Diasporic Identification', *Third Text*, 13, Winter: 3–16.

—— (1993a) *The Black Atlantic*. London: Verso.

—— (1993b) *Small Act: Thoughts on the Politics of Black Cultures*. London: Serpent's Tail.

—— (2000) *Against Race: Imagining Political Culture Beyond the Color Line*. Cambridge, MA: Belknap Press of Harvard University Press.

Gilroy, Paul, Grossberg, Lawrence and McRobbie, Angela (eds) (2000) *Without Guarantees: In Honour of Stuart Hall*. London: Verso.

Giroux, Henry (1992) 'Resisting Difference: Cultural Studies and the Discourse of Critical Pedagogy', in L. Grossberg, C. Nelson and P. Treichler (eds) *Cultural Studies*. New York: Routledge, pp. 199–211.

Goldsworthy, David (1997) 'The British Colonial Order, 1948–60', in David Lowe (ed.) *Australia and the End of Empires*. Geelong: Deakin University Press, pp. 137–160.

Gómez-Peña, Guillermo (1996) *The New World Border*. San Francisco: City Lights.

Gopalakrishnan, Raju (1998) 'Ethnic Chinese Hit again in Indonesia Strife', Reuters, 7 May (reproduced in www.huaren.org).

Ghosh, Amitav (1989) 'The Diaspora in Indian Culture', *Public Culture*, 2 (1): 73–78.

Godley, Michael R. and Coppel, Charles (1990) 'The Indonesian Chinese in Hong Kong: A Preliminary Report on a Minority in Transition', *Issues and Studies: A Journal of Chinese Studies and International Affairs*, July: 94–108.

Gray, Geoffrey and Winter, Christine (eds) (1997) *The Resurgence of Racism: Howard, Hanson and the Race Debate*. Calyton, Vic: Monash Publications in History.

Grossberg, Lawrence (1996a) 'History, Politics and Postmodernism: Stuart Hall and Cultural Studies', in D. Morley and K.-H. Chen (eds) *Stuart Hall: Critical Dialogues*. London and New York: Routledge, pp. 151–173.

—— (1996b) 'The Space of Culture, the Power of Space', in I. Chambers and L. Curti (eds) *The Post-Colonial Question*. London: Routledge, pp. 169–188.

—— (ed.) (1996c) 'On Postmodernism and Articulation: An Interview with Stuart Hall', in D. Morley and K.-H. Chen (eds) *Stuart Hall: Critical Dialogues*. London: Routledge, pp. 131–150.

Grossberg, Lawrence, Cary Nelson and Treichler, Paula (eds) (1992) *Cultural Studies*. New York: Routledge.

Gunew, Sneja (1993) 'Feminism and the Politics of Irreducible Differences: Multi-culturalism/Ethnicity/Race' in S. Gunew and A. Yeatman (eds) *Feminism and the Politics of Difference*. Sydney: Allen & Unwin, pp. 1–19.

Gunew, Sneja and Yeatman, Anna (eds) (1993) *Feminism and the Politics of Difference*. Sydney: Allen & Unwin.

Gunn, Janet V. (1982) *Autobiography: Towards a Poetics of Experience*. Philadelphia: University of Pennsylvania Press.

Habermas, Jürgen (1984) *The Theory of Communicative Action*. London: Heinemann Educational.

Hage, Ghassan (1994) 'Locating Multiculturalism's Other', *New Formations*, 24: 19–34.

—— (1998) *White Nation: Fantasies of White Supremacy in a Multicultural Society*. Sydney: Pluto Press.

Hall, Catherine (1992) *White, Male and Middle Class*. Oxford: Polity Press.

Hall, Richard (1998) *Black Armband Days*. Sydney: Vintage.

Hall, Stuart (1988) *The Hard Road to Renewal*. London: Verso.

—— (1989) 'The Meaning of New Times', in Stuart Hall and Martin Jacques (eds) *New Times*. London: Lawrence and Wishart, pp. 116–133.

—— (1990) 'Cultural Identity and Diaspora', in Jonathan Rutherford (ed.) *Identity: Community, Culture, Difference*. London: Lawrence & Wishart, pp. 222–237.

—— (1992) 'Cultural Studies and its Theoretical Legacies', in L. Grossberg, C. Nelson and P. Treichler (eds) *Cultural Studies*, New York: Routledge, pp. 277–285.

—— (1993a) 'Culture, Community, Nation', *Cultural Studies*, 7 (3): 349–363.

—— (1993b) 'Minimal Selves', in Ann Gray and Jim McGuigan (eds) *Studying Culture*. London: Edward Arnold, pp. 134–138.

—— (1996a) 'The Problem of Ideology: Marxism Without Guarantees', in David Morley and Kuan-Hsing Chen (eds) *Stuart Hall: Critical Dialogues*. London: Routledge, pp. 25–46.

—— (1996b) 'For Allon White: Metaphors of Transformation', in D. Morley and K-H. Chen (eds) *Stuart Hall: Critical Dialogues*, London: Routledge, pp. 287–308.

(1996c) 'Cultural Studies and the Politics of Internationalisation', in D. Morley and K-H. Chen (eds) *Stuart Hall: Critical Dialogues*, London: Routledge, pp. 392–410.

—— (1996d) 'New Ethnicities', in D. Morley and K-H. Chen (eds) *Stuart Hall: Critical Dialogues*, London: Routledge, pp. 441–449.

—— (1996e) 'What is this "Black" in Black Popular Culture?', in D. Morley and K-H. Chen (eds) *Stuart Hall: Critical Dialogues*, London: Routledge, pp. 465–475.

—— (1996f) 'When Was "The Post-Colonial"? Thinking at the Limit', in I. Chambers and L. Curti (eds) *The Post-Colonial Question*, London: Routledge, pp. 242–260.

—— (1996g) 'Introduction: Who Needs "Identity"?' in S. Hall and P. Du Gay (eds) *Questions of Cultural Identity*, London: Sage, pp. 1–17.

—— (1998) 'Subjects in History: Making Diasporic Identities', in Wahneema Lubiano (ed.) *The House that Race Built*. New York: Vintage Books, pp. 289–300.

Hall, Stuart and du Gay, Paul (eds) (1996) *Questions of Cultural Identity*. London: Sage.

Han Fook Kwang (1999) 'White Envy: Don't Rush to Condemn the Young', *The Straits Times*, 18 December.

Hannerz, Ulf (1996) *Transnational Connections*. London: Routledge.

Hanson, Pauline (1997a) *The Truth, On Asian Immigration, The Aboriginal Question, the Gun Debate and the Future of Australia*, Ipwich: no publisher.

—— (1997b), *Parliamentary Speech*, 3 September.

Haraway, Donna (1988) 'Situated Knowledges: The Science Question in Feminism and the Privilege of Partial Perspective', *Feminist Studies*, 14 (3): 575–599.

Harding, Harry (1993) 'The Concept of "Greater China": Themes, Variations and Reservations', *China Quarterly*, 136: 661–686

Hay, David (1996) *Claiming a Continent*. Sydney: Angus & Robertson.

Heryanto, Ariel (1998a) 'Ethnic Identities and Erasure: Chinese Indonesians in Public Culture', in Joel S. Kahn (ed.) *Southeast Asian Identities*.

—— (1998b) 'Flaws of Riot Media Coverage', *The Jakarta Post*, 15 July.

—— (1999) 'Race, Rape and Reporting', in Arief Budiman, Barbara Hatley and Damien Kingsbury (eds) *Reformasi: Crisis and Change in Indonesia*. Melbourne: Monash Asia Institute, pp. 299–334.

Ho, Ruth (1975) *Rainbow Round My Shoulder*. Singapore: Eastern Universities Press.

Ho, Chooi Hon and Coughlan, James (1997) 'The Chinese in Australia: Immigrants from the People's Republic of China, Malaysia, Singapore, Taiwan, Hong Kong and Macau', in J. Coughlan and D. J. McNamara (eds), *Asians in Australia*. South Melbourne: Macmillan Education, pp. 120–170.

Hobsbawm, Eric (1990) *Nations and Nationalism Since 1780: Programme, Myth, Reality*. Cambridge: Cambridge University Press.

Hoffman, Eva (1989) *Lost in Translation*. Harmondsworth: Penguin.

Hollinger, David (1995) *Postethnic America: Beyond Multiculturalism*. New York: Basic Books.

hooks, bell (1990) *Yearning: Race, Gender and Cultural Politics*. Boston: South End Press.

—— (1992) *Black Looks: Race and Representation*. Boston: South End Press.

Howard, John (1995a) 'The Role of Government: A Modern Liberal Approach.' National Lecture Series. Menzies Research Centre.

—— (1995b) 'Politics and Patriotism'. Grand Hyatt Hotel, Melbourne, 13 December.

—— (1997) 'Address at the Launch of the National Multicultural Advisory Council Issues Paper Multicultural Australia: The Way Forward', Melbourne Town Hall, 11 December.

Hsia, C.T. (1971) 'Obsession with China: The Moral Burden of Modern Chinese Literature', in *A History of Modern Chinese Fiction*, 2nd edn, New Haven, CT.: Yale University Press, pp. 533–554.

Huaren (1998a) 'Internet Power, the Third Force, and the Global Huaren', Editorial, 31 July www.huaren.org.

—— (1998b) 'Compassion, Humanity, Solidarity – Global Huarens Respond', Editorial, 14 August www.huaren.org.

—— (1998c) 'Internetocracy: Let a Hundred Flowers Bloom; Let a Hundred Ideas Contend', Editorial, 4 Sept www.huaren.org.

Huntington, Samuel P. (1993) 'The Clash of Civilizations', *Foreign Affairs*, 72 (3): 22–49.

—— (1997) *The Clash of Civilizations and the Remaking of the World Order*. New York: Touchstone.

Hutnyk, John (1997) 'Adorno at Womad: South Asian Crossovers and the Limits of Hybridity Talk', in P. Werbner and T. Modood (eds) *Debating Cultural Hybridity*, London and New York: Zed Books, pp. 106–136.

Ignatiev, Noel (1996) *How the Irish Became White*. New York: Routledge.

Immigration Reform Group (1962) *Control or the Colour Bar? A Proposal for Change in Australian Immigration Policy*. Melbourne: Melbourne University Press.

—— (1975) *Australia and the Non-White Migrant*. Melbourne: Melbourne University Press.

Inglis, Ken (1991) 'Multiculturalism and National Identity', in Charles Price (ed.) *Australian National Identity*. Canberra: Australian Academy of the Social Sciences.

Inglis, Christine (1998) 'Australia', in Lynn Pan (ed.) *The Encyclopedia*, Singapore: Archipelago Press, pp. 274–285.

Inglis, Christine, Gunasekaren, S., Sullivan, G. and Wu, Chung-Tong (eds) (1996) *Asians in Australia: The Dynamics of Migration and Settlement*, St Leonards: Allen & Unwin.

Ishihara, Shintaro (1991) *The Japan That Can Say 'No'*. Trans. Frank Baldwin. New York: Simon & Schuster.

Johnson, Carol (1997) 'John Howard and the Revenge of the Mainstream: Some Implications for Concepts of Identity', in G. Crowder (ed.) *Australasian Political Studies 1997: Proceedings of the 1997 APSA Conference*. Adelaide: Department of Politics, Flinders University.

Jolly, Margaret (1991) 'The Politics of Difference: Feminism, Colonialism and the Decolonisation of Vanuatu', in G. Bottomley *et al.* (eds) *Intersexions*. Sydney: Allen & Unwin, pp. 52 74.

Jupp, James (1991) *Immigration*. Melbourne: Oxford University Press.

Kaplan, Caren (1996) *Questions of Travel: Postmodern Discourse of Displacement*. Durham, NC and London: Duke University Press.

Kelly, Paul (1992) *The End of Certainty: The Story of the 1980s*. Sydney: Allen & Unwin.

Keith, Michael and Pile, Steve (eds) (1993) *Place and the Politics and Identity*. London and New York: Routledge.

Kim, Elaine (1993) 'Preface', in Jessica Hagedoorn (ed.) *Charlie Chan is Dead*. New York: Penguin.

Kirby, Vicki (1993) '"Feminisms, Reading, Postmodernisms": Rethinking Complicity', in S. Gunew and A. Yeatman (ed.) *Feminism and the Politics of Difference*, Sydney: Allen & Unwin, pp. 20–34.

Kristeva, Julia (1991) *Strangers to Ourselves*. New York: Columbia University Press.

Kwok, Yenni (1998) 'How Indonesian Am I?, *Asiaweek*, 25 May.

—— (1999) 'A Daring Leap of Faith', *Asiaweek*, 16 July.

Kyriakopoulos, Vikki (1996) 'Mixed Blessings', *The Bulletin*, 23/30 January.

Laclau, Ernesto and Mouffe, Chantal (1983) *Hegemony and Socialist Strategy*. London: Verso.

Lawrence, Peter (1983) *Australian Opinion on the Indo-Chinese Influx 1975–1979*. Centre for the Study of Australian-Asian Relations, Griffith University, Brisbane, April (Research Paper No. 24).

Lawson, Sylvia (1983) *The Archibald Paradox*. Harmondsworth: Penguin.

Lee, Leo Ou-fan (1994) 'On the Margins of Chinese Discourse: Some Personal Thoughts on the Cultural Meaning of the Periphery', in W. Tu (ed.) *The Living Tree*, Stanford, CA: Stanford University Press, pp. 221–244.

Lewis, Martin W. and Wigen, Kären E. (1997) *The Myth of Continents: A Critique of Metageography*. Berkeley, CA: University of California Press.

Liu, Hong (1998) 'Old Linkages, New Networks: The Globalization of Overseas Chinese Voluntary Associations and its Implications', *China Quarterly*, 155 (September): 582–609.

Lowe, David (ed.) (1997) *Australia and the End of Empires*. Geelong: Deakin University Press.

Lowe, Lisa (1996) *Immigrant Acts: On Asian American Cultural Politics*. Durham, NC and London: Duke University Press.

Luke, Carmen (1994) 'White Women in Interracial Families: Reflections on Hybridization, Feminine Identities, and Racialized Othering', *Feminist Issues* 14 (2): 49–72.

McGregor, Russell (1997) *Imagined Destinies: Aboriginal Australians and the Doomed Race Theory, 1880–1939*. Melbourne: Melbourne University Press.

MacKerras, Colin (1991) *Western Images of China*. Hong Kong: Oxford University Press.

Mackie, J.A.C. (ed.) (1976) *The Chinese in Indonesia*. Honolulu: The University of Hawaii Press in association with The Australian Institute of International Affairs.

Mackie, Jamie (1997) 'The Politics of Asian Immigration', in J. Coughlan and P. J. McNamara (eds) *Asians in Australia*, South Melbourne: Macmillan Education, pp. 10–48.

McLennan, Gregor (1995) *Pluralism*. Buckingham: Open University Press.

Mahathir Mohamad (1999) *A New Deal for Asia*. Subang Jaya: Pelanduk Press.

Mahathir Mohamad and Shitaro Ishihara (1995) *The Voice of Asia*. Tokyo: Kodansha International.

Mahbubani, Kishore (1998) *Can Asians Think?* Singapore and Kuala Lumpur: Times Books International.

Mani, Lata (1992) 'Cultural Theory, Colonial Texts: Reading Eyewitness Accounts of Widow Burning', in L. Grossberg, C. Nelson and P. Treichler (eds) *Cultural Studies*, New York: Routledge, pp. 392–404.

Markus, Andrew (1979) *Fear and Hatred: Purifying Australia and California, 1850–1901*. Sydney: Hale & Iremonger.

—— (1988) 'How Australians See Each Other', in The Committee to Advise on Australia's Immigration Policies, *Immigration: A Commitment to Australia. Consultants' Reports*. Canberra: Australian Government Publishing Service.

Martin, Jeannie (1991) 'Multiculturalism and Feminism', in G. Bottomley *et al.* (eds) *Intersexions*, Sydney: Allen & Unwin, pp. 110–131.

Massey, Doreen (1994) *Space, Place and Gender*. Oxford: Polity Press.

May, Jon (1996) 'Globalization and the Politics of Place: Place and Identity in an Inner London Neighbourhood', *Transactions of the Institute of British Geographers*, 21 (2): 194–215.

Mercer, Kobena (1994) *Welcome to the Jungle: New Positions in Black Cultural Studies*. London and New York: Routledge.

—— (2000) 'A Sociography of Diaspora', in P. Gilroy, L. Grossberg and A. McRobbie (eds) *Without Guarantees: In Honour of Stuart Hall*. London: Verso, pp. 233–244.

Miyoshi, Masao (1996) 'A Borderless World? From Colonialism to Transnationalism and the Decline of the Nation-State', in R. Wilson and W. Dissanayake (eds) *Global/Local*, Durhan, NC: Duke University Press, pp. 78–106.

Mohanty, Chandra (1984) 'Under Western Eyes: Feminist Scholarship and Colonial Discourses', *boundary* 2, 13 (1): 333–358.

—— (1989) 'On Race and Voice: Challenges for Liberal Education in the 1990s', *Cultural Critique*, 14: 179–208.

—— *et al.* (eds) (1991) *Third World Women and the Politics of Feminism*. Bloomington: Indiana University Press.

Morley, David and Robins, Kevin (1995) *Spaces of Identity: Global Media, Electronic Landscapes and Cultural Boundaries*. London and New York: Routledge.

Morley, David and Chen, Kuan-Hsing (1996) *Stuart Hall: Critical Dialogues*. London and New York: Routledge.

Morris, Meaghan (1992) 'Afterthoughts on "Australianism"', *Cultural Studies*, 6 (3): 468–475.

—— (1998a) 'White Panic or Mad Max and the Sublime', in Kuan-Hsing Chen (ed.) *Trajectories: Inter-Asia Cultural Studies*. London and New York: Routledge.

—— (1998b) *Too Soon Too Late: History in Popular Culture*. Bloomington: Indiana University Press.

Morris, Meaghan and Muecke, Stephen (1995) 'Editorial', *UTS Review*, 1 (1): 1–4.

Naficy, Hamid (1993) *The Making of Exile Cultures*. Minneapolis: University of Minnesota Press.

Napaul, V.S. (1980) *A Bend in the River*, Harmondsworth: Penguin.

Naisbitt, John (1997) *Megatrends Asia: The Eight Asian Megatrends That Are Changing The World*. London: Nicholas Brealey Publishing.

National Inquiry into the Separation of Aboriginal and Torres Strait Islander Children from their Families (1997) *Bringing Them Home: Report of the National Inquiry into the Separation of Aboriginal and Torres Strait Islander Children from Their Families* Sydney: Human Rights and Equal Opportunity Commission.

National Multicultural Advisory Council (1997) *Multicultural Australia: The Way Forward.* Canberra: AGPS.

—— (1999) *Australian Multiculturalism for a New Century: Towards Inclusiveness.* Canberra: AGPS.

Neilson, Brett (1996) 'Threshold Procedures: "Boat People" in South Florida and Western Australia', *Critical Arts: A Journal of Cultural Studies*, 10 (2): 21–40.

Niranjana, Tejaswini (1992) *Siting Translation: History, Post-Structuralism and the Colonial Context.* Berkeley, CA: University of California Press.

Nonini, Donald and Ong, Aihwa (1997) 'Chinese Transnationalism as an Alternative Modernity', in A. Ong and D. Nonini (eds), *Ungrounded Empires*, New York: Routledge, pp. 3–36.

Novak, Michael (1972) *The Rise of the Unmeltable Ethnics. Politics and Culture in the Seventies.* New York: Macmillan.

Ong, Aihwa (1988) 'Colonialism and Modernity: Feminist Re-presentations of Women in Non-Western Societies', *Inscriptions*, 3–4: 79–93.

—— (1999) *Flexible Citizenship.* Durham, NC and London: Duke University Press.

Ong, Aihwa and Nonini, Donald (eds) (1997) *Ungrounded Empires: The Cultural Politics of Modern Chinese Transnationalism.* New York: Routledge.

Ouyang, Yu (1997) 'Lost in the Translation', *Australian Review of Books*, 2 (9): 10–11, 35.

Palimbo-Liu, David (1999) *Asian/American: Historical Crossings of a Racial Frontier.* Stanford, CA: Stanford University Press.

Pan, Lynn (1990) *Sons of the Yellow Emperor: The Story of the Overseas Chinese.* London: Mandarin.

—— (ed.) (1998) *The Encyclopedia of the Chinese Overseas.* Singapore: Archipelago Press.

Parker, David (1995) *Through Different Eyes: The Cultural Identities of Young Chinese People in Britain.* Aldershot: Avebury.

Patton, Cindy (1993) 'Embodying Subaltern Memory: Kinesthesia and the Problematics of Gender and Race', in C. Schwichtenberg (ed.) *The Madonna Connection*, Sydney: Allen & Unwin, pp. 81–106.

Pauline Hanson's One Nation (1998) *Immigration, Population and Social Cohesion Policy Document*, July.

Pettman, Jan Jindy (1992) *Living in the Margins: Racism, Sexism and Feminism in Australia* Sydney: Allen & Unwin.

Phelan, Amanda (1997) 'Boat Figures Way Out', *Sydney Morning Herald*, 9 July.

Pratt, Marie-Louise (1992) *Imperial Eyes: Travel Writing and Transculturation.* London and New York: Routledge.

Probyn, Elspeth (1992) 'Technologizing the Self', in L. Grossberg, C. Nelson and P. Treichler (eds) *Cultural Studies*, New York: Routledge, pp. 501–511.

Public Culture (1989) 'Editors' Comment: On Moving Targets', 2 (1): 1–4.

Radhakrishnan, R. (1987) 'Ethnic Identity and Poststructuralist Difference', *Cultural Critique*, 7: 199–220.

—— (1996) *Diasporic Mediations: Between Home and Location.* Minneapolis: University of Minnesota Press.

Reid, Anthony (1997) 'Entrepreneurial Minorities, Nationalism and the State', in
 D. Chirot and A. Reid (eds) *Essential Outsiders*. Seattle and London: University of
 Washington Press, pp. 33–71.

Reid, V. (1993) 'Vietnamese girl', *Fremantle Herald*, 9 October.

Reynolds, Henry (1996) *Aboriginal Sovereignty: Reflections on Race, State and Nation*.
 Leonards, NSW: Allen & Unwin.

Ricklefs, M.C. (1985) 'Why Asians?', in Andrew Markus and M.C. Ricklefs (eds)
 Surrender Australia?, Sydney: Allen & Unwin.

Robbins, Bruce (1993) *Secular Vocations: Intellectuals, Professionalism, Culture*. London
 and New York: Verso.

—— (1999) *Feeling Global: Internationalism in Distress*. New York: New York University
 Press.

Robertson, Roland (1992) *Globalization*. London: Sage.

Rolls, Eric (1996) *Citizens*. St Lucia: University of Queenslands Press.

Rothwell, Nicholas (1997) 'Pauline's People', *The Weekend Australian*, 17–18 May.

Rushdie, Salman (1991) *Imaginary Homelands*. London: Granta Books.

Russo, Ann (1991) '"We Cannot Live Without our Lives": White Women, Antiracism
 and Feminism', in C. Mohanty (ed.) *Feminism and Third World Women*, Bloomington: Indiana University Press.

Rutherford, Jonathan (ed.) (1990) *Identity: Community, Culture, Difference*, London:
 Lawrence & Wishart.

Safran, William (1991) 'Diasporas in Modern Societies: Myths of Homeland and Return',
 Diaspora, 1 (1): 3–7.

Said, Edward (1993) *Culture and Imperialism*. London: Chatto & Windus.

Sakai, Naoki (1989) 'Modernity and Its Critique: The Problem of Universalism and
 Particularism', in Masao Miyoshi and H.D. Harootunian (eds) *Postmodernism and
 Japan*. Durham, NC and London: Duke University Press.

Sassen, Saskia (1991) *The Global City*. Princeton: Princeton University Press.

Schech, Susanne and Haggis, Jane (2000) 'Migrancy, Whiteness and the Settler Self
 in Contemporary Australia', in John Docker and Gerhard Fischer (eds) *Race, Colour
 and Identity in Australia and New Zealand*. Sydney: University of New South Wales
 Press, pp. 231–239.

Schlosstein, Steven (1989) *The End of the American Century*. Chicago, ILL: Congdon &
 Weed.

Schwichtenberg, Cathy (ed.) (1993) *The Madonna Connection: Representational Politics,
 Subcultural Identities and Cultural Theory*. Sydney: Allen & Unwin.

Scott, David (2000) 'The Permanence of Pluralism', in P. Gilroy, L. Grossberg and
 A. McRobbie (eds) *Without Guarantees*, London: Verso, pp. 282–301.

Sheridan, Greg (ed.) (1995) *Living with Dragons: Australia Confronts Its Asian Destiny*.
 St. Leonards: Allen & Unwin with Mobil Oil Australia.

—— (1999) *Asian Values, Western Dreams. Understanding the New Asia*. St. Leonards:
 Allen & Unwin.

Shiraishi, Takashi (1997) 'Anti-Sinicism in Java's New Order', in D. Chirot and A. Reid
 (eds) *Essential Outsiders*, Seattle and London: University of Washington Press,
 pp. 187–207.

Shohat, Ella (1992) 'Notes on the Postcolonial', *Social Text*, 31/32: 99–113.

Slack, Jennifer Daryl (1996) 'Articulation', in D. Morley and K-H. Chen (eds) *Stuart
 Hall: Critical Dialogues*. London: Routledge, pp. 112–127.

222

Soja, Edward (1996) *Thirdspace: Journeys to Los Angeles and Other Real-and-Imagined Places*. Oxford: Blackwell.

Sollors, Werner (1986) *Beyond Ethnicity*. New York and Oxford: Oxford University Press.

Song, Xianlin and Sigley, Gary (2000) 'Middle Kingdom Mentalities: Chinese Visions of National Characteristics in the 1990s', *Communal/Plural: Journal of Transnational and Crosscultural Studies*, 8 (1): 47–64.

Spelman, Elizabeth (1988) *Inessential Woman: Problems of Exclusion in Feminist Thought*. Boston: Beacon Press.

Spillman, Lyn (1997) *Nation and Commemoration: Creating National Identities in the United States and Australia*. Cambridge: Cambridge University Press.

Spivak, Gayatri Chakravorty (1987) *In Other Worlds*. London: Routledge.

—— (1990) *The Post-Colonial Critic*. Ed. Sarah Harasym. New York and London: Routledge.

Steedman, Carolyn (1986) *Landscape for a Good Woman*. London: Virago.

Straits Times, The (1998) 'Tragedy and Technology Makes Overseas Chinese UNITE', 20 August.

—— (1999) 'White Envy Shocks Polster', 15 December.

—— (2000) 'Speak Mandarin Campaign Goes to the Movies', 12 September.

Stratton, Jon (1998) *Race Daze: Australia in Identity Crisis*. Sydney: Pluto Press Australia.

—— (2000) *Coming Out Jewish*. London and New York: Routledge.

Stratton, Jon and Ang, Ien (1996) 'On the Impossibility of a Global Cultural Studies: "British" Cultural Studies in an International Frame', in D. Morley and K-H. Chen (eds) *Stuart Hall: Critical Dialogues*. London: Routledge, pp. 361–391.

—— (1998) 'Multicultural Imagined Communities: Cultural Difference and National Identity in the USA and Australia', in David Bennett (ed.) *Multicultural States: Rethinking Difference and Identity*. London: Routledge, pp. 135–162.

Sun, Wanning (2000) 'Internet, Memory, and the Chinese Diaspora: The Case of the Nanjing Massacre', *New Formations*, 40 (Spring): 30–48.

Suryadinata, Leo (1975) *Pribumi Indonesians, the Chinese Minority and China*. Kuala Lumpur: Heinemann.

—— (ed.) (1979) *Political Thinking of the Indonesian Chinese 1900–1977: A Sourcebook*. Singapore: Singapore University Press.

—— (ed.) (1997) *Ethnic Chinese as Southeast Asians*. Singapore: Institute of Southeast Asian Studies.

—— (1998) 'Quo Vadis, Indonesian Chinese?', *The Straits Times*, 25 February (reproduced in www.huaren.org).

Sydney Morning Herald (1997) 'Hanson: PM Has a Duty', Editorial, 6 May.

—— (1998) 'Leader Flees as Police and Protesters Fight', 23 July.

Tan, Mely G. (1997) 'The Ethnic Chinese in Indonesia: Issues of Identity', in L. Suryadinata (ed.) *Ethnic Chinese as Southeast Asians*. Singapore: Institute of Southeast Asian Studies, pp. 33–65.

Tanaka, Stefan (1993) *Japan's Orient: Rendering Pasts into History*. Berkeley and Los Angeles: University of California Press.

Taylor, Charles (1992) *Multiculturalism and the Politics of Recognition*. Princeton, NJ: Princeton University Press.

Tejapira, Kasian (1997) 'Imagined Uncommunity: The Loskjin Middle Class and Thai Official Nationalism', in D. Chirot and A. Reid (eds) *Essential Outsiders*, Seattle and London: University of Washington Press.

223

Ten, Chin Liew (1993) 'Liberalism and Multiculturalism', in Gordon Frank *et al.* (eds) *Multiculturalism, Difference and Postmodernism*. Melbourne: Longman Cheshire.

Terrill, Ross (1996) 'Is APEC worth the worry?', *Sydney Morning Herald*, 21 November.

Theophanous, Andrew (1995) *Understanding Multiculturalism and Australian Identity.* Melbourne: Elikia Books.

Thomas, Nicholas (1996) 'Cold Fusion', *American Anthropologist*, 98 (1): 9–25.

Thung, Ju-lan (1998) 'Identities in flux: young Chinese in Jakarta', PhD thesis, La Trobe University.

Tölölyan, Khachig (1991) 'The Nation-State and its Others: In Lieu of a Preface', *Diaspora*, 1 (1): 3–7.

—— (1996) 'Rethinking Diaspora(s): Stateless Power in the Transnational Moment', *Diaspora*, 5 (1): 3–36.

Torgovnick, Marianna (1994) *Crossing Ocean Parkway.* Chicago: Chicago University Press.

Trainor, Luke (1994) *British Imperialism and Australian Nationalism*, Cambridge: Cambridge University Press.

Trinh, Minh-ha (1991) *When the Moon Waxes Red*. New York and London: Routledge.

Tu, Wei-ming (ed.) (1994a) *The Living Tree: The Changing Meaning of Being Chinese Today*. Stanford, CA: Stanford University Press.

—— (1994b), 'Preface to the Stanford Edition', in Tu Wei-ming (ed.) *The Living Tree*, Stanford, CA: Stanford University Press, pp. v–x.

—— (1994c) 'Cultural China: The Periphery as the Center', in Tu Wei-ming (ed.) *The Living Tree*, Stanford, CA: Stanford University Press, pp. 1–34.

Turner, Graeme (ed.) (1993) *Nation, Culture, Text.* London: Routledge.

—— (1997) 'Two Faces of Australian Nationalism', *The Sydney Morning Herald*, 25 January.

Viviani, Nancy (1996) *The Indochinese in Australia 1975–1995: From Burnt Boats to Barbecues.* Melbourne: Oxford University Press.

Vogel, Ezra (1979) *Japan as Number One: Lessons for America*. Tokyo: Charles Tuttle Co.

Walker, David (1997) 'Australia as Asia', in W. Hudson and G. Bolton (eds) *Creating Australia: Changing Australian History*. St. Leonards: Allen & Unwin, pp. 131–141.

—— (1999) *Anxious Nation: Australia and the Rise of Asia 1850–1939*. St. Lucia: University of Queensland Press.

Wallerstein, I. (1974) *The Modern World System*. London: Academic Press.

Wang, Gungwu (1992) 'The Origins of Hua-Ch'iao', in Wang Gungwu, *Community and Nation: China, Southeast Asia and Australia*. St. Leonards: Allen & Unwin.

—— (1997) 'Migration History: Some Patterns Revisited', in Wang Gungwu (ed.), *Global History and Migrations*. Boulder, CO: Westview Press, pp. 1–22.

—— (1999) 'A Single Chinese Diaspora? Some Historical Reflections', in Wang Gungwu and Annette Shun Wah, *Imagining the Chinese Diapora: Two Australian Perspectives*. Canberra: Centre for the Study of the Chinese Southern Diaspora.

Wang, Gungwu and Wang, Ling-chi (eds) (1998) *The Chinese Diaspora: Selected Essays*, Singapore: Times Academic Press.

Ware, Vron (1992) *Beyond the Pale: White Women, Racism and History*. London: Verso.

Wasserstrom, Jeffrey N. and Perry, Elizabeth J. (eds) (1992) *Popular Protest and Political Culture in Modern China*. Boulder, CO: Westview Press.

Webb, Janeen and Enstice, Andrew (1998) *Aliens and Savages: Fiction, Politics and Prejudice in Australia*. Sydney: HarperCollins Publishers.

Werbner, Pnina (1997a) 'Introduction: The Dialectics of Cultural Hybridity', in Pnina Werbner & Tariq Modood (eds) *Debating Cultural Hybridity*. London and New York: Zed Books.

—— (1997b) 'Essentialising Essentialism, Essentialising Silence: Ambivalence and Multiplicity in the Constructions of Racism and Ethnicity', in P. Werbner and T. Modood (eds) *Debating Cultural Hybridity*, London and New York: Zed Books, pp. 226–255.

Werbner, Pnina and Tariq Modood (eds) (1997) *Debating Cultural Hybridity: Multi-Cultural Identities and the Politics of Anti-Racism*. London and New York: Zed Books.

West, Cornel (1990) 'The New Cultural Politics of Difference', in Russell Ferguson, Martha Gever, Trinh T. Minh-ha and Cornel West (eds) *Out There: Marginalization and Contemporary Cultures*. Cambridge, MA and London: The MIT Press, pp. 19–36.

—— (1994) *Race Matters*. New York: Random House.

White, Richard (1981) *Inventing Australia*. Sydney: Allen & Unwin.

Wilkinson, Marian (1998) 'Who's Afraid of Pauline Hanson?', *Sydney Morning Herald*, 12 September, p. 43.

Williams, Lea (1960) *Overseas Chinese Nationalism*. Glencoe, ILL: The Free Press.

Williams, Raymond (1961) *Culture and Society*. Harmondsworth: Penguin.

—— (1977) *Marxism and Literature*. Oxford: Oxford University Press.

Wilson, Rob and Dissanayake, Wimal (eds) (1996) *Global/Local: Cultural Production and the Transnational Imaginary*. Durham: Duke University Press.

Wiseman, Jon (1998) *Global Nation? Australia and the Politics of Globalisation*. Cambridge: Cambridge University Press.

Wood, Alan (1997) 'Short-changed?', *The Weekend Australian*, 25–26 October.

Wray, Matt and Newitz, Annalee (eds) (1997) *White Trash: Race and Class in America*. New York: Routledge.

Wu, David Yen-ho (1994) 'The Construction of Chinese and Non-Chinese Identities', in Wei-Ming Tu (ed.) *The Living Tree*, Stanford, CA: Stanford University Press, pp. 148–167.

Yang, William (1996) *Sadness*. St. Leonards: Allen & Unwin.

Yao Souchou (1997) 'Books from Heaven: Literary Pleasure, Chinese Cultural Text and the "Struggle Against Forgetting"', *Australian Journal of Anthropology*, 8, 2: 190–209.

Yeatman, Anna (1993) 'Voice and Representation in the Politics of Difference', in S. Gunew and A. Yeatman (eds) *Feminism and the Politics of Difference*, Sydney: Allen & Unwin, pp. 228–245.

—— (1995) 'Interlocking Oppressions', in Barbara Caine and Rosemary Pringle (eds) *Transitions: New Australian Feminisms*. Sydney: Allen & Unwin, pp. 42–56.

Young, Iris Marion (1990) 'The Ideal of Community and the Politics of Difference', in Linda J. Nicholson (ed.), *Feminism/Postmodernism*. New York and London: Routledge, pp. 300–323.

Young, Robert (1995) *Colonial Desire: Hybridity in Theory, Culture and Race*. London and New York: Routledge.

Zhang, Longxi (1988) 'The Myth of the Other: China in the Eyes of the West', *Critical Inquiry* 15 (Autumn): 110–135

Žižek, Slavoj (1993) *Tarrying with the Negative*. Durham, NC: Duke University Press.

INDEX

Ahmad, A. 2, 52
Allon, F. 138, 207
ambivalence 143–4; concerning Chinese
22–3, 39; feminist 186–7; of hybridity
194, 197, 200–1; of identity 56, 158,
187; of multiculturalism 143–4, 146,
147; of race 143–4; as third space
146–7
Anderson, B. 28, 63, 77, 83, 120
Anderson, I. 195–6
Ang, I. 7, 28, 63, 72, 198, 209; and
Stratton, J. 90, 100
Anthias, F. and Yuval-Davis, N. 140
Anwar, I. 6
Anzaldúa, G. 164–6, 167, 169
Appadurai, A. 70, 72, 76, 84, 89, 115,
155, 172, 199
Arnold, W. 57
Asia/Asian 158; attitude towards 140; and
Australia 7–8, 95, 102–3, 104, 105,
107, 108, 112–25; as challenge to the
West 6; economic crisis 6; feminine
image 147–9; and local/national
involvement 157–9; and modernity 7;
'not quite' status of 147; notions of
171; positive status of 155–6; re-
imagining of 171–2; as terms of identity
4–5
Asian-American 4, 123
Asianness 5–8, 9, 16, 17
Asians in Australia 172; anxieties
concerning 121–3, 126, 127, 130,
135–6; definition of 112–13; feminist
problematic 189–92; grudging
acceptance of 120; and Hanson
phenomenon 113, 114, 118–19, 123;
inclusion/exclusion of 116–23;
information concerning 123–5; issue of
112, 114; as *persona non grata* 139; as
'pet poeple' 140; positive aspect 137;

proto–racial rendering 113; and
racial/cultural homogeneity 116;
resentment of 116; symbolic
significance of 114–15
assimilation 8–11; confusion concerning
28; failure of 105; forced/voluntary 27,
29; need for 65; policies 47–8;
postcolonial process of 8–10; rapid 52,
56
Attwood, B. 187, 197
Australia 7; Anglo-Celtic 98–9, 107–11;
Asianization of 123, 133–4, 135, 136;
ethnocentrism of 190; and fear of
invasion 129–30; Hansonite politics in
126–7, 131, 133–4, 154, 156;
historical background 128–9;
hybridization of race in 194;
immigration policies 117–18, 119–20,
132, 133; as island-continent 129; as
multicultural 98–100, 138–9, 141–2,
145, 153, 171, 173; nationalism in
125; one-nation view 114–15, 118–19,
121–2, 125, 138; as part of Asia–Pacific
region 130–1, 133, 134–5; as
postmodern transnational nation 155;
psycho-geography of 129–30, 134–7;
racial/spatial singularity/separateness
130, 132–3, 134, 137; as racist society
141; and repression of 'race' 104–7;
sense of identity in 154–5; tolerant
pluralism in 141–2; White Australia
policy 101–4, 116, 117, 118, 119,
121–2, 128, 131–2; white/Western
hegemony in 188–92

Balibar, E. 49, 50
Bauman, Z. 9, 74, 147
Benjamin, G. 90
Berger, J. 156
Berry, C. *et al* 209

226